INTRODUCTION TO JUVENILE DELINQUENCY

MARY E. MURRELL
Juvenile Resource Center, Inc.

DAVID LESTER
Department of Psychology
Stockton State College

A GLENCOE Book

MACMILLAN PUBLISHING CO., INC.
New York

Collier Macmillan Publishers
London

Macmillan Publishing Co., Inc.
866 Third Avenue
New York, New York 10022

Collier Macmillan Canada, Ltd.

Library of Congress Catalog Card Number: 78-59963

ISBN 0-02-478790-6

Printing: 3 4 5 6 7 8   Year: 5 6 7 8

Contents

PREFACE   v

PART I: CAUSES OF DELINQUENCY   **1**

INTRODUCTION   **2**

1. THE SCOPE OF THE PROBLEM   **5**

Legal Definitions of Juvenile Delinquency *7*   The Extent
of Delinquency *10*   Alternatives to Official Crime
Statistics *15*   Characteristics of Delinquents *19*
Causes of Delinquency *20*

2. DELINQUENCY AND THE SOCIAL ENVIRONMENT:
AN OVERVIEW   **24**

Delinquency and the Slum Neighborhood: The Role of Social
Disorganization *26*   Delinquency and Opportunity
Structures *32*   Subcultures and Deviance *37*   Control
Theory *44*   Modern Conflict Theory *49*
Summary *51*

3. LABELING THEORY   **56**

What is Labeling Theory? *57*   Effects of Labeling *59*
Conclusions and Treatment Implications *65*

4. PSYCHOLOGICAL THEORIES   **70**

The Development of Delinquency *71*   The Personality of
Delinquents *79*   The Prediction of Delinquency *81*
Physiological Bases of Delinquency *86*

5. PATTERNS OF DELINQUENT INVOLVEMENT   98

Middle Class Delinquency *98*   Female
Delinquency *103*   The Delinquent Gang *109*
The Violent Offender *116*

6. CASE STUDY: AN INTERVIEW WITH TERRY   127

Interview *127*   An Analysis of Terry's
Delinquency *138*   Terry's Reform *140*

PART II: THE JUVENILE JUSTICE PROCESS   143

INTRODUCTION   144

7. CHILDREN AND THE JUVENILE COURT   147

Changing Perspectives on Crime and Delinquency *147*
The Child-Saving Movement *149*   The Early Juvenile
Court *151*   Constitutional Positions *153*
The Juvenile Court Today: Divergent Goals *157*
New Trends in Juvenile Justice *162*

8. REFERRAL, DETECTION, AND INTAKE   167

Referral *167*   Detention *174*   Intake Interview and
Hearing *177*

9. ADJUDICATION HEARING   182

Petitions and Determination of Jurisdiction *182*   Hearing:
The Participants *185*   Hearing: The Procedure *191*
Appeals *193*   Adjudication: Conflicting
Perspectives *193*

10. DISPOSITION   197

The Decision-Making Process *197*   Dispositional
Alternatives *199*   Probation *202*
Institutionalization *207*   Aftercare *217*

11. INNOVATIONS IN THE JUVENILE JUSTICE PROCESS   222

Removal of Status Offenders from the Juvenile Court *223*
Child Advocacy *224*   Deinstitutionalization *226*
Diversion *232*

12. INTERVIEW WITH JUDGE RICHETTE   245

AUTHOR INDEX   253

SUBJECT INDEX   259

Preface

This book is designed to provide a broad introduction to juvenile delinquency and the juvenile justice system. The nature, frequency, and possible causes of delinquency are presented in order to encourage an understanding of the behavioral, or social science, perspective on juvenile crime. With this knowledge, the student is prepared to explore the juvenile justice system from the arrest by the police of the child to his or her incarceration in a training school or reformatory.

Part I presents sociological and psychological theories and empirical research on the nature and causes of juvenile delinquency. The implications of theory for delinquency prevention and the rehabilitation of offenders are considered, and examples of specific programs are presented. In addition, topics of current interest, such as labeling theory, are discussed. Part I concludes with an interview with a former juvenile delinquent which offers the student an opportunity to apply some of the theoretical ideas about delinquency to an actual case.

Part II examines the legal response to juvenile crime, from the early days of the juvenile court until the present. The chapters are organized so that the sequence of stages in the juvenile justice process may be followed. The strengths and weaknesses of the juvenile court are considered, with attention to the use of legal and administrative controls on discretion in decision making. The response of the United States Supreme Court to the rights of juveniles is analyzed and innovations in the juvenile justice process are detailed.

Although the book is divided into two parts, we have attempted to integrate legal and behavioral information on delinquency. The ties between the juvenile justice system and the community are direct ones, and it is very important to understand the origin of the delinquent act as well as the legal response to it.

We have attempted to write a clear, concise introduction to juvenile delinquency that will be interesting and thought provoking to students. There are examples of delinquent behavior drawn from newspapers and interviews. There are also examples from court cases, probation reports, and an interview with Judge Lisa Richette, who has been an outspoken advocate for children. Each chapter is followed by discussion questions that have been designed to encourage students to review and develop a more thorough understanding of the major points made in the chapter.

M.E.M.
D.L.

PART I

Causes of Delinquency

Introduction

Part I is an introduction to the nature and extent of juvenile delinquency in the United States. It is also a consideration of the causes of delinquency. Before one can consider the causes of delinquency, it is necessary to define the term *juvenile delinquency*. How, for example, is delinquency typically defined by state law? What specific acts constitute delinquent behavior? Legal definitions vary from state to state, but, generally, delinquent conduct encompasses acts ranging from truancy and curfew violations to serious offenses such as robbery.

Another important aspect of juvenile delinquency is the frequency with which the behavior occurs in our society. How much delinquency is there? Although there are major obstacles in providing an exact number of delinquent acts committed during a given period of time, there are both the records of police departments and the research of social scientists from which some conclusions can be drawn. We will see that public concern about youth crime is not unfounded; indeed, juveniles are responsible for a large proportion of criminal acts.

The amount of juvenile delinquency is alarming, yet many youngsters do not persist in deviant acts as they grow older. Unfortunately, some people have assumed that delinquent behavior is a reliable predictor of adult criminality. Actually, only a very small number of juveniles continue to engage in serious illegal behaviors. A good description of delinquency compares it to measles: ". . . as a rule it takes a mild form, only for a few is the infection virulent, the complications serious."[1] This may be little consolation for the victims of youthful offenders, but it is important to be aware of the sporadic nature of this type of deviance.

Once delinquency has been defined and its extent measured, the possible causes of this behavior can be examined. Sociologists and psychologists have attempted to analyze the conditions that lead to delinquency, but no single explanation or theory appears adequate to explain all delinquent behavior. However, some common threads can be seen in theories of delinquency, such as poverty and problems in family relationships. The implications of these theories for the prevention and treatment of delinquency are discussed, as well as some of the shortcomings of these theories in outlining the causes of illegal acts by juveniles.

Other possible contributors to delinquency, in addition to those of the social and home environment, are considered. The effect of the juvenile justice process, from arrest to the court imposed label of delinquent, may be to increase the delinquent behavior of those juveniles who come into contact with it. Decisions of police officers, probation officers, prosecutors, and judges determine which juveniles go through the juvenile justice process and what happens to them. Perhaps the youngsters who go through this labeling process are not helped but harmed by it.

The following chapters present a review of a vast amount of literature on delinquency, ranging from theoretical explanations to the results of empirical research. The information is not exhaustive, but has been chosen to provide a balanced introduction to the field of juvenile delinquency. Such an introduction is necessary so that the reader has an understanding of the complexity of delinquent behavior prior to discussion of the juvenile justice process.

NOTE

1. Sir Leon Radzinowicz and Joan King, ''The Growth of Crime: An International Perspective,'' in L. Radzinowicz and M. E. Wolfgang, eds., *Crime and Justice: The Criminal in Society,* 2nd ed. (New York: Basic Books, 1977), p. 17.

1 The Scope of the Problem

Although children are highly valued in almost all modern-day societies, there is some evidence that concern for the welfare of the young is a relatively new phenomenon in the history of civilization. Few people would dispute the fact that juvenile delinquency is an important area for concern or that the care of children must be regulated to insure that future generations are being exposed to appropriate values and behaviors. Fortunately, the current view of juveniles emphasizes the fact that children are indeed valuable and should be protected, nurtured, and educated.

Children have not always been held in such high esteem. In fact, until the Middle Ages little distinction was made between children and slaves.[1] Both were regarded as "chattel," or property, which the head of the household could treat in any manner he saw fit. Under Roman law, the *paterfamilias* doctrine gave the father unlimited power over all members of the family, much as he had power over his slaves. This totalitarian philosophy was also found among Christian, Moslem, and Jewish civilizations.

Infanticide, or the killing of newborn infants, was widely practiced in many cultures. As late as 1890, dead babies could be seen in the streets of London and in garbage dumps. Children were regularly abandoned, sold, or given to wet nurses, who were expected to let the infants die. They were often viewed as replaceable objects, partly as a result of the high rates of infant mortality. If children died or were killed, sold, or abandoned, they could be easily replaced.

Early attitudes toward children were reflected in the legal codes, which frequently provided for very harsh punishments for their misconduct. In the code of Hammurabi in 2270 B.C., in the law of the Romans, and in old English law (924–939 A.D.), severe punishments were set down for children who defied parental authority.[2] A son could be put to death, have his tongue cut out, or be sold into slavery if his father ordered it.

During the Middle Ages children were regarded as property and in some instances were used as objects of sexual pleasure.[3] By the sixteenth and seventeenth centuries, a greater concern for modesty inspired by Catholicism and Protestantism altered this view, and it became common for children to be heavily supervised and tirelessly disciplined. Now, instead of being treated as property, the young were seen as products of sinful sexual activity and, as such, were thought to require complete control by adults lest they succumb to the temptations of living in a sinful world. Corporal punishment became an acceptable means of training the young, not only in the family but in religious and educational settings as well.[4]

Under the law children could be held responsible for criminal acts. Numerous accounts can be found in literature of children who were convicted and punished for crimes. One such account tells of a thirteen-year-old English girl who was executed for having allegedly killed her mistress.[5] Under the law children could be charged, tried, and sentenced in exactly the same manner as adults.

During the late nineteenth century, the growing child-saving movement in the United States helped stimulate public concern about the plight of children, particularly the harsh treatment children received in the adult courts.[6] The child savers advocated the establishment of an alternative court, which would be designed to protect the welfare of the young. Instead of automatically punishing a child for misbehavior, this new court would offer humane treatment and an opportunity for rehabilitation. This approach would extend to children who had committed offenses as well as to orphans and children who had been abused or neglected.

At the time of the establishment of the first juvenile court, delinquency was already considered a major problem in the United States. Reformers not only felt that children had been treated too harshly under adult law but they were also opposed to the practice of placing children in jails alongside adults to await trial and then incarcerating them in the same facilities after trial. Constant exposure to accomplished criminals was felt to be detrimental to juveniles in that it gave them opportunities to develop their skills at illegal acts and reinforced their deviant behavior patterns.

Reformers also believed that rehabilitation of children at an early age could divert them from a life of criminality by exposing them to socially acceptable values and activities. Training schools and reformatories could give children who were delinquent, neglected, or abandoned an opportunity to learn useful skills that would prepare them for productive lives. Thus the juvenile justice system would attempt to resocialize wayward youngsters and thereby decrease the likelihood of future criminality.

Children had now moved from the position of being totally controlled by their parents, as in the code of Hammurabi, to one in which the state could intervene in their lives when it was deemed necessary. As societies became more populated and increased in complexity, juvenile delinquency came to be viewed as a community problem.

Concern about the behavior of the young continues to surface as an important issue in many societies. Perhaps in a society like that of the United States, the growing concern with the welfare of children is in part due to cultural values which emphasize the virtues of youthfulness and achievement. Today the actions and life-styles of the young have a powerful influence on adults; in many ways, the young are trend setters—for example, in clothing styles, music, and so forth. Many people think of the childhood years as the happiest years of one's life. Parents hope that their children will be successful in school and later in their jobs. They strive to provide their offspring with advantages and educational opportunities they themselves did not have. Today's child-oriented family structure emphasizes the importance of the activities of the young, and parents may go so far as to subordinate their own interests and desires to those of their children.

Some people fear that childhood deviance may lead to adult criminality and therefore must be curtailed to insure that youngsters will establish appropriate positions for themselves in society. It is believed that delinquents may contaminate ''normal'' youngsters by encouraging them to engage in illicit acts; thus efforts to curb delinquency and to isolate the offenders are seen as necessary for the preservation of the future social order.

Legal Definitions of Juvenile Delinquency

Almost everyone has used the term *juvenile delinquent* on occasion, perhaps in describing someone they know or in discussing the problem of crime in society; but the term has different meanings for different people. One person may refer to youngsters who are chronically truant from school as delinquent; others may employ the term in reference to adolescents who commit homicide, rape, or armed robbery; still others may use the term to describe children who break curfew laws or engage in premarital sex.

Given these conflicting viewpoints, it is necessary to consider the legal definitions of juvenile delinquency. Legal definitions of juvenile delinquency are contained in statutory laws, which ennumerate specific actions that constitute delinquent behavior; children who are found to be engaging in these behaviors are then labeled by the juvenile justice court as delinquent. Below are some examples of statutory definitions of delinquent acts as they appear in the state laws of New York, Texas, and Pennsylvania.

New York § 712. Definitions.
>   A. "Juvenile delinquent." A person over seven and less than sixteen years of age who commits any act which, if committed by an adult, would constitute a crime.

B. "Person in need of supervision." A male less than sixteen years of age and a female less than eighteen years of age[7] who does not attend school in accord with provisions of part one of article sixty-five of the education law or who is incorrigible, ungovernable, or habitually disobedient and beyond the lawful control of parent or other lawful authority or who violates the provisions of Section 221.05 of the penal law.[8]

Texas § 51.03. Delinquent Conduct; Conduct Indicating a Need for Supervision.
A. Delinquent conduct is conduct, other than a traffic offense, that violates:
   1. a penal law of this state punishable by imprisonment or by confinement in jail; or
   2. a reasonable and lawful order of a juvenile court entered under Section 54.04 or 54.05 of this code. . . .
B. Conduct indicating a need for supervision is:
   1. conduct, other than a traffic offense, that on three or more occasions violates either of the following:
      a. the penal laws of this state of the grade of misdemeanor that are punishable by fine only; or
      b. the penal ordinances of any political subdivision of this state;
   2. the unexcused voluntary absence of a child on ten or more days or parts of days within a six-month period . . . ,
   3. the voluntary absence of a child from his home without the consent of his parent or guardian for a substantial length of time or without intent to return;[9]

* * *

Pennsylvania § 6302. Definitions.
   "Child." An individual who is:
   1. under the age of eighteen years;
   2. under the age of twenty-one years who committed an act of delinquency before reaching the age of eighteen years;

* * *

"Delinquent act."
   1. The term means an act designated a crime under the law of this Commonwealth, or of another state if the act occurred in that state, or under Federal law, or under local ordinances.
   2. The term shall not include
      (i) the crime of murder; or
      (ii) summary offenses, unless the child fails to pay a fine levied thereunder, in which event notice of such fact shall be certified to the court.

   "Delinquent child." A child ten years of age or older whom the court has found to have committed a delinquent act and is in need of treatment, supervision or rehabilitation.

"Dependent child." A child who:

1. is without proper parental care or control, subsistence, education as required by law, or other care or control necessary for his physical, mental or emotional help, or morals;
2. has been placed for care or adoption in violation of law;
3. has been abandoned by his parents, guardian, or other custodian;
4. is without a parent, guardian, or legal custodian;
5. while subject to compulsory school attendance is habitually and without justification truant from school;
6. has committed a specific act or acts of habitual disobedience of the reasonable and lawful commands of his parent, guardian or other custodian and who is ungovernable and found to be in need of care, treatment or supervision;[10]

* * *

These statutes include several characteristics that must be present in order for a child to be labeled or adjudicated delinquent. First, the age of the child determines whether he or she will come under the jurisdiction of the juvenile court. In most states this includes children between the ages of 7 and 18. Only children who fall into this age group can be processed as delinquents. Younger children are not considered legally responsible for their actions, and older children would come under the jurisdiction of the criminal court.

The second characteristic concerns the type of activities in which the child has engaged. Minor infractions such as traffic offenses may be excluded from consideration, but acts that would be considered criminal offenses if committed by adults are classified as delinquent acts. Some states exclude specific offenses from the juvenile court, such as the Pennsylvania Act, which excludes the crime of murder, but as a general rule delinquent acts are offenses that would be criminal acts if committed by adults.

In addition to crimes, juvenile delinquency often covers such acts as running away from home, truancy, and incorrigibility. For this type of offender, the New York Statutes provide a separate category known as PINS (person in need of supervision). Other states use similar categories: CHINS (children in need of supervision); JINS (juveniles in need of supervision); and MINS (minors in need of supervision).[11] Children in these categories come under the jurisdiction of the juvenile court despite the fact that the offenses they have committed would not be classified as crimes if they were committed by persons over the age of 18. These offenses are often called *status offenses* since they are considered illegal only when committed by persons who are under the age of 18.

The age and the actions of the child, then, will determine whether he or she is delinquent or in need of supervision. In some cases, the condition of the child will indicate that he or she is deprived. Of course not all youngsters who engage in delinquent behaviors are detected; only those who are found in a court of law to have committed one of these acts can be legally classified as juvenile delinquents.

In light of the legal definitions of delinquency presented here, it is clear that the juvenile court handles a wide variety of offenses. Indeed some writers have pointed out that there are few adolescent behaviors that have *not* come under the label of delinquency. Criminal acts include homicide, rape, burglary, robbery, assault, carrying a weapon, larceny, auto theft, narcotics offenses, and vandalism. In addition, the juvenile court regularly handles a number of other acts. These include (1) truancy from school; (2) association with vicious or immoral persons; (3) growing up in idleness and crime; (4) loitering; (5) use of alcohol; (6) running away from home; (7) attempting to marry without consent, in violation of law; and (8) deportment that injures or endangers the health, morals, or safety of others.[12]

Because legal definitions of delinquency are broad and often vague, the state has been given considerable leeway in deciding how and when to intervene in a youngster's life. These statutory guidelines, which were originally intended to facilitate the ability of the court to offer help to children in need, have also allowed the court to exercise virtually unlimited power over the lives of individual juveniles. Recent appraisals of the actual treatment children receive have led many critics to question whether the original humanitarian goals of the juvenile justice system are in fact being met.

The broad definitions of delinquency found in the state statutes are especially problematic for status offenders since these youngsters are often processed in exactly the same manner as more serious offenders. There is increasing support in the United States for completely removing status offenders from the jurisdiction of the juvenile court, but a survey of state statutes conducted in 1977 indicated that none of the states had entirely removed status offenders from its delinquency laws.[13] The survey found that terms such as ungovernable, runaway, incorrigible, wayward, truant, habitually disobedient, idle, dissolute, dangerous to self, and dangerous to others are still being used in delinquency statutes to describe children who are handled by the juvenile court.[14]

Perhaps the most significant change in state statutes dealing with status offenders is the fact that many states now make provisions for separate facilities for delinquents and status offenders. At the time of the 1977 survey, 16 states prohibited the placement of status offenders in facilities and institutions in which delinquents were incarcerated.

The Extent of Delinquency

Delinquent behavior occurs in all types of families, in both large urban areas and small rural communities, and in all parts of the United States. The number of delinquent acts committed is often gauged by use of official police records of crimes based on reports by witnesses or victims or detection by law enforcement officers. Police records are compiled each year by the Federal Bureau of Investigation in the *Uniform Crime Reports (UCR)*. Other agencies, such as courts or research centers, also publish information on criminal activity, but the major source of data on offenses is the *UCR*.

Several difficulties arise, however, when one attempts to use official records of offenses as indicators of the actual amount of criminal activity in society. First, many offenses go undetected by law enforcement agencies since victims or witnesses frequently fail to notify authorities of crimes. In addition, the reports filed by individual police agencies are not always accurate since some departments tend to downplay certain offenses and emphasize others. Arrest policies may also affect crime records. For example, an official increase in the number of narcotics offenses may actually reflect a new departmental policy of concentration on drug arrests. Indeed, some writers have suggested that official records should be used to describe police practices rather than the prevalence of particular types of crime in the society.[15]

Another criticism of official records is that the number of juvenile offenses reported each year is not weighted according to the number of persons in the population who fall into this particular age group. For instance, if one examines juvenile arrests over a two-year period, the rate of delinquency may appear to be increasing, but any fluctuation in the number of arrests may actually be a result of changing numbers of persons under the age of 18 in the general population during that same period. If the juvenile population has increased, then the crime *rate* (number of delinquent acts per total number of juveniles) may not have increased at all, even though the number of official arrests has increased.[16]

Although these factors must be considered when interpreting official crime statistics, they do not completely invalidate the use of official records. Trends in arrest patterns can be examined and some conclusions drawn from them. Figure 1-1 provides information on the percentage of all arrests by age groups during 1976.

The percentage of all arrests accounted for by juveniles is quite large, especially when compared to the number of juveniles in the population as a whole. If the arrests of 13-to-15-year-olds and 16-to-18-year-olds are combined, approximately one-third of the total number of arrests will be accounted for.

Table 1-1 presents data on the percentage of arrests for violent and property offenses by various age groups. Here again is evidence for concern about the involvement of juveniles in criminal activity since persons under the age of 18 account for approximately one-fifth of the arrests for violent offenses and nearly one-half of the arrests for property offenses.

In considering the number of crimes committed by juveniles, it is also important to review trends in crime rates. The reported arrests of persons

PERSONS ARRESTED
Distribution by Age, 1976*

TOTAL POPULATION
Distribution by Age, 1976†

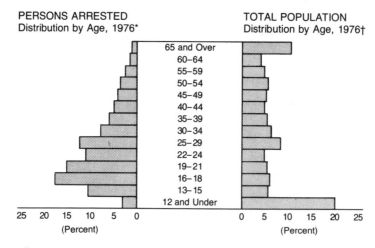

*Persons arrested is based on reports received representing 175,449,000 population.

†The total population is 214,659,000 for the United States, based on Bureau of Census provisional estimates, July 1, 1976.

Source: FBI, Uniform Crime Reports, 1976, p. 172.

Figure 1-1. Number of persons, by age, arrested in the United States compared to total population (1976).

TABLE 1-1. PERCENTAGE OF TOTAL ARRESTS OF PERSONS BY AGE GROUPS FOR VIOLENT AND PROPERTY OFFENSES, 1976

	VIOLENT OFFENSES *	PROPERTY OFFENSES:†
Under 15	6.1	18.4
Under 18	22.0	46.1
Under 21	39.6	64.4
Under 25	57.8	77.5

*Violent offenses include murder, forcible rape, robbery, and aggravated assault.
†Property offenses include burglary, larceny-theft, and motor vehicle theft.
Source: Adapted from FBI, Uniform Crime Reports, 1976, p. 183.

under 18 for a given year are not as instructive as are *crime trends* since increases or decreases in juvenile crime can only be determined with a comparison of fluctuations over a period of time. Table 1-2 presents data showing arrest trends over a five-year period.

Although there are some difficulties in interpreting official records due to problems with their accuracy, Table 1-2 does indicate large increases in arrests of juveniles for many specific offenses. When all violent crime is considered, there is a 54 percent increase. There is an increase in property

**TABLE 1-2. ARREST TRENDS FOR PERSONS UNDER 18 YEARS OF AGE
(1970–1975)**

OFFENSE	1970	1975	PERCENT CHANGE
Criminal homicide			
(a) Murder and nonnegligent manslaughter	1,017	1,301	+ 27.9
(b) Manslaughter by negligence	201	239	+ 18.9
Forcible rape	2,687	3,189	+ 18.7
Robbery	25,479	39,917	+ 56.7
Aggravated assault	18,128	28,460	+ 57.0
Burglary—breaking or entering	129,370	185,082	+ 43.1
Larceny-theft	282,804	352,715	+ 24.7
Auto theft	63,991	52,537	− 17.9
Violent crime*	47,311	72,867	+ 54.0
Property crime†	476,165	590,334	+ 24.0
Other assaults	45,298	58,838	+ 29.9
Arson	4,999	6,082	+ 21.7
Vandalism	70,531	89,328	+ 26.7
Weapons; carrying, possessing	14,445	17,870	+ 23.7
Prostitution and commercialized vice	1,054	2,215	+110.2
Sex offenses (except forcible rape and prostitution)	8,954	8,647	− 2.4
Narcotic drug laws	68,713	93,875	+ 36.6
Liquor laws	67,260	75,151	+ 11.7
Disorderly conduct	106,720	91,284	− 14.5
Curfew and loitering violations	95,696	92,993	− 2.8
Runaways	149,978	141,895	− 5.4

*Violent crime includes murder, forcible rape, robbery, and aggravated assault.
†Property crime includes burglary, larceny-theft, and motor vehicle theft.
Source: Adapted from FBI, Uniform Crime Reports, 1975, p. 184.

offenses but it is not as large as that of violent offenses, which surely is cause
for alarm. Table 1-2 indicates that juveniles are being arrested more frequently for the offenses generally considered to be the most serious in our
society.

Police records of juvenile arrests are not the only source of information
about delinquent behavior. Table 1-3 presents data on the number of cases
processed by juvenile courts between 1957 and 1974. Note that the rate of
cases is constructed by using the population of 10-to-17-year-old persons in
the United States for each year. It appears that during this period the number of cases referred to the juvenile justice system has steadily increased.

Unfortunately more data are needed in order to determine the amount of delinquent activity in society. Cases may be referred to juvenile court at the discretion of police, probation officers, or others. This discretion determines the case flow into court, which means that the rate of cases handled could be a result of both increased delinquent behavior and increased referrals to court. With the implementation of programs to divert juveniles out of the juvenile court in recent years, it seems likely that referrals to the court by police and probation staff may well have decreased; thus the rates of delinquent acts shown in Table 1-3 would reflect increased delinquency.

On the basis of the data presented here what can one conclude about the extent of delinquent behavior in the United States? No completely accurate statements about the total number of juvenile offenses committed can be made, and definite conclusions about the size of a rising delinquency rate cannot be formulated. Additional information about offenses unknown to the police as well as the population structure in 1976 is needed. Yet there is evidence to suggest that patterns of delinquent involvement are changing to some extent, with more juveniles becoming involved in serious offenses. The data from the juvenile court also suggest that delinquent behavior is increasing

TABLE 1-3. ESTIMATED NUMBER AND POPULATION-STANDARDIZED RATES OF DELINQUENCY CASES DISPOSED OF BY JUVENILE COURTS, 1957–1974

YEAR	DELINQUENCY CASES*	CHILD POPULATION 10 THROUGH 17 YEARS OF AGE (IN THOUSANDS)	RATE†
1957	440,000	22,173	19.8
1958	470,000	23,443	20.0
1959	483,000	24,607	19.6
1960	510,000	25,368	20.1
1961	503,000	26,056	19.3
1962	555,000	26,989	20.6
1963	601,000	28,056	21.4
1964	686,000	29,244	23.4
1965	697,000	29,536	23.6
1966	745,000	30,124	24.7
1967	811,000	30,837	26.3
1968	900,000	31,566	28.5
1969	988,500	32,157	30.7
1970	1,052,000	32,614	32.3
1971	1,125,000	32,969	34.1
1972	1,112,500	33,120	33.6
1973	1,143,700	33,377	34.2
1974	1,252,700	33,365	37.5

*Data for 1957–69 estimated from the national sample of juvenile courts. Data for 1970–74 estimated from all courts who have responded for two consecutive years. These jurisdictions included more than two-thirds of the population of the United States.

†Based on the number of delinquency cases per 1,000 U.S. child population 10 through 17 years of age.

Source: National Center for Juvenile Justice, "Juvenile Court Statistics, 1974," 1976, p. 13, Table 6 (preliminary draft).

in the United States, with more and more juveniles coming into contact with the juvenile justice system.

Alternatives to Official Crime Statistics

Criminologists and other social scientists have long been interested in measuring the "dark figure" of undetected and unreported offenses.[17] Two techniques have been developed for measuring these offenses—self-report surveys and victimization surveys. Self-report surveys request that subjects record the number of times they have committed specific offenses. Victimization surveys ask respondents how many times they have been victims of a crime during a given period of time. Both techniques have indicated that large numbers of delinquent and criminal acts are not reflected in official crime statistics.

Self-Report Studies

Self-report techniques were first used in the United States in the 1940s. Porterfield administered questionnaires to college students who were asked to acknowledge behaviors in which they had engaged. These questionnaire reponses were anonymous, and the results indicated that every subject had committed at least one delinquent act, either a criminal offense or a status offense.

Many other researchers began to utilize the self-report method for collecting data on delinquent behavior, and found offense patterns that differed from those typically seen in official records. One of the major differences concerned the prevalence of delinquency among children from lower socioeconomic status backgrounds. Official records of delinquent behavior show high

---

TABLE 1-4. BEHAVIORS USED IN SELF-REPORT STUDY

1. Skipped class when you were in school
2. Stayed out later than your parents said you should
3. Gone onto someone's land when he didn't want you there or without permission
4. Gone into a house or building when you were not supposed to be there
5. Played on a school athletic team
6. Threatened to hurt someone
7. Gotten something by telling a person something bad would happen to him if you did not get what you wanted
8. Done something your parents told you not to do
9. Done something in a class so that other kids couldn't do their work
10. Been told to bring your parents to school for something you did wrong
11. Damaged or messed up something not belonging to you
12. Hurt someone badly enough for him to need bandages or a doctor

TABLE 1-4. BEHAVIORS USED IN SELF-REPORT STUDY (CONTINUED)

13. Gotten on the honor roll for good grades in school
14. Argued or fought with your mother
15. Told a lie to your parents
16. Taken some part of a car or some gasoline
17. Hit your father
18. Taken something not belonging to you worth between $2 and $50
19. Not been allowed to go to school until the suprintendent or principal or someone like that told you that you could go again
20. Gotten something by lying about who you are
21. Gotten something by lying to a person about what you would do for him
22. Taken something not belonging to you worth less than $2
23. Earned over $50 a year
24. Gotten something by lying about your age
25. Drunk beer or liquor
26. Run away from home
27. Skipped a day of school without a real excuse
28. Been sent to the school principal's office for bad behavior in class
29. Been elected officer of a club
30. Carried a gun or knife
31. Worked on the school newspaper
32. Taken something not belonging to you worth over $50
33. Done something around the house or for your family that really pleased your parents
34. Taken part in a fight in which a bunch of your friends was against another bunch
35. Not done something your parents said you were supposed to do
36. Argued or had a fight with a teacher
37. Been elected to the student council
38. Set fire to someone else's property
39. Used or threatened to use a weapon to get something from a person
40. Broken windows of the school
41. Taken something from a store without paying for it
42. Argued or fought with your father
43. Smoked without your parent's knowing it or without their permission
44. Worked free for a charity organization (example, March of Dimes, Red Cross, etc.)
45. Been elected as a class officer
46. Won a prize or award for doing something outside of school
47. Made so much noise that people were angry
48. Hit your mother
49. Taken a car without permission of the owner (even if auto returned)
50. Gone all the way with a boy (girls)
    Gone all the way with a girl (boys)

Source: Delinquent Behavior in an American City by M. Gold, p. 16. Copyright © 1970 by Wadsworth Publishing Company, Inc. Reprinted by permission of the publisher, Brooks/Cole Publishing Company, Monterey, California 93940.

concentrations of poor, black males who are arrested by the police and processed through the juvenile justice system. Self-report studies indicate either that 1) there is no correlation between social status and delinquency;[18] or 2) social status is not as strongly related to delinquency as official records suggest.[19] Self-report studies also reveal that differences between black and white delinquency are smaller than official records indicate.

The self-report technique has been refined by researchers so that the behaviors listed on the questionnaires more closely resemble acts that would result in official handling. (See Table 1-4.) Earlier studies had included vague definitions of certain acts or had included extremely trivial offenses. Efforts have also been made to validate the reports that subjects give, for there is the possibility that some respondents may either exaggerate or minimize their delinquent involvement. Cross-checks with police records or juvenile informants have been utilized to determine the accuracy of the responses. Some types of offenses are more likely to be concealed than others, such as breaking and entering, carrying weapons, and sexual activity, but Gold concluded that the reports from juveniles in his study were accurate for about 70 percent of the subjects.[20]

Self-report studies have shown that many more offenses are committed by juveniles than are known to the police. Between 11 and 16 percent of those children who report delinquent involvement report detection and prosecution,[21] so it appears that those children who become "official delinquents" are a very small proportion of all delinquent offenders. However, there is evidence that official delinquents commit more serious and more frequent offenses than do other juveniles (see Table 1-5), which suggests that the juvenile justice system generally handles those children who are the most seriously delinquent.

This type of information suffers from the same general inaccuracies as those found in official crime statistics, but it does help to put the incidence of delinquent behavior in perspective. Self-report studies provide an estimate of unreported behavior and allow comparisons of "official" and "unofficial" delinquents. It can also be seen from these studies that comparisons between delinquents and a nondelinquent control group needs careful scrutiny since so many respondents acknowledge involvement in deviant acts. (See Table 1-5.)

Victimization Studies

Victimization studies attempt to measure the amount of crime unknown to officials by asking subjects to recall the number of times during a given period that they were victims. Unlike self-report studies, victimization surveys have been used to measure the incidence of all types of crimes. They have been very helpful in exploring reporting practices since victims can be questioned about their failure to notify the police of crimes.

TABLE 1-5. EXTENT OF DELINQUENT ACTS BY STUDENTS AND TRAINING SCHOOL BOYS BY AREA

DELINQUENT ACT	ADMIT ACT			ADMIT ACT MORE THAN ONCE OR TWICE		
	Midwest Students (in percent)	Western Students (in percent)	Training School Boys (in percent)	Midwest Students (in percent)	Western Students (in percent)	Training School Boys (in percent)
Driving a car without a license	81.1	75.3	91.1	61.2	49.0	73.4
Skipping school	54.4	53.0	95.3	24.4	23.8	85.9
Fist fighting	86.7	80.7	95.3	32.6	31.9	75.0
Running away	12.9	13.0	68.1	2.8	2.4	37.7
School probation or expulsion	15.3	11.3	67.8	2.1	2.9	31.3
Defying parents' authority	22.2	33.1	52.4	1.4	6.3	23.6
Stealing items worth less than $2	62.7	60.6	91.8	18.5	12.9	65.1
Stealing items worth from $2 to $50	17.1	15.8	91.0	3.8	3.8	61.4
Stealing items worth more than $50	3.5	5.0	90.8	1.1	2.1	47.7
Gang fighting	24.3	22.5	67.4	6.7	5.2	47.4
Drinking beer, wine, or liquor	67.7	57.2	89.7	35.8	29.5	79.4
Using narcotics	1.4	2.2	23.1	0.7	1.6	12.6
Having sex relations	38.8	40.4	87.5	20.3	19.9	73.4

Source: James Short, Jr., and F. Ivan Nye, "Extent of Unrecorded Juvenile Delinquency: Tentative Conclusions," Journal of Criminal Law, Criminology & Police Science, 49, no. 4 (1959): 297. Reprinted by special permission of the Journal of Criminal Law, Criminology & Police Science. Copyright © 1959 by Northwestern University School of Law, Vol. 49, No. 4.

Victimization reports confirm that many offenses are unknown to the police. The percentage of offenses that are reported to law enforcement agencies fluctuates according to the offense category. The National Crime Panel program conducted in the United States in 1974 revealed that burglaries and completed motor vehicle thefts were among the crimes most commonly reported to police; the crime of larcency was least likely to be reported.[22] This still left almost half of the rapes, robberies, and assaults unknown to officials.

Reasons for not reporting offenses abound. Most victims stated that they did not report offenses because they felt that nothing would be achieved by notifying the police. Others expressed negative attitudes toward the police or a fear of reprisals from their assailant. The inconvenience of appearing in court, a desire to "not get involved," or sympathy for the offender may discourage notification of authorities.

Of course this method of gathering data on the amount of crime has its drawbacks, for subjects may forget offenses, exaggerate the seriousness of a crime, or inflate the number of times that an offense occurred. Even with these problems, the victimization surveys do present information that underscores the difficulty of drawing conclusions about crime and delinquency from official crime statistics.

The National Crime Panel program also gathered information about how victims perceive the offender. Of particular interest here is the percentage of offenses attributed to offenders from 12 to 20 years of age. Purse snatchers were most commonly described as belonging to this age range, and crimes with multiple offenders were also frequently attributed to youngsters. Over half of the simple assaults with injury and 41 percent of the robberies were perceived to have been committed by young offenders. Thus victimization surveys mirror the findings of self-report studies and official statistics—that young people are responsible for large proportions of the crime in the United States.

Characteristics of Delinquents

What kinds of characteristics can one conclude are common among juvenile delinquents? Contrasts between the results of self-report surveys and official records of crime require some qualifications in the description of the typical delinquent. To some extent, the use of the term "typical delinquent" is misleading because there is so much diversity among juveniles who commit delinquent acts. One might even say that at some time in their lives nearly all children have engaged in behaviors that *could have been* termed delinquent. There are some general patterns that can be noted in delinquent behavior, however, and below is a brief summary of these. (These characteristics are not representative of *all* delinquents but rather are characteristics of *many* juveniles who commit such acts.)

Sex: Delinquency occurs more frequently among males than among females. Part of this difference is certainly due to sex-role definitions in our society, which encourage aggressive, adventurous behaviors from males and passive, emotional behaviors from girls. There is some evidence that the difference between males and females is narrowing, but self-report surveys still indicate that the ratio of male to female offenses is approximately 2 to 1.[23]

Social Status: Official records indicate that delinquency is primarily found among lower-socioeconomic status youngsters. This finding has been qualified by self-report studies that show middle- and upper-class juveniles confess to delinquent acts but do not appear to get caught. There is evidence that lower-class youngsters report more serious offenses, and this may partially account for their high concentrations in the juvenile justice system.[24]

Race: Minority group members are found more frequently in official records than one would anticipate on the basis of their numbers in the population at large. Self-report studies have indicated that the differences between minority and white involvement in delinquency are smaller than those found in official records, but they do nonetheless exist.[25] It must be emphasized that race and social status are strongly related in the United States, and so it becomes difficult to isolate the effects of these two variables from each other. It may well be the case that social status is the crucial variable in determining the causes of delinquency.

Other characteristics of offenders could be considered in addition to these three, but they will be discussed in greater detail in subsequent chapters. An exploration of possible causes of delinquency is also needed before any conclusions about offenders can be drawn from the characteristics described here.

Causes of Delinquency

So far we have considered the legal definitions of delinquency and the extent to which delinquent behavior occurs in our society. It is important to understand what the term *juvenile delinquent* means not only from a legal perspective but also from the perspective of a social scientist. The number of juvenile offenses that occur is also a crucial issue for the welfare of society and for the allocation of resources for curbing delinquent acts.

Once the need to decrease delinquency is recognized, it becomes necessary to explore the causes, or etiology, of delinquent behavior. If the causes of delinquency can be determined, then steps can be taken to correct these causal factors. Thus, for example, if one discovers that poor school performance is related to high rates of delinquency, then perhaps new approaches to education would be a possible measure for curbing delinquency.

A second reason for considering the possible causes of delinquency is to guide the development of rehabilitative techniques for juveniles who have already been labeled delinquent. Treatment strategies must be devised so that the initial causes of the behavior can be overcome or made inoperative in order to prevent further delinquency.

Unfortunately, the determination of the causes of delinquent behavior is very complicated, and it is difficult to verify that a particular characteristic or factor will *always* lead to juvenile offenses. For example, not all children who grow up in homes with limited incomes become delinquents, yet poverty may play an important role in the lives of many juveniles who do engage in such acts. If the causes of delinquency could be isolated with a high degree of accuracy, then the prevention and treatment of the behavior would be possible. Many theories have been proposed to explain the causes of delinquent behavior. In the following chapters, we will examine some of these explanations.

Theories of human behavior fall roughly into three categories—sociological, psychological, and physiological (or biological). Sociological theories emphasize the role of social structure and social environment in the etiology of juvenile delinquency. Psychological theories concentrate on how early experiences within the family contribute to the development of deviant behavior patterns and antisocial personality traits. Physiological theories of delinquency examine the relationship between deviant behavior and inherited genetic traits, the basic assumption being that delinquency may have a biological basis.

In the following chapters, major emphasis will be given to a review of the sociological and psychological theories of delinquency. Sociological theories are by far the most numerous and have been used as the basis for large-scale delinquency prevention projects. Psychological theories have been frequently applied in institutional settings for the treatment of juvenile offenders. Few conclusive findings on purely biological causes of delinquency exist, and here biological factors are mentioned only in relation to those theories of delinquency which combine psychological and biological factors.

An alternative perspective on delinquency is provided by the theory known as "labeling theory." Labeling theory rejects the sociological and psychological explanations of delinquency and emphasizes the role of the juvenile justice system in choosing those children who are labeled "delinquent." Labeling theory describes delinquency as primarily a result of the decisions of those in power—for example, police decisions concerning whom to arrest—and the effects these decisions have on the child's self-concept.

DISCUSSION QUESTIONS

1. Why are the activities and attitudes of children considered to be so important in the United States today? What cultural values does this attitude reflect?

2. What common elements can be found in legal definitions of juvenile delinquents and status offenders?

3. How do official crime records, self-reports, and victimization surveys differ?

4. Describe the characteristics of delinquents discussed in this chapter. Why are these particular factors thought to be related to delinquency?

5. Why is it important to measure the amount, or rate, of delinquent activity in society?

NOTES

1. For an account of the position and treatment of children throughout history, see Graeme Newman, *The Punishment Response* (Philadelphia: Lippincott, 1978).

2. Ruth S. Cavan and T. N. Ferdinand, *Juvenile Delinquency,* 3rd ed. (Philadelphia: Lippincott, 1975), pp. 2–3.

3. Newman, *Punishment Response,* p. 62.

4. Ibid., p. 63.

5. Rollin Perkins, *Perkins on Criminal Law* (Mineola, N. Y.: The Foundation Press, 1969), p. 838.

6. Anthony Platt, *The Child Savers* (Chicago: University of Chicago Press, 1969), pp. 101–136.

7. The age difference for males and females in noncriminal acts was struck down in New York in 1972. See *In re Patricia A.,* 31 N.Y. 2d 83, 286 N.E. 2d 432, 335 N.Y.S. 2d 33 (1972).

8. Family Court Act § 712, *McKinney's Consolidated Laws of New York, Annotated* (1979).

9. Family Code § 51.03, *Vernon's Texas Codes Annotated* (1980), Vol. 2, Title 3.

10. § 6302, *Pennsylvania Consolidated Statutes* (1978), Title 42.

11. Ronald Goldfarb, *Jails* (New York: Anchor Books, 1974), p. 313.

12. Sol Rubin, *Crime and Juvenile Delinquency: A Rational Approach to Penal Problems* (New York: Oceana Publications, 1961), p. 49.

13. L. Teitelbaum and A. Gough, *Beyond Control: Status Offenders in the Juvenile Court* (Cambridge, Mass.: Ballinger Publishing, 1977), pp. 297–309.

14. Ibid.

15. John I. Kitsuse and Aaron Cicourel, "A Note on the Uses of Official Statistics," *Social Problems,* 11 (Fall 1963): 131–139.

16. Don C. Gibbons, *Society, Crime, and Criminal Careers* (Englewood Cliffs, N.J.: Prentice-Hall, 1973), p. 103.

17. See R. Hood and R. Sparks, *Key Issues in Criminology* (New York: McGraw-Hill, 1970), Chapter 1, pp. 11–45.

18. James Short and F. Ivan Nye, "Extent of Unrecorded Juvenile Delinquency: Tentative Conclusions," *Journal of Criminal Law, Criminology, and Police Science*, 49, no. 4 (1958): 296–302; R. L. Akers, "Socio-Economic Status and Delinquent Behavior: A Retest," *Journal of Research in Crime and Delinquency*, 1, no. 1 (1964): 38–46; Travis Hirschi, *Causes of Delinquency* (Berkeley: University of California Press, 1969).

19. Martin Gold, *Delinquent Behavior in an American City* (Monterey, Calif: Brooks/ Cole, 1970), pp. 72–78.

20. Ibid, p. 23.

21. Ibid.

22. M. Hindelang et al., *Sourcebook of Criminal Justice Statistics* (Washington, D.C.: Government Printing Office, 1977), p. 358.

23. M. Hindelang, "Age, Sex, and the Versatility of Delinquent Involvement," *Social Problems*, 18 (1971): 552–533.

24. Gold, *Delinquent Behavior in an American City,* p. 73.

25. Hirschi, *Causes of Delinquency,* pp. 75–81.

2 Delinquency and the Social Environment: An Overview

Sociologists emphasize the role of the social environment in the etiology, or causes, of delinquent behavior. The major characteristics of societies with high rates of juvenile misconduct are industrialization, modernization, and urbanization.[1] These societies are characterized by particular family structures and youth cultures that are thought to be influential in the behavior of youth. Moreover, the increased affluence brought about by industrialization is also believed to encourage criminal activity.

The type of family structure most frequently found in industrialized nations is the "nuclear" or "conjugal" family.[2] In these societies, the family is based on the husband-wife tie and their offspring, and there is a relative independence of other kinship ties. This type of family structure is useful to an industrialized social system because it increases mobility; when households are set up independently, a move to a new location necessitated by one's job does not need the approval of large numbers of relatives. The cost of living in the society makes the maintenance of extended kin networks very difficult, if not impossible, so that the extended family system, with several generations residing in a common residence, is very uncommon.

This change in the family structure is paralleled by changes in the socialization process children undergo. Nuclear families have less control over their young because there are fewer adults to act as socialization agents; in addition, there is competition from other groups for influence over the family members. Peer groups and educational institutions consume much of the child's time and interest and may serve to undermine the power of parents.[3]

The type of youth culture found in these countries also may encourage misconduct. Homogeneous age groups are common in many societies and serve a valuable function. Some writers have pointed to the important role these groups play in bridging the gap between childhood dependence and adult independence.[4] There is also the possibility that these groups might inadvertently lead to delinquent behavior by encouraging children to oppose adult values.

The existence of a "youth culture" is made possible through the increased length of dependency on one's parents. Instead of having to become productive members of society at the age of 12 or younger, as in some social systems, the child does not become an adult until the age of 18 or even later. The emphasis on educational achievement in industrialized nations further encourages this extended period of childhood. Because young people are not expected to take on adult responsibilities, they have a great deal of free time, which is often unstructured and unsupervised.

Affluence is another contributor to crime among youth. Obviously there is more opportunity for theft when members of a society enjoy material wealth. The rising expectation of ownership in wealthier countries provides an additional motivation for theft.[5] Affluence also creates an adolescent market that purchases goods and services and that influences what types of goods and services will be most profitable.[6] Rock music stars, television shows, clothing styles, and cosmetics are only a few of the areas over which teenage consumers exercise control through their purchasing power. Distinctive clothing and activities may become symbols for one's identification with and membership in the youth culture.

Affluence may also weaken the ties within the nuclear family. Divorce and separation rates are higher in industrialized nations, which makes it even more likely that family control over offspring will be decreased.[7] Since women can support themselves and extended family ties are weak, marriages can be dissolved more easily. There is some evidence that broken and/or inadequate family backgrounds are related to delinquency in affluent, industrialized societies. This is not the case in societies with extended family structures, however, since other relatives may act as surrogate parents even if the mother or father is absent.[8]

The following theories of the causes of juvenile delinquency refer to American delinquency, although there is evidence of a youth crime problem in other countries.[9] Traditionally, Americans have been more concerned about the problem of delinquency than have other countries. As Bloch and Geis suggest, the so-called open-class system of our country encourages concern over youth.[10] The possibility of upward movement in the social structure makes the behavior of children, who are thought to be able to attain goals that have been beyond the reach of their parents, more significant.

The theories discussed in this chapter explore the relationship between social structure and delinquent behavior in terms of the role of the family, the influence of subcultures, and the effects of social status. Only one of these theories rejects social status as the most important determinant of youth crime, and it is important to note the difference in the data sources which were employed. Hirschi's control theory, which will be discussed later in this chapter, utilizes information from self-reported delinquency questionnaires, whereas other theorists generally rely on the social-status distribution of delinquent offenses found in official statistics.

Although there is much overlap between the different theories, there are also some discrepancies. No one theory appears to be broad enough to encompass all types of delinquents and all types of delinquent acts. In this chapter we will consider the particular weaknesses of each theoretical position and its implications for purposes of treatment and prevention.

Delinquency and the Slum Neighborhood: The Role of Social Disorganization

One of the earliest studies of delinquent behavior was conducted by Frederic M. Thrasher in 1936 in Chicago, Illinois.[11] Thrasher studied the gang areas of the city, which consisted primarily of the slums and central business districts. A total of 1,313 juvenile gangs found in these areas was considered.

The gang was described as a manifestation of "interstitial areas," which are those neighborhoods in which the structure of social organization has broken down. Thrasher felt that a lack of economic, moral, and cultural structures existed in these areas, which were primarily populated by immigrants. He believed that delinquency and delinquent gangs evolved as a result of efforts by youngsters to create a social order where little or none existed. The "society" of the delinquent gangs provided a means through which juveniles could form meaningful relationships. Considerable emphasis was placed on gang loyalty and mutual support. The gang also served as a means of filling leisure time and relieving monotony.

Thrasher believed delinquency to be the direct result of a failure on the part of immigrant parents to control their children. The difficulties faced by the parents of these youngsters were indeed great. The disorganization created by conflicting cultures and poverty left children to their own devices in amusing themselves and developing relationships.

> Since about two-thirds of the parents of delinquent boys in Chicago are peasants from rural areas and villages in Europe, it is not strange that they do not know how to manage their children in such a totally new and different environment. The language difficulty is only one part of the cultural discrepancy that grows up between parents and children. Family discipline cannot be maintained because of the lack of tradition in the American community to support it, and the constant coming in and going out (immigrant succession) in many of the immigrant areas further increases the difficulty of developing any consistent tradition with reference to family control. In this sense, then, the gang becomes a problem of community organization.[12]

Thrasher felt that delinquency was not only dangerous in its demoralizing powers, which had an effect on the child's later behavior, but also in the potential threat it posed to the lives and property of those who lay in its wake. A means of becoming assimilated into American culture was sorely needed by these gang members. Thrasher recognized this need and concluded his study by recommending that alternative activities (for example, Boy Scouts) be provided for children living in these interstitial areas of the city. Such activities would offer constructive, conventional alternatives to delinquent behavior and provide a means by which juvenile gang members could be integrated into society.

In Thrasher's view, then, delinquency is a result of disorganized neighborhoods and family disintegration. The children of immigrants turn to delinquency because of a lack of parental control over their behavior. According to him, efforts to increase community organization and provide alternative means of cultural assimilation would effectively serve to decrease delinquency.

Shaw and McKay

The concern over urban delinquency was again apparent in a study conducted by Clifford Shaw and Henry McKay. In their book titled *Juvenile Delinquency and Urban Areas*, they examined the ecology of delinquency in Chicago and other large urban areas.[13] The ecology of delinquency was concerned with the relationship between neighborhood characteristics and delinquency rates. By dividing the city into specific zones and examining the official records of juveniles in terms of their home locations, data on the delinquent rate by zone were obtained.

Shaw and McKay adopted the concept of concentric urban zones that had been suggested earlier by Ernest Burgess in *The Urban Community*.[14] According to Burgess the pattern of city growth resulted in five concentric zones. Zone I consisted of the central industrial and business district. Zone II was the "zone in transition" since it was in the process of changing from a residential to business/industrial area. (It was often known as a slum area.) Zone III consisted of working-class homes, and Zone IV was strictly residential. The final zone, Zone V, was that area beyond the city limits where commuters live. The zones were not viewed as static but rather as subject to change as the city grew. When more room was needed in a zone its members invaded the zone nearest to it and thus moved outward.

Zones I and II were the least desirable residential areas and also the least expensive in terms of rent. Those persons who lived in Zones I and II were most often the poor, including immigrants and migrants. Segregation occurred throughout the city on the basis of economic status so that there was some degree of homogeneity among persons residing in each zone. Working- and middle-class families would be financially capable of residing in zones situated farther away from the central parts of the city.

Shaw and McKay examined the official records of male delinquents brought before juvenile court, juveniles whose cases had been disposed of by a law enforcement officer without a court appearance, and school truants. In examining the home backgrounds of these youngsters they determined that the distribution of delinquency was related to location of the city's industrial and commercial areas. Analyses of these rates over a period of time indicated that the distribution by zone was relatively constant.

Delinquency rates were highest in those areas of the city in which the poor and the immigrants were concentrated. An array of other social problems, such as truancy, infant mortality, and mental illness, also flourished in Zones I and II. The social pathology found in this study supported an earlier study conducted in Chicago in 1929 and pointed to the environment as an important factor in the etiology of delinquent behavior.

Those areas of the city with high rates of delinquency were distinguished from the low-rate areas in terms of population characteristics as well as physical and economic conditions. These obvious differences, however, do not in themselves serve to explain the high rates of juvenile misconduct in certain areas of the city. Shaw and McKay suggested that other, less obvious characteristics, such as "differences in values, standards, attitudes, traditions, and institutions," must also be examined.[15]

Residents of high- and low-delinquency areas were found to have different moral and social values. Those neighborhoods with low rates of juvenile offenses tended to be supportive of conventional values. For example, there was a consistency and uniformity of attitudes and beliefs about how children should be cared for and the importance of conformity to the law. In contrast, high-delinquency areas were found to harbor a variety of moral values that were often competing and conflicting. The values of different groups within the area ranged from strictly conventional to overtly criminal. Illegal economic activity often appeared as a viable means of financial gain and prestige.

In low-delinquency areas there were often no deviant role models. The child growing up in a high-delinquency area was exposed to conventional models such as the family or church but also was exposed to adult criminal gangs and illegal rackets. The contradictions in both values and actions appeared to create difficulties for the juvenile faced with choosing appropriate behaviors. Neighborhood access to criminal opportunities enhanced the possibility of delinquent acts since specific techniques such as "jackrolling" (robbing drunks) and shoplifting could be easily learned, and knowledge of activities like fencing operations was widespread.

Neighborhood organizations and institutions in low-delinquency areas served to reinforce constructive values. Women's clubs, service clubs, churches, neighborhood centers, and parent-teacher associations all contributed to control of juvenile behavior. In the high-delinquency neighborhoods the organizations that existed tended to be nonindigenous and therefore much less effective. Organizations staffed by "outsiders" tended to lack community support. In addition, because many people living in these areas saw themselves as transients their concern with neighborhood activities was minimal. The power of the family as a controlling force in the behavior of the young was greatly diminished in the high-delinquency neighborhoods. Family members might provide both conventional and deviant role models so the juvenile would be exposed to illegal activities in the home as well as in the greater community. The opposition to criminality maintained by one's parents was often neutralized by the fact that at least some family members profited from illegal activities.

Attachment to peers also served to weaken parental control. Loyalty to members of one's delinquent group was strong. Parental attitudes and values were typically those of persons with an "old-world" perspective. Their children became "Americanized" much more rapidly and often saw their parents' values as old-fashioned, outmoded, or inappropriate to the new environment. Peers offered knowledge of a new society and a means whereby children could become assimilated into a subculture, albeit a delinquent one, composed of their contemporaries.

The problems confronting these families were often new and challenging ones for which their previous culture had no solutions. Whereas leisure time had not been a problem in societies in which work responsibilities began at an early age, urban life in America provided an abundance of free time. As a result, many youngsters turned to their peers, who offered diversion and initiation into new activities.

Rates of delinquency by area of the city were found to be consistent over a period of time. One could hypothesize that delinquency flourished because it was an adaptive response to the conditions of one's environment. Shaw and McKay noted that in addition to this a process took place that served to transmit the delinquent tradition. Youngsters were exposed to other juveniles in their neighborhoods who were skilled in delinquent techniques. New boys were initiated into these pursuits and would eventually initiate others. The records of the juvenile court showed patterns of older boys who were involved in delinquent acts with younger boys; these boys would in turn become involved with even younger boys. The consistency of rates and types of delinquency over time could then be explained as resulting from a transmission of acts, values, and attitudes from one generation to the next.

Shaw and McKay viewed the causes of delinquent behavior as a complex combination of social and economic conditions. Illegal activities enabled the poor to attain the goods valued by society when other, legitimate means were unavailable. The fact that delinquency flourished in those urban areas that had the greatest amount of poverty, conflicting value systems, and social disorganization was well established by their research, not only in Chicago but in many other urban areas as well.

Differential Association

Shaw and McKay noted that the transmission of a delinquent set of values, attitudes, and actions occurred from generation to generation in the slum areas of cities. This served to explain the stability of delinquency rates over time in the central urban zones. In 1939 Edwin Sutherland formulated a more elaborate explanation of this process, which became known as a theory of "differential association."[16]

The nine statements of the theory as presented in the 1947 edition of *Principles of Criminology* are as follows:

1. Criminal behavior is learned.
2. Criminal behavior is learned in interaction with other persons in a process of communication.
3. The principle [*sic*] part of the learning of criminal behavior occurs within intimate personal groups.
4. When criminal behavior is learned, the learning includes (a) techniques of committing the crime, which are sometimes very complicated, sometimes very simple, (b) the specific direction of motives, drives, rationalizations, and attitudes.
5. The specific direction of motives and drives is learned from definitions of the legal codes as favorable or unfavorable.
6. A person becomes delinquent because of an excess of definitions favorable to violation of law over definitions unfavorable to violation of law.
7. Differential associations may vary in frequency, duration, priority, and intensity.
8. The process of learning criminal behavior by association with criminal and anticriminal patterns involves all of the mechanisms that are involved in other learning.
9. While criminal behavior is an explanation of general needs and values, it is not explained by those general needs and values since noncriminal behavior is an explanation of the same needs and values.[17]

According to Sutherland, all behavior was learned, whether deviant or nondeviant. Through a process of interaction with other persons, criminal values or actions were communicated. Most of this communication occurred within "intimate personal groups," so one could anticipate that family members or close associates might have a great impact on the origin of deviant behaviors. One not only learned actual techniques for committing crimes but also how to rationalize the behavior. In neighborhoods and environments where there is an "excess of definitions favorable to violation of law over definitions unfavorable to violation of law," deviant behavior was most likely to result.

Thus delinquent acts and nondelinquent acts coexisted in the same area of a city because some youngsters were exposed to an excess of pro-delinquent values and actions whereas others had role models (parents or friends) who presented them with nondelinquent values. The process of differential association would also explain the high rates of delinquency consistently found in some areas of a city and the longevity of the subcultures later described by Cohen and Miller.

Criticisms of Social Disorganization and Differential Association

Thrasher and Shaw and McKay relied on official records of delinquent acts in formulating their theories of the causes of delinquency. Differential law enforcement practices may have had a major role in defining the children of the poor and immigrants as official delinquents and in shielding children from privileged backgrounds from arrest.[18] Thus the social class and ecological distribution of urban delinquency may be a reflection of police and social agency policies.

Another point that must be emphasized is that a lack of traditional, or middle-class, social organization in a neighborhood does not necessarily produce a state of "social disorganization." In fact, as Matza points out, *the social organization* of deviant life is actually described in these works.[19]

A question that is left unanswered by these theories is, why do some children in these areas avoid delinquent involvements? A lack of parental control over juvenile behavior is thought to be the precipitating factor in delinquent involvement, but it is unclear why some of these children *do not* become delinquent. If social disorganization and parental inadequacy cause deviance, then what factors prevent or counteract it? Why do some children conform whereas others do not?

Sutherland's theory of differential association provides a possible answer to this question. By noting the role of an excess of definitions favorable to delinquency in the etiology of deviant behavior, Sutherland suggests that those children who avoid delinquency have an excess of definitions *unfavorable* to delinquency. Thus factors in one's social milieu may insulate the child from deviance.

The theory of differential association is not without its critics. One of the major flaws of the theory is the difficulty of testing it empirically. The nine statements are difficult to operationalize. One attempt to test the influence of differential association on delinquent behavior found less than conclusive results for the theory.[20]

Treatment Implications

The Chicago Area Project begun in 1932 was an attempt to utilize the ideas about the causes of delinquency that Shaw and McKay outlined in *Juvenile*

Delinquency and Urban Areas.[21] The project was designed to work with delinquent and predelinquent youngsters in the "delinquency areas" of the city. The theoretical basis of the project was essentially what we have described above as *social disorganization and cultural transmission*. Young people growing up in these high-delinquency areas were subject to less control over their behavior due to a breakdown in the sources of such control, especially the family. Thus delinquent behavior was to some extent unopposed. These children also were exposed to criminal role models that encouraged the learning of deviant values and techniques.

With this as its theoretical base, the Chicago Area Project undertook to set up neighborhood organizations designed to strengthen controls over the behavior and to provide opportunities for juvenile exposure to appropriate adult role models. The neighborhood organizations for youth welfare were composed of indigenous persons who were encouraged to take active leadership roles in the community groups. Resident involvement and responsibility was a major characteristic of the program, since the goal was to enlist the efforts of the neighborhood population in improving the organization of their communities.

These neighborhood organizations included three elements. First, recreational programs, operated by resident volunteers, were made available to children in the area. Second, campaigns for overall community improvement, such as better law enforcement services and schools, were undertaken. And third, assistance was made available to the police and juvenile court in providing supervision for delinquent youth. Work with incarcerated juveniles and adult parolees was also undertaken and included efforts to help these people in problems of community reintegration.

Kobrin analyzed the impact of the Chicago Area Project after twenty-five years of operation. He concluded that perhaps the most significant aspect of the project was that it encouraged actual residents of the neighborhoods, rather than outsiders, to take active leadership roles in the delinquency prevention programs.[22] Unfortunately, there is no information in his evaluation about the reduction of delinquency rates in the problem areas, so it is not clear whether these neighborhood organizations were effective in decreasing deviant juvenile behavior.

The Chicago Area Project provides a good example of the types of steps one would take to prevent and treat delinquency if the ideas of Thrasher, Shaw and McKay, and Sutherland were utilized. Community organization and mechanisms of social control must be encouraged and children must be given increased exposure to appropriate role models and values.

Delinquency and Opportunity Structures

The influence of social structure on deviant behavior has been examined by many theorists. One of the first theories of deviance was outlined by Emile Durkheim in his description of the social phenomenon of *anomie*.[23] Anomie is the term Durkheim used to describe the state of society when old forms of order have broken down and a state of lawlessness, or normlessness, exists.

Durkheim saw the solidarity, or cohesion, of the social order as determining a society's legal and moral value systems. A primitive society with homogeneous members was held together by *mechanical solidarity*. Mechanical solidarity resulted in repressive laws, which punished societal members for acts that were seen as harmful to society as a whole. As society became more complex, and its members became more heterogeneous and numerous, mechanical solidarity no longer worked. As a result, another type of solidarity, known as *organic solidarity*, emerged. Unlike mechanical solidarity, which is based on similarities, organic solidarity is a form of cohesion based on differences. The division of labor within a society served to increase the strength of organic solidarity since specialization of tasks necessitated interdependence among its members. For example, a farmer became dependent on owners of markets to sell his goods. This organic solidarity resulted in laws that were restitutive; that is, laws that govern the interrelationships among members of society, such as civil and commercial law. Organic solidarity was often not as strong as mechanical solidarity because diversity and heterogeneity of populations made it more difficult to develop. Economic crises and social change can upset organic solidarity and there may be a sense of isolation among people who live in a highly differentiated social order. The outcome of such problems would be a state of anomie, which leads to an erosion of conforming behavior and an increase in deviant behavior, such as suicide or crime.

In addition to the concept of anomie, Durkheim noted that crime or deviance is a normal occurrence in society. Although anomie results from problems in social solidarity, there will always be some deviance in a society. Durkheim saw this as functional for society since deviance indicated flexibility and the possibility of social change. Deviance may also serve to strengthen the collective conscience of society by reinforcing its value systems. The deviant may provide an opportunity for people to reaffirm their shared definition of appropriate behavior.[24]

Social Structure and Deviance

Robert K. Merton expanded on Durkheim's ideas of deviance and focused attention on the role of social structure in the etiology of deviance.[25] Society communicated *goals* that its members were to attempt to obtain. For example, people in the United States were taught to strive for material possessions, which were considered indicators of success. A new car, a color television set, and a home in the suburbs are all examples of the material goals one might be expected to attain. At the same time, society communicated appropriate *means* of attaining these goals. Hard work, responsibility, and long-term planning were the socially acceptable means of acquiring goods, yet there was no guarantee that those who worked hard and planned ahead would succeed financially, particularly if their salaries were modest or their dependents numerous. Obviously access to scarce and valued resources was not distributed equally throughout the social structure. There were times when efforts that once resulted in success no longer worked, such as during an economic depression. It was this disparity between means and goals that resulted in strain and frustration for some members of society. Strain could not only weaken one's commitment to the dominant social order but also to those means of success that were considered acceptable. It could also cause the goals of society to be questioned. This weakening process resulted in the state of anomie, or normlessness, described above.

Deviant behavior then was a possible adaptation to the disjuncture between goals and institutionalized means. By considering one's acceptance or rejection of these goals and means, typical modes of adaptation could be delineated. Merton's modes of adaptation are described in the following chart.[26]

		CULTURE GOALS	INSTITUTIONALIZED MEANS
I.	Conformity	+	+
II.	Innovation	+	−
III.	Ritualism	−	+
IV.	Retreatism	−	−
V.	Rebellion	±	±

Conformity is exemplified by those persons in society who accept the cultural goals and institutionalized means. All of the other adaptations involve some type of deviant behavior. The innovator looks for alternative ways of attaining cultural goals and might include criminal offenders such as organized crime members, pimps, or delinquents who steal items and "fence" them. The ritualists would be those persons who become primarily involved in the means but who lose sight of the ultimate goal in the process. For example, the person who attends church regularly but has no clear concept of its purpose, other than that it is socially acceptable, would fit into this category. The retreatist would be in a sense a double failure, for here we would find those persons who have attempted to succeed using both legitimate and illegitimate means, and have failed at both. This method of adaptation involves rejecting both the means and the goals of society. Drug addicts and skid-row drunks would be examples of retreatists. The last category, rebellion, involves a rejection of current means and goals and attempts to replace them with new ones. Instead of adapting to the social order, the rebel would make an active attempt to change it.

For our purposes the most significant modes of adaptation are those of innovation and retreatism. The social position of some groups serves to block their access to legitimate means of goal attainment. Lack of cultural sophistication or educational achievement by minority-group members precludes opportunities to find employment that offers high remuneration. At the same time, all members of the social order are pressured to achieve financial success. Thus high rates of crime in poverty areas should be expected since it is these people who have the least access to legitimate means of success. The retreatist may be the youngster who owing to lack of skill or socialization is not able to succeed in criminal behavior. A retreat to a different value system, such as the subculture of the heroin addict, may appear the only avenue left open.

Opportunity Theory

The concepts of anomie and structural strain were explored further by Cloward and Ohlin in their book, *Delinquency and Opportunity*.[27] They focused their attention on the delinquent behavior found in lower-class urban neighborhoods. Their explanation of juvenile misconduct focused on the lack of access to legitimate avenues of success for the poor. Since opportunities for legitimate success were greatly limited, juveniles from the lower class tended to engage in delinquent behavior as a means of obtaining status, prestige, or wealth.

Cloward and Ohlin emphasized the disparity between the goals of American society and the delinquent's access to legitimate means of attaining these goals. Industrial societies defined success goals as accessible to everyone, so that motivation for success was widespread. In reality, the access to means of attaining the goals was narrow for some. The cultural and structural barriers that existed in our society were much more prevalent among the poor. Thus a lower-class adolescent might look forward to moving up the social ladder, only to find that his ignorance of middle-class manners and values and his lack of educational achievement serve to erect barriers that are virtually insurmountable. This discrepancy between one's aspirations and the opportunities available to actualize them could lead to a search for alternative responses. Since deviant responses could result in some form of success, delinquency became the means of coping with pressure to achieve.

Cloward and Ohlin noted that delinquents had been taught to hope and to see themselves as competent, but did not succeed.

> It is our impression that a sense of being unjustly deprived of access to opportunities to which one is entitled is common among those who become participants in delinquent subcultures. Delinquents tend to be persons who have been led to expect opportunities because of their potential ability to meet the formal, institutionally established criteria of evaluation. Their sense of injustice arises from the failure of the system to fulfill these expectations.[28]

Surely a feeling of such injustice could account for much hostility and opposition to conventional values. Success and status among one's peers were possible, though, and the delinquent gang became a collective problem-solving technique for these youngsters.

Delinquent subcultures persisted because they became a viable means of adaptation to limited opportunities. Over time new members were recruited and neighborhood structures remained conducive to deviant behavior. Only through major community change aimed at providing access to legitimate opportunity could delinquent acts be decreased.

Criticisms of Anomie and Opportunity Theories

Merton's theory of anomie provides a good framework for considering the role of social structure in the etiology of deviance. It is not exhaustive, however, because it fails to take into account forms of deviance that occur among people who *do* have access to legitimate means but choose illegitimate means anyway. An example of this would be middle-class delinquency.

Another problem with both theories is that neither takes into account non-utilitarian acts. Delinquency is treated only as a means to an end—namely, wealth or prestige. Might a youngster break out the windows of an abandoned house simply because it's fun? Might a juvenile turn to violence as a result of boredom?

Treatment Implications

A lack of access to legitimate opportunities for attaining the goals of society is the key concept of these theories of deviance and delinquency. A community prevention program based on this idea was implemented in the early 1960s. A survey of residents of the lower East Side of New York City placed teenage behavior high on the list of problems in their neighborhood. This finding led to the implementation of a demonstration project known as Mobilization for Youth.

The goal of the project was to decrease delinquency by providing those resources necessary for conformity.[29] Mobilization included four major areas: education, work, individual and family services, and community organization. By increasing access to job opportunities through education and training and by providing mechanisms for resident involvement in community improvement and activism, social and psychological resources would become available to neighborhood residents and conformity would be encouraged.

Some of the same techniques employed in the Chicago Area Project were utilized in the New York project. Indigenous organizers and employees ran many of the mobilization services. Once again, an attempt was made for organization to come from within the community itself. The emphasis on self-government and action-oriented strategies created opposition from some factions in the city, particularly from those who were already in positions of leadership in existing neighborhood organizations. These people felt that the projects should be placed under their control, which would have served to perpetuate middle-class dominance of the community. Lower-class residents would have been discouraged from participation. The activation of minority groups was not accepted by other factions in the city and intensive investigations of mobilization resulted from external allegations and criticisms.[30]

The community organization portion of Mobilization also included projects specifically designed to deal with the delinquent and the predelinquent. A detached worker project was developed in order to redirect group energies toward constructive activities for juveniles, such as competitive sports. An Adventure Corps for 9 to 13-year-olds provided recreational activities that would compete with the attractiveness of delinquency.

Individual and family services programs provided referral to public-assistance agencies and mental-health professionals. Family counseling was also included, as were efforts to reintegrate released juvenile offenders. The issue of a client's "right to public services" was emphasized and programs to teach the skills necessary to realize these rights were implemented.[31]

Educational opportunities were enhanced through projects aimed at making educational institutions more responsive to the community they served. This included enhanced parent-school relations, preschool and guidance opportunities, and additional teacher training. The special educational problems of many of the youngsters necessitated curriculum development and teaching skills geared toward remedial and enriched learning.

Work opportunities were increased through a variety of techniques. Job training and extensive vocational counseling were used to increase the employability of the young. Aggressive placement and efforts to make young people aware of existing opportunities were conducted. An Urban Youth Services Corps for young people 16 to 21 years old was organized and provided jobs on neighborhood-improvement projects, such as the construction of playgrounds.

Mobilization was an attempt to organize community members and to develop self-help skills among the poor. It was also an attempt to provide opportunity structures for people who had little access to them and thereby to encourage conformity to legitimate means of achievement.

A comprehensive and expensive program, Mobilization had a large impact on the lower East Side as far as providing new opportunities for the poor and encouraging social change. As for delinquency rates, however, significant decreases in official juvenile misconduct during the period between 1962 and 1966 were not apparent. Although there was a slight decrease in delinquency rates in the mobilization area, it was not large enough to conclude that the project was particularly successful in delinquency prevention.[32]

Subcultures and Deviance

The importance of "subcultures" in the etiology of delinquent behavior was explored by Albert Cohen in his work, *Delinquent Boys*.[33] Cohen defined subculture as "cultures within cultures" that exist throughout society. These subgroups include specific "ways of thinking and doing that are in some respects peculiarly [their] own."[34] The role of a delinquent subculture in juvenile offense patterns would then be one of encouragement; children exposed to delinquent subcultures would learn values, norms, and behaviors that were conducive to delinquent acts.

Cohen noted that delinquency was not exclusively a working-class or lower-class phenomenon but in fact was found among adolescents at all levels of society. The gang-affiliated delinquent was found primarily in the lower class and appeared to be the most serious and frequent offender. Thus offenders of this type and the subcultures to which they belong must be examined.

Role of Subcultures

How do subcultures evolve? Cohen suggested that people who interact with each other frequently and who have shared problems may develop group solutions which take the form of subcultures. The shared problems of working-class youth were primarily ones of status and success. The youngster from a lower-socioeconomic background was measured by a "middle-class measuring rod." Although some of these children managed to do well in the measuring process, the majority did not.

Differences in socialization practices in middle- and lower-class families served to prepare the middle-class child for success in school and the lower-class child for minimal success or failure. Since educational achievement was an important tool for moving upward in society, the child who did not succeed in school knew that legitimate avenues to success would not be readily available.

Cohen described the school as a middle-class institution where the manners, dress, and demeanor of a child are important in the teacher's evaluation and response to him. The youngster from a middle-class home was more likely to have received close parental supervision. In addition, these youngsters had been exposed to "educational" books and toys and had been taught the value of neatness and punctuality. Love-oriented punishment techniques were also more likely to have been employed, thus strengthening the child's attachment to the parent.

Cohen's description of lower-class socialization practices was quite different from those of the middle class. An easygoing approach and a lesser degree of parental control characterized the lower-class child's family. Skills, values, and motivation for learning were not as heavily emphasized. The reliance on physical punishment was thought to encourage less emotional dependency on the parent than the middle-class use of love-oriented techniques, and as a result peer relationships were more important to these children. The working-class child-rearing practices did not teach the values, behavior, and skills necessary for success in school.

Role of Middle-Class Values

The values and success criteria of the middle class might not be important to the youngsters themselves, but as Cohen noted, these ". . . are the norms of people who *run things* in politics, religion, and education."[35] An inability to realize the values of the middle class was manifested in a loss of a sense of self-worth by the child. This was not the only response available, however, for one may reject these values and follow a different set. This is what Cohen described as happening among lower-class boys. Through a process of "reaction formation," the youngsters rejected the middle-class values and adopted completely opposite ones. For example, the respect of the middle class for property and its concern for material possessions were replaced by respect for vandalism and stealing. To attain status with one's peers in the delinquent subculture, the adolescent engaged in what Cohen described as nonutilitarian acts, which are malicious and negativistic. Thus delinquent behavior evolved as an alternative means of attaining status in a middle-class world, and ultimately subcultural support for this solution developed in lower-class neighborhoods.

A delinquent adaptation is not the only one that was found under these circumstances. Cohen referred to the stable corner-boy and the college boy as alternative roles. The college boy adopted middle-class values and elected to play the status game by middle-class rules. This made it difficult for him to continue associations with other boys in his neighborhood. Cohen assumed that this type of adaptation was very difficult for lower-class youth and thus was rare. The stable corner-boy response involved an acceptance of one's community and a degree of withdrawal from middle-class institutions. Cohen suggested that this was the most frequent mode of behavior among these juveniles. It allowed acceptance by the adults in one's environment, did not produce anger among middle-class adults, and did not entirely close off opportunities for upward mobility.

The delinquent response provided youngsters with an alternative means of attaining status and an outlet for their hostility. Instead of perceiving themselves as a failure by middle-class standards, they could evaluate themselves as successful in terms of their own values and those of their peers.

Why do some young people choose this path whereas others do not? Cohen answered this question by emphasizing the role of reference groups and models. Delinquency was legitimated and approved in some subgroups of society. Those children who were exposed to delinquency among others or who grew up in an area with an already-existing delinquent subculture easily adopted delinquent behavior. The social chemistry of the gang served to reinforce the values of these juveniles and in some instances functioned as a "sort of catalyst which releases potentialities not otherwise visible."[36]

The influence of middle-class values and measures of success was given an important position in all of the theories examined thus far. Thrasher and

Shaw and McKay pointed to the problems of immigrant families in socializing their children and the lack of controls found in their neighborhoods. Children from these backgrounds coveted the affluence enjoyed by the middle class but learned illegal techniques for acquiring the desired possessions or services. The strongest statement on the role of middle-class values in the etiology of delinquent behavior was proposed by Albert Cohen. The reaction formation *against* these values that occurred among working- or lower-class youngsters resulted in delinquent behavior. Values and actions which were in direct opposition to the traditional middle-class ones but were conducive to delinquency developed since these children realized they could never attain success by middle-class standards. Cloward and Ohlin reiterated the theme of middle-class values by pointing to the lack of legitimate opportunities available to children of the poor. The disparity between motivations to succeed and avenues that one might legitimately take to attain this goal resulted in the adoption of alternative means of achievement.

In all of these theories we see the role of middle-class standards. They encourage achievement or upward social mobility, even among those persons who occupy the lowest position in the social hierarchy. Motivation is discouraged by limited opportunities or is channeled into avenues of success that are illegal. Delinquency then is a response to value systems held most strongly by persons outside of one's own group.

Miller's Focal Concerns

Walter Miller proposed an analysis of lower-class delinquency that differed from other explanations. Miller viewed the lower-class culture itself as the generating force behind juvenile offenses.[37] Rejecting the ideas of other writers, who had described lower-class values as "middle class standards 'turned upside down,'"[38] Miller emphasized the context of lower-class culture as the major determinant of juvenile behavior.

Miller noted that the cultural milieu in which a juvenile lives exerts the primary influence on behavior. The culture of the lower class evolved on its own and has a long-established set of patterns, traditions, and "focal concerns." Focal concerns are found in all cultural groups and represent issues and areas of life that are important to the members of the group. According to Miller, the focal concerns of the lower class were such that delinquent behavior was encouraged by them.

Trouble was a focal concern in this culture, both in terms of getting into it and staying out of it. A desire to avoid illegal acts was often based less on moral beliefs than on a wish to avoid the complications it would create, such as arrest. Although getting into trouble created difficulties and lowered one's status within the social group, it also served as a means of obtaining status with others, such as a gang. Trouble was a means to other focal concerns such as excitement. An individual's trouble potential was a major criterion used to gauge his or her position in the culture whereas in middle-class neighborhoods, symbols of achievement would be a major concern.

Toughness indicated a concern for overtly masculine behavior by males in the culture. The stereotypic male sex role, which characterized men as physically strong, fearless, and aggressive, exemplified the idea of being "tough." Miller suggested that the female-centered, or matriarchal, households found in these areas made the adoption of sex roles more difficult for male children. The importance of masculinity in the lower class was perhaps a reaction-formation against appearing feminine.

Smartness was a concern involving the ability to be clever, which usually meant being able to outsmart or "con" others. Miller described this as a "capacity to achieve a valued entity—material goods, personal status—through a maximum use of mental agility and a minimum use of physical effort."[39] Smartness in the sense of traditional definitions of the term (achievement in school, specialized knowledge, or appreciation of the arts) was not valued because it was related to effeminacy. The lower-class child who is "street wise," for example, was highly valued and respected.

The daily boredom of life resulted in an active seeking out of *excitement*. In lower-class cultures, excitement involved widespread use of alcohol and gambling. Making the rounds of local bars, attempting to "pick up" women, and engaging in fights constituted a major part of one's activities. Excitement, thrills, and a flirtation with danger temporarily replaced other, relatively passive activities such as "hanging out" on a street corner.

The concept of *fate* was related to several of the other focal concerns. There was a belief in fate as the controlling force in life, and one's efforts toward achieving goals were often seen as futile. Since there was a strong belief that people were either lucky, unlucky, or without control over their lives, gambling became a legitimate means of obtaining financial reward. Smartness and toughness may be needed to develop gambling skills and provide excitement. In playing the numbers, fate determines the outcome.

The focal concern of *autonomy* must be considered on two levels—the overt evaluation of freedom and that state which is covertly sought. There might be much verbalization of resentment of authority and external controls, such as, "No one's gonna push me around."[40] However, authority and nurturance were also related so that being strictly controlled is seen as being cared for.

> Many lower class people appear to seek out highly restrictive social environments wherein stringent external controls are maintained over their behavior. Such institutions as the armed forces, the mental hospital, the disciplinary school, the prison or correctional institution, provide environments which incorporate a strict and detailed set of rules, defining and limiting behavior.[41]

Although there might be much complaining about the restrictions of the environment, Miller pointed out that the behavior exhibited after release often assured recommitment. The discrepancy between that which was overtly desired and that which was covertly desired was directly related to a desire for nurturance.

The motivation of the delinquent was directly related to the focal concerns of the culture. Juveniles desired a sense of belonging (which a same-sex peer group or gang provided), status, or a feeling of importance. Being tough or smart allowed the juvenile to affirm his or her membership in the group and to attain status by acting "adult." Adult activities or interests as outlined in the focal concerns served to encourage behaviors that may ultimately be labeled delinquent. Gang fights, sexual experimentation, gambling, or any other quest for excitement provided entertainment and an enhanced reputation with one's peers.

Lower-class culture was the dominant factor in the delinquent's career. Instead of striking out at a predominantly middle-class social order, delinquents were responding to the cultural milieu of their daily lives. Lower-class culture existed with "an integrity of its own,"[42] and through conformity to it juveniles became involved in delinquency.

Criticisms of Subcultural Theories

Cohen and Miller explain the origin of the value systems of the lower-class in different ways, but both agree on the central role of cultural values in the etiology of delinquent behavior. The lower- or working-class youngster is presented with solutions to problems of status, prestige, and financial success that are often illegal or at least conducive to delinquency. These "solutions" have developed in response to the social situation and have been transmitted from generation to generation.

This explanation of delinquency is more applicable to lower-class delinquency than to middle-class deviance. If different values cause juvenile misconduct then middle-class children, with their middle class values, should be immune to such illegal acts. We know this is not the case from self-report studies of delinquency.

Another criticism of subcultural theories is that values among juveniles may not differ to the extent that Cohen and Miller suggest. A study of delinquent attitudes indicated that the delinquent does not evaluate middle-class values negatively. Delinquents and nondelinquents, lower-class boys and middle-class boys, and blacks and whites all considered working hard for good grades as beneficial.[43] If we assume that value differences are not as pronounced as the subcultural theorists contend, then other factors must be considered in order to explain the higher rates of delinquency in lower-class urban areas.

Treatment Implications

The subcultural theories indicate several methods of implementing prevention and treatment programs in high-delinquency neighborhoods. One area that would need change is the social environment. This would involve setting up programs for both adults and children that would facilitate upward mobility in the social structure. The Chicago Area Project and the Mobilization for Youth project are both examples of this approach. In effect, the aim is to reorganize communities from within and to provide constructive activities and adult role models for children who live in these areas. Opportunities in education are enhanced through remedial programs and opportunities in employment are created through vocational training and job counseling.

Another implication of the subcultural theories is that delinquent behavior must be redirected into acceptable channels. The gang offers enjoyment, prestige, and a sense of belonging; perhaps the gang itself can be redirected and its members encouraged to pursue alternative activities. The Midcity Project conducted in Boston from 1954 to 1957 was designed to effect such a change in delinquent gangs.[44]

Each gang was assigned a detached worker who developed a relationship with the gang members in order to help them modify their behavior. At the end of the project, the gang worker's role was terminated. The behavior modification phase of the project played the most important role in decreasing delinquent behavior. Attempts were made to organize the informal street gang into a more formal group—say, a club or an athletic team. Club meetings, athletic contests, dances, and fund-raising dinners were held in order to provide experience in a "rule-governed" atmosphere and to reward harmonious relations within and outside of the group. Workers also served as role models for the juveniles by presenting "law-abiding, middle-class-oriented adults" who supported a particular value system. Unfortunately efforts to measure the impact of the project on behavior did not reveal significant results from the project. The Midcity Project provides an example of the type of approach subcultural theories suggest in decreasing delinquency, but it may be that the appeal of the subculture overwhelms the effects of such a project.

Another suggestion for dealing with the effects of subcultural value systems was suggested by Wolfgang and Ferracuti in *The Subculture of Violence*.[45] They propose an assimilation of the subculture into the greater social structure. Isolation and residential segregation serve to strengthen subcultures since little interaction occurs with persons on the outside. By decreasing this isolation, alternative behaviors and values may become apparent and ultimately the subculture will break down.

If this technique were applied to the working-class subculture, programs of relocation would be necessary. Low-income housing projects located in primarily middle-class areas would be needed in order to expose these children to different cultural norms. Of course there is the possibility that these

people will not be integrated into the community and will continue their isolation, but residential segregation may be overcome by such efforts.

Control Theory

Most studies of delinquent behavior focus on the question, "Why do they do
it?" Travis Hirschi, in his control theory, proposed a different approach.[46]
Instead of emphasizing the characteristics of delinquent youngsters, Hirschi
examined the forces that serve to prevent certain youngsters from turning to
delinquency. Thus the question he asked was, "Why *don't* they do it?" This
perspective led to an examination of the controls exerted on behavior that
served to inhibit or prevent delinquent acts.

Control theory is based on the assumption that delinquency occurs when
the bond between the individual and society is weakened. It should be remembered that one of the major elements of this bond is *attachment,* which
Hirschi defined as concern for the wishes and expectations of others. This
corresponds to the idea that internalized social norms result in conformity.
The norms and values in a society are shared by members of that social order.
If one cared about the reactions of those people, then there would be good
reason to follow the norms. If one was *not* concerned about the opinions of
others, deviation might occur since in effect there would be no boundaries.

The second major part of the bond was *commitment.* Hirschi pointed out
that most people have interests or a stake in society that would somehow be
endangered by deviance. A possible prison term or arrest record has tremen-
dous negative implications for those who are committed to conventional values and activities. If such commitment was weak, then the price one pays for
delinquency may appear substantially smaller since there is less to lose.

Another aspect of one's bond to the social order was *involvement.* The
person who is very active in conventional activities not only has little desire
to risk public censure but also has less time to become involved in illegal
acts. Many community efforts to provide recreational programs for juveniles
are based on this idea since busy youngsters will have fewer opportunities
and certainly less time for delinquency.

The final aspect of the bond was *belief.* Many theories of delinquency have
pointed to value systems as the cause of deviance. Lower-class focal concerns
are thought to actually encourage illegal behavior.[47] Other writers have suggested that the delinquent rationalizes away guilt feelings and can thus be
free to break those rules in which he believes.[48] Hirschi proposed a third
alternative to the issue of delinquent values. Instead of different value systems
or techniques for removing guilt, the delinquent has a weaker belief in the
"moral validity of norms."[49] A person may accept the values of the conventional order as "good" and "correct" yet still refuse to see how they
apply to his or her own behavior.

In order to test the assumptions of control theory, Hirschi gathered data from a large sample of male junior and senior high-school students in California. A questionnaire was administered and school and police records were obtained. Delinquent activity was measured through the use of a self-report scale and police data.

The social distribution of the sample when examined in relation to delinquent acts indicated that differences in delinquent involvement by social class were minimal. The use of self-report techniques by other researchers has resulted in a much smaller difference in delinquent acts than is found in official records, and Hirschi's findings underscore this. When delinquent behavior in racial groups was examined, higher rates of offenses among black juveniles was indicated. The discrepancy by racial grouping is not very large, certainly not as large as that found in the police data.

Control theory assumed that *attachment* to others in society will decrease the possibility of deviant acts. The relationship between parent (who is either conventional or unconventional according to Hirschi) and child was strongly related to delinquency. Personal communication and strong emotional identification with the parent were associated with low delinquency. When those juveniles with delinquent friends were considered, the attachment to the parent remained an important factor in behavior. The child with delinquent associates and friends was less likely to commit deviant acts if attached to the parent.

Attachment to school was also found to be greatest among the nondelinquent and low-delinquency subjects. Those children who enjoyed and were successful in school avoided delinquency. Students who were unsuccessful academically and disliked school were more often involved in illegal behavior. Hirschi presents data that support the causal chain shown in Figure 2-1. The relationship between poor performance in school and delinquency has been explored by many researchers.[50] Hirschi's data served to underscore the importance of success in school. Because school consumes such a large portion of the child's day and is a primary means of attaining status, failure or low performance in school removes some of the control over one's behavior. Lack of attachment to school was also found to be characteristic of subjects who had weak affectional ties to parents, suggesting that lack of attachment may be transferred from one area of the juvenile's life to another.

Peer influence was also examined to detect the effect of attachment to friends who were delinquent. The greater the attachment to one's peers, the

Figure 2-1. Hypothetical causal chain of delinquency.

less the child engaged in delinquent behavior. Although not as strong as attachment to parents, attachment to peers is related to more conventional behavior. Juveniles with low stakes in conformity were more likely to have committed delinquent acts when they had delinquent friends, which suggests that peer influence is a stronger factor with some children than with others.

Commitment to conventional activities was strongest among the low-delinquency subjects. Juveniles with high educational and occupational aspirations tended to conform to socially acceptable standards of behavior. High aspirations and achievement motivation were very uncommon among the delinquents. Actual *involvement* in conventional activities, such as time spent in homework, was related to delinquency, but the effects of involvement appeared to be overstated in the original theory. Perhaps, as Hirschi noted, this problem resulted from the assumption that delinquency requires more time that it actually does.

The final part of the bond, *belief*, was also considered. Research results indicated that youngsters who have committed delinquent acts tend to evaluate middle-class values as highly as do nondelinquents. Surprisingly, 62 percent of those youngsters who had committed delinquent acts did not agree with the statement, ''It is alright to get around the law if you can get away with it.''[51] These juveniles have violated laws which they see as morally valid. Apparently one can believe in laws and values but feel that they have little or no bearing on one's personal behavior.

The parts of the bond are not, however, mutually exclusive. Children who are attached to parents and school and who are committed to conventional activities are least likely to be delinquent regardless of race or social status. Attachment to parents was a strong factor in relation to delinquency, which even overcame the effects of delinquent friends. Commitment to conventional activities affected the degree to which delinquent friends influenced one's behavior. Attachment to parents was also found to be related to positive belief in the legal system and nondelinquency. Delinquents with weak ties believed in conventional values but did not apply them to their own lives.

Control theory and Hirschi's test of it question some of the assumptions that previous theorists drew upon. Social-class differences in values are not pronounced. According to Hirschi's data, lower-class children do not differ in frequency of delinquent acts to the extent that had been suggested. Attachment to parents and commitment to conventional activity serve to insulate some children from peer influence, even when the peers are delinquent.

The attempt to test control theory indicated some weaknesses in the theory. For example, involvement was not as important a factor as had been hypothesized. There was also evidence that the role of companions had been underestimated in the initial theory. The basic concepts of the theory were supported, however, and there is reason to believe that a weakened bond between the individual and society allows deviance to occur more easily.

Criticisms of Control Theory

Hirschi notes that the original theory underestimates the impact of the group process or the influence of companions on behavior. Surely a youngster's peers may serve as a strong situational inducement even for the child who has a strong attachment to parents and school. The influence of immediate situational factors on behavior were considered by Briar and Piliavin, who suggested that

> acts are prompted by short-term situationally induced desires experienced by all boys to obtain valued goods, to portray courage in the presence of, or be loyal to peers, to strike out at someone who is disliked, or simply to 'get kicks'.[52]

They also point out that such acts depend on a variety of contingencies, such as likelihood of detection, attractiveness of the activity, and the ease with which the act can be performed. Peers may not only make a delinquent act appear more attractive but may also facilitate the commission of it. For example, drug use may be encouraged by peers who are knowledgeable about drugs and who also have easy access to them.

Another criticism of control theory is that it does not adequately explain all types of delinquency. Because behaviors like vandalism, "joyriding," or drug use may be enjoyable for most young people, unusual motivations or circumstances are not needed to explain their occurrence. Other types of delinquency, such as armed robbery or gang activities, are not so well treated by control theory.

A final criticism of Hirschi's work concerns the manner in which delinquency was measured. The self-report scale of delinquent acts consisted of the following questions:

1. Have you ever taken little things (worth less than $2) that did not belong to you?
2. Have you ever taken things of some value (between $2 and $50) that did not belong to you?
3. Have you ever taken things of large value (worth over $50) that did not belong to you?
4. Have you ever taken a car for a ride without the owner's permission?
5. Have you ever banged up something that did not belong to you on purpose?
6. Not counting fights you may have had with a brother or sister, have you ever beaten up on anyone or hurt anyone on purpose?[53]

Although these questions measure petty and grand larceny, auto theft, vandalism, and battery, they fail to address the more serious offenses such as rape, burglary, and armed robbery. The measure of self-reported delinquency is then biased in the direction of less serious offenses.

Treatment Implications

Control theory focuses on the role of one's bond to society in inhibiting delinquent behavior, which suggests that attempts to treat delinquents or predelinquents must consider means of strengthening this bond. Since strength of attachment was found to be an important element in the etiology of juvenile misconduct, it is in this area that treatment programs should be concentrated.

Many researchers have explored the family in their attempts to understand delinquency. Hirschi's study emphasizes the importance of affectional ties between the child and parents in inhibiting misconduct. One may then assume that delinquent children have greater problems within the family setting and thus the affectional ties to the parent (or a parent surrogate) must be strengthened if further delinquency is to be prevented.

Although the broken home has frequently been cited as a major contributor to delinquency, there is some evidence that the broken home has differential effects upon children. Studies have placed more emphasis on the association between delinquency and the outward structure of the family than on that between delinquency and the "internal" structure. The effect broken homes have on juvenile behavior may encourage deviance, but other factors, such as whether the family is "psychologically broken," must be considered. Parental marital adjustment, discipline patterns and techniques, and affection toward the child affect the quality of the home environment to a large extent.[54] A positive family environment may lead to greater attachment between parent and child.

Parental discipline has been found to be an important factor in the causation of delinquency. Consistency of punishment and the "fairness" with which it is dispensed are also important. Children who feel they have received "fair" discipline in the home are more likely to conform to conventional norms. Lax and erratic discipline has been found to be more common among the families of delinquents.[55]

Another aspect of the parent-child relationship, patterns of affection, is also related to juvenile delinquency. Cold, rejecting parents are more likely to produce delinquent children. There is also evidence that internalization of parental values is related to affection. The affectionate parent encourages the internalization of values that may insulate the child from delinquency.[56]

Treatment techniques aimed at strengthening attachment between the child and parents, such as family therapy, must then aim at teaching parents new ways of interacting with their children. Consistency and fairness of punishment in an atmosphere of affection may serve to insulate the child from delinquent acts in both broken and unbroken home environments. Of course there are children whose parents are uncooperative or who do not have parents at all. Substitution of a relationship with a parent surrogate, such as a foster parent, detached gang worker, or probation officer, could be attempted in these situations.

Another aspect of attachment, education, could also be included. Educational experiences have been found to be associated with delinquency by many researchers. Remedial programs, specially trained instructors, and parental involvement may all help to break the chain of events leading from educational failure to delinquency. These techniques are very similar to those utilized in the Mobilization for Youth project discussed earlier in this chapter, the main difference being that such programs would be aimed at all children with such problems, not only those in lower-socioeconomic groups.

Hirschi finds a relationship between social status and delinquency that is much smaller than that found in official statistics. The role of social status in official delinquency has long been explained in terms of differences in child-rearing techniques and parent-child relationships. The middle-class parent is warmer to the child and more likely to use loving types of punishment whereas the lower-class parent is more likely to use loud reprimands or physical punishment.[57] There is also evidence that middle-class parents encourage the development of cognitive capacity and verbal skills that will enable their children to do well in school.[58] Thus the child-rearing techniques and interaction patterns between parent and child in lower-socioeconomic groups do not always encourage a strong bond between the child and society. Some middle-class children develop stronger bonds with the social order. Hirschi's findings that the differences between status groups are not as great as once thought to be suggests that parental techniques are not specific to one's social status. There are many parents, regardless of social status, whose children do not succeed in school and who become delinquent. The common factors in these families must be dealt with if we are to prevent and treat delinquency.

Modern Conflict Theory

Major sociological explanations of deviance in general and delinquency in particular are based on an assumption of consensus in society and on a functional interpretation of social structure. Durkheim concentrated on the "normal" aspects of crime and deviance and the functions that such behaviors perform for the social order. Law developed as a regulatory mechanism and also as a statement of value consensus. Sanctions were applied to those who overstepped the boundaries of acceptable actions, providing control over unwanted behavior and a mechanism for reaffirmation of common values by nondeviants.

The theories presented so far in this chapter focus on the role of community organization, opportunity structures, value systems, and socialization differences as causes of delinquency. These causes are viewed as variables that can be changed in order to decrease delinquency. Community reorganization, creation of new opportunities, and resocialization are the types of solutions that are thought to be most effective in overcoming crime-producing forces.

Conflict theorists take a dim view of the idea of consensus.[59] Instead of agreement among society members, they see an ongoing conflict among people over power and resources. The inequality that exists in society, which is most evident in social stratification and social classes, encourages conflict because no group wants to remain on the lower rungs of the status ladder. Law emerges as a means of controlling conflict; it is the instrument of the ruling classes and "prevents the dominated classes from becoming powerful."[60] Law then is not an indicator of consensus but is an indicator of the interests of those in power.

The social-class distribution found in official records is to be expected from the conflict viewpoint. Lower-class youngsters are more likely to be taken into custody and channeled into the juvenile court system because they are members of a politically weak class. The results from self-reported delinquency studies have shown that much juvenile deviance is not detected, especially among middle- and upper-class youngsters. Their positions in the social hierarchy insulate them from official attention. The courts, police, and correctional institutions all control the behavior of the weak in society and do so for the benefit of the powerful.

Criticisms of Conflict Theory

The main criticism of the conflict perspective is that it fails to explain the nondeviant poor or the deviant wealthy. If capitalism breeds crime, then why do some of the poor become delinquent while others who are in very similar circumstances do not? Why do some members of the powerful classes in society commit offenses that cause them to be reprimanded by their own system of social control?

Another problem with conflict theory is that it implies that deviance should be concentrated in countries with capitalistic economic systems. Although it is difficult to compare rates of delinquency cross-nationally due to very poor crime statistics, there is evidence that delinquency is common in communist countries. In fact, recent accounts of juvenile crime in the Soviet Union attest to the seriousness of the problem, with children committing offenses ranging from vandalism to murder.[61]

Treatment Implications

According to conflict theorists, the efforts at treatment that have taken place in the United States have been little more than attempts to further control the poor.[62] In their view, pacification may result from programs that offer "piecemeal reform."[63] Striking out at poverty in a neighborhood through organization agencies or detached gang workers may offer opportunities for some people, but as long as the underlying structure of society remains the same, deviance will persist.

To effectively tackle the problems of crime and delinquency, radical social change is necessary. Conflict theorists see the economic system as the cause of inequality and crime and believe that capitalism is the part of society that must change. Quinney advocates a socialist society in place of the present one, but unfortunately he does not elaborate on what this new society will be like.

> It is not my purpose here to outline a socialist society, including details about law. Rather, the exact nature of the society and its own forms of regulation will be worked out in the struggle of building a socialist society.[64]

Another offshoot of the conflict perspective which calls for less sweeping change is the labeling perspective. The labelists acknowledge the differential selection of juveniles who are officially involved as deviants, or delinquents. They advocate a position of "radical nonintervention" which means that the smallest possible number of juveniles should go through the juvenile justice system. This perspective will be explored in greater detail in the next chapter.

Summary

The sociological theories presented in this chapter have, with the exception of control theory, focused on social status as a key variable in the etiology of delinquent behavior. Early writers explored the slum neighborhood and its lack of traditional organization, and gave the environment of the poor a major role in the origins of deviance. Merton and Cloward and Ohlin pointed to the disparity between the goals set for society members and the means available to attain them, which resulted in a state of anomie. Subcultural theorists emphasized the importance of value systems of the lower class, which functioned to encourage and approve of delinquency. Regardless of the particular focus of any single theory, the social structure and the effects of occupying a position on the lower strata of the hierarchy are seen as primary determinants of deviance. Some form of social change is necessary to mitigate the criminogenic influences found in the lower class. Social change efforts cited here were limited to community reorganization.

Control theory shifted the emphasis away from social class and instead explored the effects of family relationships and the commitment of children to conformity. Although social-class differences in delinquency were not very large according to Hirschi's data, there was a slight relationship between low socioeconomic status and frequency of delinquent acts. Control theory suggested a possible explanation of delinquency that cuts across social status, and served to explain middle- and upper-class delinquency. The importance of the relationship between parent and child and its role in delinquent behavior appeared to be similar throughout the social structure.

Conflict theorists pointed to the role of the basic structure of society in the etiology of crime. The capitalist system and the inequality it engenders create conflict between the social classes of society. To decrease and eventually eliminate crime, the economic system must be changed completely and replaced with one that offers equality to all members of society. They do not share the optimism of the other theorists who suggested reform *within* the existing social order would decrease delinquency.

DISCUSSION QUESTIONS

1. What basic assumptions about social status and juvenile delinquency do most sociological theories share?

2. What are the major shortcomings of the sociological explanations of delinquency?

3. Discuss the similarities between the ideas of Cloward and Ohlin, Albert Cohen, and Walter Miller. What are the common themes?

4. Conflict theory emphasizes causal factors in delinquency that might actually explain the status hierarchy in society. How might conflict theory complement other explanations of delinquency?

5. Hirschi's theory of delinquency should explain upper-, middle-, and lower-class delinquency. What common characteristics are present in the backgrounds of all delinquent children, regardless of social class?

NOTES

1. T. C. N. Gibbens and R. H. Ahrenfeldt, *Cultural Factors in Delinquency* (Philadelphia: Lippincott, 1966).

2. William J. Goode, "The Role of the Family in Industrialization," in Robert F. Winch and Louis W. Goodman, *Selected Studies in Marriage and the Family* (New York: Holt, Rinehart & Winston, 1962), pp. 64–70.

3. William F. Ogborn, "The Changing Functions of the Family," in Winch and Goodman, *Selected Studies,* pp. 58–63.

4. S. N. Eisenstadt, *From Generation to Generation* (New York: Free Press, 1956).

5. Jackson Toby, "Affluence and Adolescent Crime," in the President's Commission on Law Enforcement and Administration of Justice, *Task Force Report: Juvenile Delinquency and Youth Crime* (Washington: Government Printing Office, 1967), pp. 132–144.

6. Ibid., p. 140.

7. Ibid.

8. Ibid.

9. Don C. Gibbons, *Delinquent Behavior* (Engelwood Cliffs, N. J.: Prentice-Hall, 1976), pp. 202–220.

10. Herbert A. Bloch and Gilbert Geis, *Man, Crime, and Society* (New York: Random House, 1970), p. 351.

11. Frederic M. Thrasher, *The Gang* (Chicago: University of Chicago Press, 1936).

12. Ibid., pp. 489–490.

13. Clifford Shaw and Henry D. McKay, *Juvenile Delinquency and Urban Areas* (Chicago: University of Chicago Press, 1942).

14. Ibid., pp. 18–20.

15. Ibid., p. 164.

16. Edwin H. Sutherland, *Principles of Criminology*, 4th ed. (Philadelphia: Lippincott, 1947), pp. 6–7.

17. Ibid., pp. 6–7.

18. Shaw and McKay, *Juvenile Delinquency and Urban Areas*, p. 140.

19. David Matza, *Becoming Deviant* (Engelwood Cliffs, N. J.: Prentice-Hall, 1969), p. 46.

20. Albert Reiss and A. Lewis Rhodes, "An Empirical Test of Differential Association Theory," *Journal of Research in Crime and Delinquency*, no. 1 (January 1964): 12.

21. Solomon Kobrin, "The Chicago Area Project—A 25 Year Assessment," *The Annals of the American Academy of Political and Social Science*, no. 322 (March 1959): 19–29.

22. Ibid., p. 29.

23. Emile Durkheim, *The Division of Labor in Society* (New York: Free Press, 1964).

24. For a detailed example of this process, see Kai Erikson, *Wayward Puritans* (New York: John Wiley, 1966).

25. Robert K. Merton, "Social Structure and Anomie," *American Sociological Review* (October 1938): 672–682.

26. Ibid., p. 676.

27. Richard Cloward and Lloyd Ohlin, *Delinquency and Opportunity* (New York: Free Press, 1960).

28. Ibid., p. 117.

29. George Brager and Francis Purcell, eds., *Community Action Against Poverty* (New Haven, Conn.: College and University Press, 1967), pp. 17–26.

30. Ibid.

31. Richard A. Cloward and Richard Elman, "The Storefront on Stanton Street: Advocacy in the Ghetto," in Brager and Purcell, eds., *Community Action*, pp. 253–279.

32. M. Appleby and H. Heifetz, "Legal Challenges to Formal and Informal Denials of Welfare Rights," in Harold Weissman, ed., *Justice and the Law in the Mobilization for Youth Experience* (New York: Association Press, 1969), pp. 88–105.

33. Albert Cohen, *Delinquent Boys: The Culture of the Gang* (Glencoe, Ill.: Free Press, 1955).

34. Ibid., p. 12.

35. Ibid., p. 86.

36. Ibid., p. 156.

37. Walter Miller, "Lower Class Culture as a Generating Milieu of Gang Delinquency," *Journal of Social Issues,* 14, no. 3 (1958): 5–19.

38. Ibid., p. 19.

39. Ibid., p. 9.

40. Ibid., p. 12.

41. Ibid., pp. 12–13.

42. Ibid., p. 19.

43. Travis Hirschi, *Causes of Delinquency* (Berkeley: University of California Press, 1972).

44. Walter Miller, "The Impact of a 'Total-Community' Delinquency Control Project," *Social Problems,* 10, no. 2 (Fall 1962): 168–191.

45. Marvin Wolfgang and Franco Ferracuti, *The Subculture of Violence* (New York: Tavistock, 1969), p. 299.

46. Hirschi, *Causes of Delinquency.*

47. Miller, "Lower Class Culture," pp. 5–19.

48. Gresham M. Sykes and David Matza, "Techniques of Neutralization: A Theory of Delinquency," *American Journal of Sociology,* 22 (December 1957): 664–670.

49. Hirschi, *Causes of Delinquency,* p. 26.

50. See for example: Marvin Wolfgang et al., *Delinquency in a Birth Cohort* (Chicago: University of Chicago Press, 1972), pp. 53–64; and Kenneth Polk and Walter Schafer, eds., *Schools and Delinquency* (Engelwood Cliffs, N. J.: Prentice-Hall, 1972).

51. Hirschi, *Causes of Delinquency,* p. 215.

52. Scott Briar and Irving Piliavin, "Delinquency, Situational Inducements, and Commitment to Conformity," *Social Problems*, 13, no. 1 (Summer 1965): 36.

53. Hirschi, *Causes of Delinquency,* p. 54.

54. Hyman Rodman and Paul Grams, "Juvenile Delinquency and the Family: A Review and Discussion," in the President's Commission on Law Enforcement and Administration of Justice, *Task Force Report: Juvenile Delinquency and Youth Crime* (Washington: Government Printing Office, 1967), pp. 132–144.

55. Ibid., p. 198.

56. Ibid., p. 199.

57. Wesley Becker, "Consequences of Different Kinds of Parental Discipline," in M. L. Hoffman and L. W. Hoffman, eds., *Review of Child Development Research* (New York: Russell Sage Foundation, 1964), p. 171.

58. H. L. Bee et al., "Social Class Differences in Maternal Teaching Strategies and Speech Patterns," *Developmental Psychology*, 1, no. 6 (1969): 726–734.

59. I. Taylor, P. Walton, and J. Young, *The New Criminology* (New York: Harper Torchbooks, 1973), pp. 237–267.

60. Richard Quinney, ed., *Criminal Justice in America* (Boston: Little, Brown, 1974), p. 18.

61. David K. Shipler, "Rising Youth Crime in Soviet Troubles Regime and Public," *New York Times* (March 5, 1978), p. 1.

62. Stephen Spitzer, "Toward a Marxian Theory of Deviance and Control," *Social Problems*, 22 (1975): 638–651.

63. Edwin Schur, *Radical Non-Intervention* (Engelwood Cliffs, N. J.: Prentice-Hall, 1973), p. 106.

64. Richard Quinney, *Critique of Legal Order* (Boston: Little, Brown, 1974), p. 190.

3 Labeling Theory

Traditionally, sociologists have explained delinquent behavior in terms of childhood environment. They then consider the relationships between these environmental factors and later juvenile misconduct. Another perspective, which holds a quite different view of delinquent behavior, is labeling theory. [1] This approach has received considerable attention in recent years and is often included in criticisms of the juvenile justice process.

Recent evaluations of the juvenile justice process have indicated that its original goals of humane treatment and rehabilitation, set forth in the 1900s, are not often met. Instead of rehabilitating or reforming children, the system may in fact make them worse. In a report on juvenile delinquency published in 1967, the President's Commission on Law Enforcement and Administration of Justice warned of this possible outcome.

> Official action may actually help to fix and perpetuate delinquency in the child through a process in which the individual begins to think of himself as delinquent and organizes his behavior accordingly. That process itself is further reinforced by the effect of the labeling upon the child's family, neighbors, teachers, and peers, whose reactions communicate to the child in subtle ways a kind of expectation of delinquent conduct. [2]

Investigations into the actual functions of the juvenile justice process indicate that a series of decisions has been made by persons exercising large amounts of discretionary judgment with little regard for the child's legal rights. Decisions such as these can and do have a long-term impact on the lives of many youngsters.

What Is Labeling Theory?

Labeling theory attempts to evaluate the impact of the social control process on the etiology or causes of delinquent behavior. In a broader sense, it is concerned with the total process through which a child becomes officially labeled as a juvenile delinquent and how this process affects the individuals who experience it. This includes a consideration of how and why specific behaviors become defined as necessitating intervention by a government agency.[3] The manner in which these definitions are applied (or translated into enforcement practices) is also important for labeling theory. Finally, it considers the effects of such labels on the individual's self-concept and subsequent behavior.

How does society decide which behaviors are unwanted or socially dangerous? We know that the definitions of status offenses as well as delinquent acts are often vague and allow much room for discretion by the police and the courts. Labeling theory asks why those definitions are so broad.

The Application of Labels

In addition to questioning the formulation of definitions of delinquency, labeling theory is also concerned with the *application* of these definitions. How are decisions made in enforcing the juvenile delinquency statutes? Are they applied equally at all levels of society? Do certain population groups in our society experience the effects of selective enforcement? To answer these questions, we must realize that there is much discretion in decision making by police, probation officers, and juvenile judges in the juvenile justice process. This discretion works to decide which juveniles will go through the system and which will not.

Empirical studies of these decision-making processes reveal certain patterns. We know, for example, that the label "delinquent" is most likely to be applied to offenders who are poor, male, and members of minority groups. (See Chapter 1, "The Scope of the Problem.") Labeling theorists would point to this type of selective enforcement as an example of how the process creates deviance; by definition, juvenile delinquents are only those persons to whom the specific, official label has been applied. Because only "official" delinquents are considered by labeling theorists, it is important to examine the policies, attitudes, and assumptions of those who apply the labels if we are to obtain a balanced, realistic picture of delinquents.

Although there are certain sociological and psychological factors that may influence the likelihood of contact with social control agents, labeling theory is not so much concerned with these as with the manner in which the system of social control works and the effects it has on the juveniles who pass through it. Unlike the other theories or explanations of delinquency presented so far in this book, labeling ideas are not primarily concerned with the causes of the initial deviant behavior. Rather, labelists are interested in the process by which an offender becomes an official delinquent *after* the primary deviation has been detected.

Stigmatization

Being labeled a delinquent places the juvenile in a category which our society views as negative. The official delinquent suffers from the "stigma" of his or her label. Goffman defines stigma as "an attribute that is deeply discrediting."[4] The youngster is discredited, or seen by others as "bad," a "troublemaker," or "incorrigible." Teachers, schoolmates, and neighbors begin to view the child who bears this label as deviant, and may well react differently to the juvenile as a result of his or her new status. Stigmatized youngsters are more likely to be held responsible for the noise in the classroom or the broken window in the corner store. They may be excluded from school functions and ostracized from their peers. Parents may discourage their children from playing or being seen with "delinquents."

According to labeling theory, the stigma of the label can have a profound effect on the delinquent. The child who has been evaluated by an authority— the juvenile court—as a deviant will begin to notice changes in the attitudes of others. These changes take the form of subtle and not-so-subtle messages suggesting to delinquents that they are indeed expected to continue acting in a deviant way and that reform is considered unlikely. The strength of the stigma combined with the expectations of others may result in the adoption of a deviant self-image by the child, who now begins to accept the externally applied labels as true. Thus after contact with the police or juvenile court, the juvenile's self-concept is altered, the stigmatized role as deviant is accepted, and delinquent behavior begins to occur with greater frequency.[5]

Lemert termed this increase in deviance "secondary deviation."[6] As a result of the initial act that led to the labeling process, as well as the stigma the child suffers and the subsequent reactions of other people, he or she is now denied access to nondelinquent activities. Thus secondary deviation, or increased deviance, is extremely probable in that it is consistent with the child's self-image, is expected by others, and is encouraged by the child's exclusion from legitimate activities. According to this analysis one would expect the child who commits an act and *is not caught* to outgrow the behavior whereas the child who commits an act and *is caught* may only get worse.[7]

Although many of the ideas of labeling theory seem consistent with other observations on the effects of stereotypes and labels, it is important to examine the research findings that support or refute this perspective on delinquency. Labeling theory is often used as a basis for the strongest criticism of the juvenile justice process. If its assumptions are accurate, the implications for major change in the juvenile justice system cannot be ignored.

Effects of Labeling

The labeling perspective assumes that the initial contact with a police officer is traumatic for the youth and may inadvertently encourage further deviant behavior. As a juvenile progresses through subsequent stages of the process—from the probation department to juvenile court to incarceration—the stigma of the official label is reinforced. The negative social attributes of the delinquency label alter the reactions of others to the now-official delinquent. Teachers, peers, and parents may encourage the juvenile in the belief that the negative label is indeed appropriate. The acceptance of a delinquent self-concept then serves to solidify further deviance. (See Figure 3-1.)

Encounters with the Juvenile Justice Process

We will now examine the research findings on how contact with the juvenile process affects the self-concepts and attitudes of delinquents. Does the stigma of a label, whether given out by the local police officer or by the juvenile judge, alter the delinquent's subsequent behavior? Afterward, do other people begin to react unfavorably to the youngster, thereby reinforcing his or her acceptance of the label? Do juveniles themselves ultimately accept the label as true? Are there differences among individual delinquents in the effects that labeling has? Are some children more susceptible to this process than others?

Police   In recent years the role of the police officer in the juvenile justice process has received wide attention. The use of police discretion in dealing with juvenile offenders is a particularly important issue since the criteria used for deciding who to take into custody are not as clearly prescribed as they are for adult offenders. Juvenile officers are given a wide latitude of choice in deciding how a case should be handled—that is, whether informally or formally. Naturally, the effects of police discretion on the juvenile can be far reaching. If the officer decides on an informal disposition the child may receive only a verbal reprimand; but if the officer thinks a formal disposition is in order, the child may be referred to juvenile court and risk possible incarceration.[8]

As we mentioned earlier, labeling theorists assume that contact with the police is traumatic for a youngster. Such encounters are thought to serve as

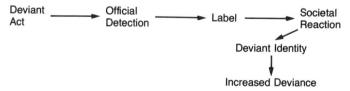

Figure 3-1. The labeling process.

the first indicator to the child that he or she is delinquent, and may also serve to reinforce negative feelings toward the police.

Many juveniles view the police negatively, regardless of what their own experiences have been. In a study of 10,000 school children conducted by Bouma, it was found that children tend to evaluate the police in a positive light until the age of 11.[9] A shift toward more negative evaluations occurs between ages 11 and 15. Children who are male, black, and from low social-status backgrounds were found to be less favorable in their opinions than were the other subjects studied.

Bouma's work is supported by the findings of other researchers, several of whom have reported that black youngsters tend to see the police as unfair and insulting.[10] All of these studies point to the fact that young people who are male, black, and from low socioeconomic backgrounds are more likely to perceive law enforcement personnel as unfair and unfriendly, regardless of their personal experiences.

Labeling theory suggests that contact with the police would encourage even stronger negative feelings. Indeed, several researchers have found that official delinquents display stronger anti-police sentiments than do nondelinquents.[11] We must be careful, however, not to interpret this finding as supporting the hypothesized labeling process. It may well be that those same youngsters who are most anti-police are also more likely to be officially labeled.

Research conducted in England has indicated that critical attitudes toward the police were more likely to follow official convictions but that negative attitudes were associated with future delinquency even among subjects with no prior convictions.[12] It appears that negative attitudes toward the police may influence a youngster's chance of official contact and that such attitudes do not then result solely from one's personal experiences.

The youngster who when stopped and questioned by the police is polite and cooperative stands a much better chance of receiving unofficial treatment—that is, a verbal reprimand. On the other hand, a youth who responds in an antagonistic or uncooperative manner runs a greater risk of being taken into custody. Although the same act may have been committed in both cases, the quality of the interaction with the officer has been an important factor in determining the eventual outcome. It may be that these differences in attitude result from the juvenile's prior feelings about law enforcement personnel.

Studies have indicated that some delinquents have a higher opinion of police who were juvenile officers than of other persons encountered in the juvenile justice system. These youngsters feel that the juvenile officers tried to help them whereas the court and correctional personnel did not.[13] Other research has indicated that delinquents did not feel mistreated by the police; in fact, most of them pointed out that they had received less harsh treatment than expected.[14]

The negative attitudes of young people toward the police are not simply a result of unpleasant experiences with individual officers. Some officers treat juveniles in such a way that the youngsters actually perceive them as more helpful and fair than other juvenile justice personnel. Thus instead of denigrating the officer after an interaction and becoming more entrenched in the delinquent role, the youngster may appreciate the treatment received or at least be pleasantly surprised at the officer's fairness.

The final question we must ask about the police role is, how does contact with the police affect a youngster's later behavior? If these encounters are traumatic and if they do set the labeling process in motion, we can assume that juveniles who experience such contacts will become more delinquent. There is some evidence that juveniles who are apprehended by the police increase their delinquent acts,[15] but there is not enough support for this finding to draw any definite conclusions. Perhaps the problem lies in separating the effects of the juvenile's experiences with the police from the effects of contact with the rest of the juvenile justice process.

Juvenile Court   The decisions of the juvenile court determine the official label the juvenile will bear. Adjudication as a delinquent surely makes rationalizations and defenses about one's identity more difficult. Once a record of delinquent behavior is established, the seriousness of the charges may become more apparent to the child. Although juvenile court proceedings are structured in an informal manner so as to avoid resembling criminal court proceedings, an appearance before a judge must have a serious impact on a youngster.

An appearance in court may be particularly traumatic because of the stigma associated with a possible official delinquent label. Whereas contact with the police can be easily hidden from others, a court appearance cannot. Thus the potential social harm of this stage of the process may be great by making one's peers, family, and teachers, as well as members of the community, more aware of the juvenile's behavior.

In addition to this stigma, the juvenile may fear the disposition of his or her case by the judge. The naive, first offender, who is unfamiliar with juvenile court proceedings, may fear incarceration. Actual incarceration or training school will further exacerbate the stigma by making the child acutely aware of the seriousness of his or her behavior. Once the juvenile's identity as a delinquent is made public, attempts to rationalize or justify the deviant behavior will be unconvincing to others.

Research on how formal court hearings affect youngsters reveals that most children are more concerned with their immediate fate than with the long-term social consequences of their actions. The built-in safeguards designed to protect the child's reputation are perceived by juveniles as working much more effectively than they actually do.[16] Most juveniles are primarily concerned with the disposition of their cases. Schur quotes one such youngster's reaction to court.

> I couldn't understand anything he [the judge] said. The only thing I understood
> was 'you're committed.' Everything else was a bunch of mumble-jumble. He
> went on and on a mile a minute and you sit there twiddling your thumbs and
> waiting for what he says . . . you're just listening for the main word, you're
> either committed or you're going home.[17]

These youngsters perceive their future in terms of whether they will be free,
not in terms of the potential social consequences of being labeled an official
delinquent.

It has also been assumed that a court hearing serves to amplify deviant
behavior. Because an official label may be more damaging than an unofficial
one, youngsters who experience a court appearance are thought to be more
likely to adopt a delinquent self-concept. Such a self-concept would naturally
increase the probability that further delinquent acts, or secondary deviations,
will occur.

Researchers who have examined the effects of informal versus formal disposition on the future behavior of juveniles have found a correlation between
formal disposition and later delinquent acts.[18] Although this finding would
seem to lend support to the labeling perspective, we must be careful in drawing conclusions.

The relationship between a court hearing and recidivism is still unclear.
Most juveniles, with the exception of those who commit serious offenses, are
not referred to court until they have had several contacts with the police.
However, it may be that those same juveniles who experience formal hearings
are also the most serious and frequent offenders. It must be remembered that
youngsters who receive formal treatment are not necessarily representative
of *all* juveniles who commit offenses. Instead, the juvenile justice process
succeeds in isolating the "hard-core" offenders among the delinquent population. If this is the case, then the higher recidivism rates for this group
reflect not only the effects of formal treatment but also a preexisting tendency
toward delinquent behavior.

This interpretation was considered by Wolfgang et al., in their cohort study
of delinquents in Philadelphia. Among the variables they found to be associated with a referral to court were:

> . . . being nonwhite, being of low socioeconomic level, committing an index
> offense, being a recidivist, and committing an offense with a relatively high
> seriousness score.[19]

Although each of these variables was found to be related to the ultimate disposition of juveniles, the most strongly related variable was "being nonwhite." Thus the juvenile who is nonwhite is more likely to be processed
through the entire juvenile system. This suggests that not all youngsters processed through the juvenile court are "hard-core" offenders. Because of se-

lective referral, many of the youngsters who end up in court are not among the most serious offenders. Using the data from the cohort study, which indicate an increase in the incidence and severity of offenses *after* court contact, it is possible to conclude that in some cases youngsters may be made worse as a result of their exposure to the system.

One must question whether it is the court referral itself that causes such outcomes. Unfortunately, it is very difficult to separate the effects of a court hearing from the effects of the resulting disposition. Since a formal hearing may result in probation, incarceration, fines, or dismissal, it is difficult to know whether future delinquency is more strongly influenced by the juvenile court labels or by the particular disposition. Incarceration in a training school may overshadow the effects of encounters with other parts of the system. An unpleasant relationship with a probation officer, for example, may serve to increase the youngster's sense of alienation whereas the labeled juvenile who goes untreated may resolve to mend his or her ways. Thus the type of disposition received as a result of court must be considered in addition to the court appearance itself.

Disposition   The dispositional alternatives available to the juvenile court judge include incarceration, probation, fines, or dismissal of the charges. Other alternatives may be available as well, depending on community resources. We will focus our attention on the effects of incarceration and probation since these dispositions intervene in the child's life to the greatest degree. According to the labeling perspective, we would assume that in either case, both self-concept and future behavior would be altered. However, incarceration would probably have the most extreme effect since it implies a seriousness that probation does not. Removing the child from the community would confer a more serious label than would participation in a community-treatment program. It can also be assumed that imprisonment is much more emotionally traumatic for a youth than is probation.

The impact of incarceration on a youngster's self-evaluation has been studied by Hall,[20] who compared the self-evaluations of incarcerated delinquents, delinquents on probation, self-reported delinquents, and nondelinquents. From his research he concluded that the incarcerated youngsters viewed themselves in the most unfavorable light. These juveniles who finally end up in a correctional institution have experienced the effects of labeling at all points in the juvenile justice process.

In addition to considering the effects of incarceration on the youngster's self-evaluation, we must also consider how incarceration affects the child's later behavior. Does incarceration amplify delinquent behavior? Is it more damaging than community-treatment approaches?

The high recidivism rates among institutionalized juveniles are well known, which lends support to the labeling hypothesis that more, rather than less, deviant behavior occurs as a result of official intervention. The idea has been emphasized recently that institutionalized youngsters can be better helped in community-treatment programs, such as probation or community group homes. Labeling theory would readily embrace this alternative since it has been shown that youngsters who experience the most stigmatizing disposition— incarceration—are also among those most likely to commit future offenses.

Deviant Identities

So far in this chapter we have examined the basic ideas of labeling theory and have identified the specific points in the juvenile justice system where labeling occurs. The final question we will consider is, what impact does labeling have on a youngster's identity? The traumatic nature of encounters with the juvenile justice system and the reactions of others to delinquents are thought to encourage these youngsters to see themselves as "delinquent" or "bad." Such identity changes are thought, in turn, to increase delinquent behavior. If we accept this view, we would have to expect high-offense rates among those youngsters who evaluate themselves as delinquent. We would also expect the most negative or delinquent self-evaluations to come from juveniles who have been officially labeled by the juvenile court. But this is not always the case.

A delinquent label may not necessarily have the denigrating effects which labeling theory suggests. Although most juveniles *do* feel stigmatized by an official label, in some instances a delinquent "record" may be used to impress peers and to bolster one's feelings of self-worth. In such cases, the label becomes a symbol of prestige. In a delinquent subculture, for example, or a neighborhood in which juvenile offenses are a common event, the label may even serve as a status symbol through which the child gains the respect and acceptance of his or her peers.

Short and Strodtbeck conducted an interesting study to determine how subculture values influence the way juveniles evaluate their own behavior.[21] To examine the self-evaluations of delinquent gang members, they had the subjects choose words that they thought best described them. They found that differences in self-concepts among individual gang members did not reflect the degree of personal involvement in delinquent activities. In fact, the most conventional self-descriptions were offered by the *most* delinquent boys. All of the subjects were members of urban gangs. In this type of environment, or subculture, delinquent behavior *is* normal behavior, and so the positive self-evaluations given are not surprising. It is clear that we must take into account the environment of the juvenile in assessing the effects of labeling since to a large extent it is the environment that determines which behaviors are appropriate and which are not.

Other research has indicated that labeling has different effects on different racial groups.[22] Black juveniles, for example, though in more frequent contact with the juvenile justice system, are less likely to see themselves as delinquent. Indeed, among black juveniles of low-social status, official records were found to be related to higher self-esteem.[23]

The studies described above indicate that the effects of labeling are variable over different racial and socioeconomic groups. Thus social-status and racial differences provide a key to understanding how contacts with the juvenile justice system affect the juvenile's self-esteem and his or her acceptance of the delinquent label. We have seen that, in some cases, labeling does not lead to a delinquent identity, may not make the child feel stigmatized, and may not serve to increase deviance.

Conclusions and Treatment Implications

We have seen that official contacts with the juvenile justice system do not always result in stigma, deviant identity, or increased delinquency. In fact, some juveniles in our society are not as susceptible to the labeling process as others. Indeed, youngsters who are most likely to experience contact with the juvenile justice system may be the least affected by labeling.

It may be that youngsters who enter the juvenile system are often the most seriously delinquent. Their subsequent delinquent behavior may be the combined result of an already-established pattern of delinquent behavior and official labeling. Those youngsters who come into contact with the courts are typically the most disadvantaged. Wolfgang et al. note that:

> The nonwhite delinquent boy is likely to belong to the lower socioeconomic group, experience a great number of school and residential moves (that is, be subject to the disrupting forces of intracity mobility more than the nondelinquent) and have the lowest grade completed, the lowest achievement level, and the lowest I. Q. score.[24]

This combination of factors suggests that a degree of social stigma is present even before the official labeling occurs. School experiences may have served to identify these youngsters as troublemakers, nonperformers, or hoodlums. These students' reputations suffer both in their own eyes and in the eyes of their peers. Thus the sense of being different or excluded may have been present long before these juveniles became officially labeled as delinquent.[25] That such youngsters are not particularly concerned about their official records is therefore not surprising since the role of outsider is not a new one in their lives.

Recognizing the Effects of Labeling

Labeling does have an impact on the lives and self-concepts of many youngsters. The difficulty lies in determining which youngsters are most affected, how strong the impact is, and what the long-term effects may be. Our original model of the labeling process (see Figure 3–1) now needs some elaboration and revision. Labels may elicit minimum response from some youngsters and have a profound impact on others. Labeling may increase deviance, have no effect, or deter further deviant behavior. For some juveniles contact with the police or the court may actually inhibit future delinquent acts. (See Figure 3–2.)

A more critical appraisal of the labeling perspective must be made and more empirical research conducted to determine exactly how labeling works. From our review of the available literature, we have seen that to assume that all contacts with the juvenile justice system have negative effects on juveniles is not appropriate. We have seen that labeling is not necessarily traumatic or detrimental for all youngsters. In fact, some juveniles derive a sense of prestige and a more positive self-concept as a result of having an official record. The most extreme form of intervention—disposition by the court—does appear to be related to the frequency and severity of future offenses. Other experiences, such as police contact, may not have such consistently negative results. Generally, we can assume that the more involved a child becomes with the system, the more damage he or she is likely to experience.

Diversion

The implications of the labeling perspective for treatment center around a process called "diversion." Labelists believe that juveniles should be diverted into other community agencies or organizations, especially cases involving minor infractions, such as status offenses. As Schur points out, "the basic injunction for public policy becomes: *leave the kids alone wherever possible.*"[26]

In the *Task Force Report: Juvenile Delinquency and Youth Crime,* precourt handling of juveniles by community agencies is strongly encouraged. One of the major advantages of this process is that it may lessen some of the stigma associated with official handling. Moreover, it increases community responsibility for delinquency problems. The report includes an outline for

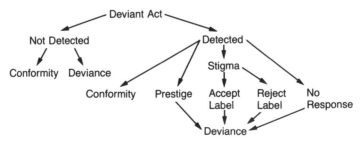

Figure 3-2. The effects of labeling.

a proposed Youth Services Bureau which would serve both delinquent and nondelinquent youth and their families. Counseling, foster-home placements, programs of work and recreation, and educational programs would be available to juveniles on the local level. Referrals would be made by the police, social agencies, or schools, and participation would occur on a voluntary basis.

Prejudicial diversion would serve to lighten the case load in juvenile court while at the same time protecting youngsters from the detrimental effects of possible court dispositions. Through alternative measures such as these, many youngsters who might otherwise go on to join the "hard core" among the delinquent population would be able to avoid further (and potentially harmful) contacts with law enforcement agents.

Although diversion of juveniles is often presented as a positive alternative to the present juvenile justice system, there are problems with this approach, too. A more detailed critique of diversion is presented in Chapter 11.

DISCUSSION QUESTIONS

1. According to labeling theory, what steps would have to be taken in order to implement the changes needed to decrease the incidence of delinquency in our society?

2. In addition to those bestowed on them by the juvenile court, what other labels may juveniles have to bear?

3. Labeling theory assumes that the label of "juvenile delinquent" is stigmatizing to most juveniles. Under what conditions would this be the case? Under what conditions would this *not* be the case?

4. Discuss the attitudes that children have toward the police. What are some of the reasons for these negative feelings, even among children who have not had personal contact with law enforcement officers?

5. Discuss the idea of diversion. What problems might this approach present?

NOTES

1. See for example: Howard S. Becker, *Outsiders: Studies in the Sociology of Deviance* (New York: Free Press, 1963); Aaron Cicourel, *The Social Organization of Juvenile Justice* (New York: John Wiley, 1968); David Matza, *Becoming Deviant* (Englewood Cliffs, N.J.: Prentice-Hall, 1969); Richard Quinney, *The Social Reality of Crime* (Boston: Little, Brown, 1971); Edwin Schur, *Labeling Deviant Behavior* (New York: Harper Row, 1971); Frank Tannenbaum, *Crime and the Community* (New York: Columbia University Press, 1938).

2. President's Commission on Law Enforcement and Administration of Justice, *Task Force Report: Juvenile Delinquency and Youth Crime* (Washington, D.C.: Government Printing Office, 1967), p. 7.

3. Quinney, *Social Reality of Crime,* pp. 15–25.

4. Erving Goffman, *Stigma* (Englewood Cliffs, N.J.: Prentice-Hall, 1963), p. 3.

5. Simon Dinitz et al., eds., *Deviance: Studies in the Process of Stigmatization and Societal Reaction* (New York: Oxford University Press, 1969), p. 19.

6. Edwin M. Lemert, *Social Pathology* (New York: McGraw-Hill, 1951), p. 23.

7. A. R. Mahoney, "The Effects of Labeling upon Youths in the Juvenile Justice System: A Review," *Law and Society Review,* 8, no. 4 (1974): 583–614.

8. Frank J. Remington et al., *Criminal Justice Administration* (Indianapolis: Bobbs-Merrill, 1968), pp. 959–976.

9. Donald Bouma, "Youth Attitudes Toward the Police and Law Enforcement," in *Police and Law Enforcement,* eds. A. Curran, J.T. Fowler, and R.H. Ward (New York: AMS Press, 1973), pp. 219–238.

10. Angus Campbell and Howard Shuman, "Police in the Ghetto," in *Who Rules the Police?,* ed. L. Ruchelman (New York: NYU Press, 1973), pp. 135–140; Robert Wintersmith, *Police and the Black Community* (Toronto: Lexington Books, 1974), pp. 87–106.

11. Ames Chapman, "Attitudes Toward Legal Authorities by Juveniles," *Sociology and Social Research,* 40, no. 3 (1956): 170–175; Gordon Waldo and Mason Hall, "Delinquency Potential and Attitudes Toward the Criminal Justice System," *Social Forces,* 49, no. 2 (1971): 291–298.

12. D. J. West and S. P. Farrington, *Who Becomes Delinquent?* (London: Heinemann, 1973), pp. 177–180.

13. Brendan Maher and Ellen Stein, "The Delinquent's Perception of the Law and the Community," in *Controlling Delinquents,* Stanton Wheeler, ed. (New York: John Wiley, 1968), pp. 187–224.

14. Jack Foster, "The Labeling Hypothesis and Perceptions of Social Liability Following Delinquent Behavior" (Ph.D. diss., Ohio State University, 1971).

15. M. Gold, *Delinquent Behavior in an American City* (Monterey, Calif.: Brooks/Cole, 1970), pp. 106–107.

16. Martha Baum and Stanton Wheeler, "Becoming an Inmate," in *Controlling Delinquents,* Stanton Wheeler, ed. (New York: John Wiley, 1968), pp. 153–186.

17. Edwin Schur, *Radical Nonintervention* (Englewood Cliffs, N.J.: Prentice-Hall, 1973), p. 162.

18. M. Wolfgang, R. Figlio, and T. Sellin, *Delinquency in a Birth Cohort* (Chicago: University of Chicago Press, 1972), p. 252; Anthony Meade, "The Labeling Approach to Delinquency: State of the Theory as a Function of Method," *Social Forces,* 53, no. 1 (1974): 83–91.

19. Wolfgang et al., *Delinquency in a Birth Cohort,* p. 252.

20. Peter Hall, "Identification with the Delinquent Subculture and Level of Self-Evaluation," *Sociometry,* 29 (1966): 146–158.

21. James Short and Fred Strodtbeck, *Group Process and Gang Delinquency* (Chicago: University of Chicago Press, 1965).

22. Leroy Gould, "Who Defines Delinquency: A Comparison of Self-Reported and Officially Reported Indices of Delinquency for Three Racial Groups," *Social Problems,* 16, no. 3 (1969): 325–335.

23. Gary Jensen, "Delinquent and Adolescent Self-Conceptions: A Study of the Personal Relevance of Infraction," *Social Problems,* 20, no. 1 (1972): 84–103.

24. Wolfgang et al., *Delinquency in a Birth Cohort,* p. 246.

25. K. Polk and W. Schafer, *Schools and Delinquency* (Englewood Cliffs, N.J.: Prentice-Hall, 1972).

26. Schur, *Radical Nonintervention,* p. 155.

4 Psychological Theories

Delinquency takes different forms and occurs at different rates depending on the particular society as well as groups, or subcultures, within that society. As we learned in Chapter 2, sociologists attempt to explain delinquency in terms of these differences. Their primary focus is on the role of social, or environmental, factors in the development of deviant behavior patterns.

Psychologists, on the other hand, are more concerned with what happens at the individual level—that is, what developmental factors make some children turn to delinquency while others choose more conventional, or socially acceptable, forms of behavior. Generally speaking, psychologists view delinquent behavior as symptomatic of deeper psychological problems, which are thought to stem from faulty developmental processes. From the psychological perspective, then, the first step in understanding the origins of deviance is to analyze the child's early life experiences. Considerable emphasis is placed on the child-rearing practices of parents and how these practices affect the child's later behavior and personality. Among the questions psychologists might ask are, what types of rewards and punishments were used with the child? What unusual events or traumas did the child experience? What type of emotional climate was the child exposed to in the home?

Normal psychological development occurs when parents are warm, loving, and genuinely concerned about their children's welfare. Separation from one's family, parental cruelty, or conflicts within the home can disrupt this process and may push the child toward deviant or delinquent behavior. Psychological theories have much in common with sociological theories in that both place considerable emphasis on the role of the family environment in causing delinquency. The major difference between the two perspectives is that psychologists are less concerned with the impact of the greater social environment and more concerned with how individual factors influence behavior.

Psychologists are also interested in identifying the different types of delinquents. Their research has included efforts to describe juveniles using standard psychological tests. In this manner children can be classified into groups on the basis of individual characteristics. This is useful for purposes of treatment since some therapeutic techniques have been found to be more effective with certain types of offenders than with others.

Genetic factors have also been examined for their relevance to crime, and some evidence exists to support the influence of genes on behavior. For example, some males are born with an extra sex chromosome (the XYY syndrome), and research has shown that these males are more often found in mental and penal institutions than in society at large. Studies of identical twins have shown that when one twin displays criminal behavior, the other twin is also likely to display this behavior whereas in nonidentical twins, this is not the case. Evidence such as this has led some psychologists to argue that genetic factors play a strong role in determining whether or not a youth becomes delinquent.

In this chapter, we will discuss the possible role of both learned and inherited personality traits in delinquency. We will also examine the various treatment techniques that are based upon these explanations of delinquent behavior.

The Development of Delinquency

The personalities and behavior patterns of children are often explained as a result of early experiences within the family. Because interactions with parents and siblings dominate the first years of a child's life, many psychologists have pointed to these formative relationships as the crucial determinant of later behavior. Systems of values, control of one's impulses, and a concern for the opinions of other people are usually learned during this period. Thus in studying the causes of delinquency, psychologists ask the following questions: What unusual events occurred during the early years of the delinquent's life that may have contributed to later deviant behavior? Why do some children fail to adopt acceptable patterns of behavior?

Psychoanalytic Theory

One of the classic explanations of the development of personality is psychoanalytic theory, originally proposed by Sigmund Freud around the turn of the century.[1] Freud continually sought to modify his theory, and many of his followers suggested variations on it. Below we will examine the basic ideas of Freudian theory.

Psychoanalytic theory attempts to explain how all people function psychologically. It focuses upon the structure of the personality and the wishes, desires, and motives behind behavior. These wishes and desires are not always apparent to a person; in fact, they are often *unconscious*. These basic drives or wishes make up the part of the personality that Freud called the *id*.

The id represents wishes or drives that are primitive, aggressive, and unorganized. To some extent, id drives are identified with the type of behavior seen in small children. When a child is angry, for example, there is often an immediate verbalization of the feeling. He may say something like "I'm going to smash you with a big truck." The drives of the id demand instant gratification, and as the child grows up, parents begin to punish the child for direct expressions of these drives.

Freud assumed that everyone is born with basic id drives and that socialization of the young is a process of redirecting or controlling the expression of these desires. The other two parts of the personality, *ego* and *superego*, result from the socialization process and serve to mediate between and constrain the desires of the id.

The *superego* is the child's internalized parent. It consists of concepts of "right" and "wrong," which are inherited from others in the child's environment. Mother tells her child that he must defecate in the toilet and that feces are dirty and disgusting. In time he comes to agree with her, and obediently uses the toilet. By internalizing the values of one's parents, the child also experiences feelings of guilt when these values are broken. These guilt feelings are thought to either prevent inappropriate acts (according to the parental definition of inappropriate) or to discourage a recurrence of the behavior.

The *ego,* which is the executive of the personality, serves as a mediator between the values of the superego, the desires of the id, and the demands of the external world. Compromises are made between id cravings and the acceptability of satisfying the craving at a particular time and in a particular social setting. The child learns to control overt expressions of anger toward a teacher but may express much hostility toward peers on the school playground. The ego must be strong enough to keep the id and the superego functioning and in balance. If the ego is weak, behavior is difficult to control. In the previous example, a dominant superego might have prohibited any anger expression whereas a dominant id might have led to an attack on the teacher.

Under ideal family conditions, each part of the personality would develop normally and the child would exhibit acceptable behavior in most situations.

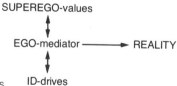

Figure 4-1. Personality structures.

Ultimately the ego would manifest itself in the child's ability to consider the needs and demands of other people. According to psychoanalytic theory, delinquent behavior can be seen as symptomatic of faulty personality structures, but what causes these faulty structures?

Faulty Ego Structure

An extensive description of the delinquent personality has been provided by Redl and Wineman, who developed an interesting program for treating delinquent youngsters using the concepts of psychoanalytic theory. In their view, the major problem shared by all delinquent children is that of an ego deficit. The patients Redl and Wineman treated had committed a variety of offenses, ranging from assault and theft to lying and truancy. At times their patients, all of whom were boys, appeared to be completely uncontrollable.

Redl and Wineman suggested that the ego of the delinquent cannot adequately perform its normal functions. In contrast to the healthy ego, which perceives and judges the external environment, mediates id and superego, and adjusts behavior in such a way as to insure appropriate actions, the ego of the delinquent fails in several ways.

1. The delinquent ego cannot tolerate the emotions resulting from frustration and insists on complete gratification of desires.
2. The emotions of insecurity, anxiety, and fear cannot be tolerated. When faced with these emotions, the delinquent either withdraws or becomes aggressive.
3. The delinquent ego fails to resist temptation. Excitement in the environment quickly spreads from one child to the next, and results in an extremely low threshold for group intoxication. If one child in the group jumps onto the dining table, for example, the others quickly follow.
4. The delinquent ego is easily flooded by memories of the past. If a counselor struggles with a boy in an attempt to control him, the child might respond as though the counselor, who has now come to represent his own father, were trying to kill him.
5. The delinquent ego cannot cope with the emotion of guilt. Children who experience guilt react in much the same manner as they do when faced with anxiety.
6. In some respects the delinquent ego is interpersonally blind. Delinquent children are unable to predict the outcome of their behavior.[2]

Thus the delinquent ego is deficient in that it is unable to control id drives and unable to deal with the external world in an adaptive fashion. Yet the delinquent ego may also have its peculiar strengths. For example, it functions to keep guilt feelings under control and enables the child to rationalize behavior. It is resistant to change and may be quite skillful at recognizing a counselor's weak spots. It is also good at ferreting out other youngsters who will provide support for antisocial acts. Although the ego of the delinquent may have difficulty coping with day-to-day events and normal emotions, it is unusually resourceful in aiding and abetting delinquency.

The two vignettes below are given by Redl and Wineman to illustrate delinquent ego deficits and delinquent strengths:

> The kids burst out of the station wagon in their usual exuberant mood and barged madly up the steps into the house. Luckily, this time the door was open so the usual pounding, kicking of door, etc., wasn't necessary. I was in my office tied up in a phone call and the door was closed. Mike yelled for me, shouting something about his jackknife which I was keeping in the drawer for him. I put my hand over the receiver and said "O.K., come on in." But the lock had slipped on the door and he could not open it. Before I even had a chance to excuse myself from my phone conversation and say "Just a minute, I'll be back," he was pounding on the door, kicking it, calling me a "sonofabitch" repetitively. I opened the door and gave him his knife. Even this failed to quiet his furor and, when I commented on the obvious fact that I hadn't even meant to make him wait, that the lock had slipped, all I got was a snarling, contemptuous "Shit." (Entry: 4/7/47, David Wineman.)[3]

> On one occasion the whole Pioneer group had been involved in a very dangerous and destructive episode of throwing bricks from the top of the garage. We decided to have individual interviews with each of the boys to "rub-in" the total unacceptability of such behavior. Andy, especially, was fascinating in his real indignation at even being approached on the subject. Tearfully he shouted at the Director who was doing the interviewing, "Yeah, everybody was doing it and you talk to me. Why is it my fault?" When it was pointed out to him that we were not saying it was all his fault but that he was responsible for his individual share in the matter, he was still unable to admit the point: "But we were all in on it. Why talk to me?"[4]

Faulty Superego Structure

Redl and Wineman also felt that the delinquent superego was faulty. The healthy superego consists of societal and parental values and standards and gives warning signals when issues concerning conscience and morality are involved. The superegos of the delinquents Redl and Wineman treated appeared to contribute to the delinquent life-style. They noted that the values of the delinquent superego were those of a delinquent subculture and stood in opposition to the values of society. Even when the superego did function in these children, it often served to produce only post-act guilt rather than pre-act or anticipatory guilt.

Another problem that has been related to delinquent or deviant behavior is the failure of the superego to develop at all. The person who seems to have no sense of right and wrong and who therefore experiences no guilt feelings is often labled "psychopathic."[5] In the case of the psychopath, deviance results from desires which are not controlled by a moral code.

The overdeveloped superego can also contribute to deviance in that the child's behavior is excessively inhibited. There are no real outlets for many drives and so after periods of buildup, the child may develop neurotic symptoms, such as anxiety attacks.[6] Another possible outcome of this buildup is aggression. Megargee has described two types of violent personalities, the *undercontrolled* and the *overcontrolled*.[7] The undercontrolled person displays a lack of inhibitions and is perhaps the most common type of violent offender. The overcontrolled offenders exhibit excessive amounts of control, but at some point their drives toward aggression build up and swamp their well-constructed control mechanisms. Megargee suggests that this model can be used to explain the "extremely polite and soft-spoken" murderer who has had no previous assaultive episodes.

Development of Faulty Personality Structures

The egos and superegos of delinquents have been described, but the question that remains is, how do these peculiarities develop? Developmentalists believe that the superego fails to develop normally when there are no adequate role models for the youngster during early childhood. When parents behave inconsistently or brutally, the child never comes to love and develop a healthy respect for them. Even when the child *does* identify with his or her parents, it is often the case that the parents themselves exhibit disturbed or antisocial behavior. Thus the child fails to learn appropriate behavior patterns.

Children also need to be helped to develop a strong ego. They have to be taught how to deal with frustration as well as with emotions of anxiety, fear, and guilt. Left to their own resources children will not develop these skills. If they are abused, neglected, or hated, they will have even more difficulty in learning such skills. This, in fact, is a general principle in psychoanalytic theory—namely, that all disturbed behavior is a result of severe frustration (or trauma) that takes place during the child's early years, from birth to the age of six or seven.

Other researchers have explored the differences between the life experiences of delinquents and nondelinquents in an attempt to isolate important factors in the development of antisocial behavior patterns. Redl and Wineman emphasized the quality of the parent-child relationship, and research evidence supports their ideas. Parental rejection and cruelty and the absence of appropriate adult role models are commonly found in the backgrounds of serious offenders.[8]

The home environments of delinquent youngsters include a wide range of negative characteristics. A comparison study of 500 delinquents and a matched sample of 500 nondelinquents from underprivileged neighborhoods in Boston, Massachusetts, revealed some of these characteristics.[9] It was found that the parents of delinquents were more likely to be indifferent or openly hostile to their children. Disciplinary practices ranged from mothers who were permissive to fathers who were overstrict and who used physical punishment.

The family of the delinquent child was found to be less stable than that of the nondelinquent. Divorce and separation rates were higher and reliance on welfare was common. Parents of these children were more likely to have been labeled delinquent or criminal themselves, and often there was a history of mental illness in the family.

A dramatic example of the influence of childhood experience on criminal behavior was presented by Stuart Palmer.[10] Palmer conducted a study in which he compared the childhoods of men who had been convicted of murder with the childhoods of their brothers. Using this approach, he was able to go beyond general family characteristics to consider individual differences within the same family. He found that in almost all cases the murderers had suffered many more childhood frustrations and traumas than their brothers. These included difficult births, injuries from forceps during delivery, serious operations and illnesses, and beatings by people other than the parents. In addition, the murderers more often had a history of physical deformities, severe toilet training, difficulties in school, and disturbed behaviors such as bedwetting, stuttering, and nightmares.

Palmer felt that all of these experiences created frustrations for the child, both physical and psychological. These frustrations and traumas in turn contributed to the child's inability to control aggressive impulses, which later resulted in violent behavior. The fact that one child in a family can become deviant while the others do not has always presented a problem for developmental explanations of delinquency, but Palmer's study indicates a possible solution. The early life experiences of children, even those who grow up in the same family, vary greatly. The child who experiences the greatest amount of frustration will be the most likely to become delinquent. What is needed in addition to this information is a greater understanding of how different kinds of trauma lead to deviant behavior, and whether specific types of trauma are more likely to lead to particular kinds of delinquent behavior.

Comments on Developmental Approaches

The developmental approach focuses on the impact of early childhood experiences on later behavior and places considerable emphasis on the parent-child relationship. A strict interpretation of this perspective would lead one to assume that an individual's past experiences are almost entirely responsible for his or her present-day behavior. The problem with this approach is that it ignores one's present environment and recent life experiences. Of course, other psychological theories, which take present events into account, have been postulated, but Freudian theory does not.

Developmental theories also fail to provide information about the causes of different types of delinquent behavior. What factors distinguish the violent offender from the status offender, for example? How do the early experiences of male delinquents differ from those of female delinquents? Developmentalists fail to address themselves to these important questions.

Another issue that must be addressed is why so many juvenile delinquents eventually cease their involvement in delinquent behavior. Implicit in psychoanalytic theory is the notion that without some type of treatment intervention, the delinquent youngster will continue to exhibit inappropriate behaviors. Although delinquent children may continue to engage in antisocial behavior as adults, it is not appropriate to assume that all delinquents will go on to become adult offenders.[11]

Treatment Implications

The treatment techniques most frequently associated with Freudian theory involve the use of psychoanalysis. This technique is rarely used with delinquents, however, because it is a long process and one that is also very expensive. Treatment programs for juveniles that are based on Freudian theory typically consist of therapeutic communities in which past traumas are resolved by exposing the child to healthy experiences in the present.

Redl and Wineman developed a treatment environment in a group home setting.[12] The delinquents, all of whom were boys, lived with staff members who had been fully trained to protect the children from the kinds of traumatic handling they had experienced in their early lives. The staff members acted as warm parent surrogates who provided the youngsters with an emotional climate that resembled that of a healthy parent-child relationship.

Initially, the major therapeutic emphasis was on building up ego strength. To strengthen the child's superego without giving him a means of handling guilt was considered premature, so ego development was the first goal. One technique used to help the boys develop alternative strategies for behavior was recreation, an activity that allowed them to discharge impulses within a structured and appropriate setting. In addition, staff members acted as full-time role models for the youngsters and served as exemplars of self-control and socially approved values.

Another implication of developmental theory is that not all delinquents have the same problems. One child may have a weak ego that cannot control id impulses; another may have a delinquent ego that tends to gratify the id yet does possess some strength; still another may have a functioning superego, but its values may be those of a deviant subculture. The best method for treatment may depend on the level of development of the individual delinquent.

This idea is best illustrated by the work of Warren, who has devised a developmental analysis of interpersonal behavior.[13] According to this model, three levels commonly characterize delinquents:

Level A: These people feel that the world should take care of them. They view others as givers and cannot understand or predict the behaviors or reactions of people around them. There are two subtypes.
  Asocial aggressive: These people make active demands and become aggressive when frustrated.
  Asocial passive: When frustrated, they withdraw and complain.

Level B: These people understand that their behavior affects whether they get what they want, and so they manipulate the environment and people in order to satisfy their needs. They do not have an internalized value system, but conform to the external structure. They can play a few stereotyped roles, but have no solid understanding of the needs and feelings of people who are different from themselves. There are three subtypes.
  Immature conformists: They comply with whoever is in power at the moment.
  Cultural conformist: They conform to a specific authority, such as particular delinquent peers.
  Manipulator: They try to undermine the authority figure.

Level C: These people have a set of internalized standards and can understand other people. They are influenced by people they admire and are concerned about status. There are four subtypes.
  Neurotic acting out: They respond to guilt by committing further delinquent acts.
  Neurotic anxious: Their feelings of inadequacy and guilt produce symptoms of emotional disturbance.
  Situational-emotional reaction: Immediate and specific crises lead to delinquent behavior.
  Cultural identifiers: They identify with a deviant value system and live by this system.

These three levels correspond to the observations of Redl and Wineman about ego and superego deficits. By classification of delinquents into Warren's levels, specific treatment techniques can be used according to their appropriateness for each level. Warren has conducted research indicating that community-based treatment programs work best for the acting-out neurotic, the cultural conformist, and the manipulator. The cultural identifier benefits from institutionally based programs whereas the situational-emotional reaction subtype does well in either type of program. Warren also found that mixing the different types of delinquents in treatment programs was less effective than separating them.

The Personality of Delinquents

The developmental ideas concerning delinquency emphasize the structure of the personality and the child's early experiences. Other research on delinquency has explored the types of personality traits found among adolescent offenders.

A common research strategy in psychology involves taking a group of people of special interest, in this case, delinquents, giving them a psychological or behavioral test, and then comparing their responses to those of a comparison group, in this case, nondelinquents. Psychologists who conduct such research are sometimes guided by a particular psychological theory. Other times they are merely exploring to see whether any differences exist that are worth studying in greater detail. Thus, if one were to review the research on delinquents one would find a complex assortment of research into many different behavioral and personality traits. Because it would be impossible to summarize all this research, we will look at representative samples of some of the more significant studies that have been done on the delinquent personality.

Intelligence and Delinquency

One topic that has been explored in depth is the relationship between intelligence and juvenile delinquency. Much of the interest in the role of intelligence in delinquent behavior stems from the assumption that intellectual functioning may serve as a form of impulse control.[14] Instead of acting on impulse, one may use intellectual processes to consider alternative and socially acceptable means of gratification. The impulse to physically strike an antagonist may be controlled and redirected into a more socially appropriate act, such as making a derogatory remark to the person. Intelligent youngsters may have a wider repertoire of alternative behaviors at their disposal, and as a result they may be less prone to engage in destructive, antisocial behavior. One would then expect delinquents to be less intelligent than nondelinquents.

Researchers have attempted to compare the intelligence levels of delinquent and nondelinquent subjects. In the early 1900s Goddard adapted the then-newly developed intelligence test of French psychologist Alfred Binet and gave it to a group of incarcerated delinquents.[15] Finding almost half of them to be mentally retarded, Goddard proposed that mental retardation was a major cause of antisocial behavior. He also believed that high intelligence was an inherited trait and was not affected by one's experiences. Goddard's views have long since been rejected as inaccurate but his work was important in that it stimulated some 450 studies on the intelligence of delinquents over the next 50 years.

Early research found that delinquents had intelligence-test scores that were 15 to 20 points lower than those of the general population, but more recent research finds a difference of only about 8 IQ points. For example, Siebert, who tested over 8,000 court cases, found a mean IQ of 91.[16] (The average for the general population is 100.) It is difficult to interpret these results literally, however, since delinquents generally come from areas in which many children, regardless of their delinquent involvement, have low IQ scores. For example, a study of grade-school children in an area of Chicago in which delinquency was very common indicated that the average IQ was 91.[17] Thus the lower scores of delinquents may not differentiate them from nondelinquents when children from similar environments are compared.

When taking intelligence tests, delinquents have been observed to perform carelessly and haphazardly, disregarding instructions and displaying poor workmanship.[18] This suggests that basic motivational differences may exist between delinquent and nondelinquent children, and these differences may account for the variation in intelligence-test scores.

Other factors may also contribute to intelligence-test scores. Caplan noted that differences in these scores may easily be a result of the already-detected delinquency.[19] That is to say, a boy who becomes delinquent may then neglect his intellectual development, thereby lowering his intelligence-test score. Delinquent samples may also be highly selected, for not every delinquent gets caught or ends up in a clinic or courtroom. Institutionalized delinquents will be expected to perform poorly on tests as a result of the generally impoverished environment in such institutions.

Among delinquents themselves there is a wide variation in intelligence-scores. One study conducted with children from a juvenile court population yielded interesting results. When children who had high scores (120 and above) were compared with those who had average scores (90 to 100), it was found that there was some variation in adjustment and offense patterns across the two groups. Not only were the more intelligent children found to be better adjusted but their delinquent acts appeared to be focused on specific sources of discontent.[20] Other research has indicated that higher intelligence is more likely to be found among runaways whereas lower intelligence is more frequently found among juveniles who commit assaults.[21]

In light of these findings, then, we cannot assume that low intelligence is a common trait among all delinquents. If intelligence does play a role in delinquency, it appears to be important in relation to the type of offense committed. Studies of the relationship between intelligence and delinquency have not provided any conclusive evidence to suggest that high intelligence provides greater impulse control, but it *may* have some bearing on the type of delinquent acts committed by the youngster.

Empirical Classifications of Delinquents

Attempts to describe the "typical" delinquent have led researchers to conclude that there are actually many different types of offenders. Some psychologists have suggested that these different types of delinquents may simply represent different types of personalities. A number of investigators have attempted to classify delinquents into groups, or personality types, on the basis of their behaviors, psychiatric symptoms, and responses to psychological tests.

Quay examined a sample of 122 male delinquents who had been placed in an institution.[22] Using ratings made by the boys' teachers and classroom supervisors as well as case histories compiled by their social workers, Quay developed three basic clusters of behaviors. He labeled them unsocialized psychopathic, disturbed neurotic, and socialized subcultural.

The behaviors found clustered in the *unsocialized psychopathic* type included boisterousness, disobedience, and impertinence among other traits. This cluster describes the aggressive and uncontrolled child who frequently transgresses the law because of his own uncontrolled impulses and his general disregard for others.

The *disturbed neurotic* cluster described behaviors ranging from self-consciousness to depression and feelings of inferiority. These boys engage in solitary delinquent acts and do so as a result of psychological disturbance.

The *socialized subcultural* cluster referred to boys who were, in effect, following the norms and values of their peers. Because their peers happened to be delinquent, antisocial behaviors were viewed as acceptable.

As Quay points out, these clusters simply refer to certain behaviors or personality traits that are most often found to be present in certain types of offenders. Because many offenders are actually mixed types, it may not be possible to classify all delinquents into one or the other of the categories.

Quay also notes that these clusters are found in general samples of adolescent males and thus may not serve as viable *explanations* of why some youngsters become delinquent. This classification system, then, is primarily useful as a means of separating delinquents into groups for treatment purposes *after* delinquency has occurred, but it does not specify which personality types are more prone to delinquency in general.

The Prediction of Delinquency

Perhaps the most important step in the prevention of delinquency is to develop an effective means of predicting which children are most likely to become delinquent. Unless and until we are able to predict delinquency, we will be forced into the passive position of waiting until youngsters are detected and brought into the juvenile court, and then trying to prevent them from repeating their delinquent behavior. Of course, by this time it may be too late to intervene.

If, on the other hand, we could identify the predelinquent, it would be possible to intervene with some therapeutic technique that might prevent the child from becoming involved in delinquent activities. Ideally we could prevent children from developing delinquent habits and from being labeled by society as delinquent.

Is it possible to predict delinquency? Briggs and Wirt noted that "there are no present systems for the prediction of delinquency."[23] In this section we will examine two major studies that attempted to develop methods of predicting delinquency. One of these studies was conducted by Glueck and Glueck and the other was conducted by Hathaway and Monachesi. The method proposed by the Gluecks appears to have considerable potential. Their predictive scale is somewhat simple, but in the 20 years since it was proposed it has proven to be reasonably valid.

The Glueck Scale

Prediction can focus on the individual, the family, the neighborhood, or the entire culture. There is little need to use complex tests to predict which neighborhoods have high-delinquency rates since reliable crime statistics are available to identify these areas. Of course, not all youths who live in high-crime neighborhoods become delinquent. It is here, in detecting which youths will become delinquent and which will not, that prediction is most critical.

Sheldon and Eleanor Glueck studied 500 delinquent boys and compared them with 500 nondelinquent boys.[24] They found a number of differences between the two groups, and on the basis of these differences proposed five aspects of family life that might serve to distinguish between the two groups of boys.

The five family factors, together with the weighted scores given to them, are as follows:

1. *Discipline of boy by father*
Firm but kindly	9.3
Lax	59.8
Erratic or overstrict	71.8

2. *Supervision of boy by mother*
Suitable	9.9
Fair	57.5
Unsuitable	83.2

3. *Affection of father for boy*

Warm or overprotective	33.8
Indifferent or hostile	75.9

4. *Affection of mother for boy*

Warm or overprotective	43.1
Indifferent or hostile	86.2

5. *Cohesiveness of family*

Marked	20.6
Some	61.3
None	96.9

This scale clearly differentiated between the delinquents and the non-delinquents.

WEIGHTED SCORE	CHANCE OF DELINQUENCY (in percent)
Less than 250	16.0
250–299	63.5
More than 300	89.2

However, the critical test of any scale is whether it can accurately predict *who* will become delinquent. How successful is the Glueck scale in accomplishing this task?

Glick studied 303 first-grade boys in New York City and followed their progress over a ten-year period.[25] A modified version of the Glueck scale was used to predict future delinquency. Despite the modification of the scale, it appeared to predict delinquency quite well. Results of this study are summarized below.

PREDICTION OF DELINQUENCY	PERCENT DELINQUENT
Low	2.9
Even chance	36.0
High	84.8

Another study conducted in Washington, D. C., focused on children ages 11 to 14, who had serious behavioral problems in school. The children, who numbered 151 in all, were followed up until they had reached the age of 18. Using the Glueck scale, delinquent behavior was predicted with accuracy.

PREDICTION	DELINQUENT BY AGE 18			
	Yes		No	
Delinquent	102	(76%)	32	(24%
Nondelinquent	5	(29%)	12	(71%)

n=151

It is clear from these studies that the Glueck scale can predict with reasonable accuracy whether a youth will subsequently become delinquent. But it must also be noted that the Glueck scale tends to overpredict delinquency, even when applied to a sample of children chosen because of their behavioral problems in school. This tendency to overpredict—that is, to incorrectly identify an individual as predelinquent—has led many psychologists to be extremely wary of these prediction techniques. In the Washington, D. C., study, for example, prediction of future delinquent behavior was incorrect in 24 percent of the cases. Surely many people would consider a technique with such a high margin of error inappropriate. In addition to practical considerations, the potentially harmful effects of labeling a child as predelinquent must be emphasized. This is a particularly thorny ethical issue when the prediction technique labels *many* children predelinquent.[26]

MMPI

Hathaway and Monachesi utilized the Minnesota Multiphasic Personality Inventory (MMPI) to predict delinquent behavior.[27] This test was originally developed to differentiate groups of psychiatric patients from samples of normal people. It consists of 566 statements to which the subject responds by indicating whether they are true or false as applied to himself. The items on the test deal with a variety of issues, ranging from social attitudes and personal interests to physical and mental health. In recent years this test has become the most commonly used objective psychological test in the diagnosis of psychiatric patients.

In 1948 Hathaway and Monachesi administered the MMPI to 3,971 ninth graders in Minneapolis. Then, in 1954 it was administered to 11,329 ninth graders. All of the subjects were followed up three years later and their delinquent involvement recorded.

The responses to statements on the MMPI that were found to be most different for delinquent and nondelinquent subjects were used to construct a prediction scale for delinquency. Some of these statements are shown in Table 4-1. Unfortunately, when this scale was used with another sample of boys, it did not differentiate between the delinquent and nondelinquent subjects very accurately. This is especially interesting since the MMPI is still a widely used, standard psychological test; yet it fails to clearly differentiate between the two groups.

TABLE 4-1. DELINQUENCY SCALE

ITEM	DELINQUENT RESPONSE
At times I have very much wanted to leave home.	True
When someone does me a wrong I feel I should pay him back if I can, just for the principle of the thing.	True
During one period when I was a youngster I engaged in petty thievery.	True
As a youngster I was suspended from school one or more times for cutting up.	True
I believe women ought to have as much sexual freedom as men.	True
In school I was sometimes sent to the principal for cutting up.	True
Most people will use somewhat unfair means to gain profit or an advantage rather than to lose it.	True
I do not worry about catching diseases.	True
When I was a child, I belonged to a crowd or gang that tried to stick together through thick and thin.	True
I have the wanderlust and am never happy unless I am roaming or traveling about.	True
I am afraid when I look down from a high place.	False
I liked school.	False

Conclusions

Although psychologists have examined a variety of personality traits and behaviors in delinquents, they have had little success in identifying specific traits that characterize all delinquents. For example, the notion proposed earlier in this century—that delinquents have low intelligence-test scores—has not stood up well in recent research studies.

A more useful approach has been to compare the different types of offenders in order to show how they differ from one another in their personalities and behavior. Herbert Quay and his colleagues have expanded this idea and identified three clusters of traits in delinquent boys: the unsocialized psychopathic cluster; the socialized subcultural cluster; and the disturbed neurotic cluster. These three clusters, which were derived from empirical studies of delinquents, match the varieties of delinquency that will be discussed in Chapter 5. Because research findings support Quay's theory, we can safely assume that there is some validity to the categories he has identified.

We have seen that it is possible to predict delinquency within certain bounds. The Glueck scale has proven to be reasonably accurate and thus can serve as a useful addition to whatever other predictive tool a counselor might care to use. But we must consider whether it is wise to attempt to predict delinquency.[25] Prediction and labeling might only serve to aggravate the problem. By stigmatizing certain youths, we may be increasing the likelihood that they will become delinquent. For example, when teachers and parents learn of the label, they may begin treating the child differently, thereby contributing to making him or her delinquent. Of course, such information could be withheld from people who interact with the children, but then ethical problems would arise.

In addition, one might ask whether early identification of potential delinquents is even necessary. If one subscribes to a social theory of delinquency, which places emphasis on social conditions such as poverty and social class (with its consequent frustrations), then to identify potential delinquents would have little utilitarian value. Rather, the social conditions would have to be changed, not the individuals. On the other hand, if one subscribes to theories that focus on the individual, it becomes necessary to identify the potential delinquent and intervene therapeutically in a selective fashion. As Tait and Hodges noted, it is not uncommon for one sibling in a family to become delinquent while the other siblings remain law abiding; thus we cannot argue that social factors alone suffice to explain delinquency. Since individual factors do exist, we must decide how much weight to give them when attempting to prevent delinquency.

One final comment on the prediction of delinquency is necessary. The research indicated that a standard psychological test of personality, the Minnesota Multiphasic Personality Inventory, was of little help in predicting delinquency. A scale based on the home environment of the youth was found to be much more effective, which suggests that the family environment is critically important in determining whether or not a child will become delinquent.

Physiological Bases of Delinquency

Developmental explanations of adolescent delinquency generally stress the role of early childhood experiences and family interactions in the development of personality. These theories are built on the assumption that all children are basically similar but that because they are reared under different circumstances they will develop different types of personalities in response to their surroundings. But we must also consider the possibility that an additional factor might be involved in delinquent behavior, one that could explain why two children raised in similar homes often turn out so differently. This additional factor may be a physiological (physical) one rather than a psychological one.

Physiological processes undoubtedly underlie all behavior in some complex way. It may be that individual differences in personality and physical makeup interact with socialization experiences in such a way as to produce specific behaviors. In this section we will consider how this combination of physical and psychological factors might contribute to delinquent behavior.

Body Types and Personality

It is commonly believed that the way people look can tell something about their personality and their behavior. William Sheldon focused on physique and argued that the same genes that determine a person's body type might also determine his or her personality.[28] Consequently, in Sheldon's view, physique is directly related to personality.

Sheldon identified three primary components of physique. *Endomorphy* refers to the degree of fat. It is associated with softness of the figure and a spherical appearance. Bone and muscle are underdeveloped and the stature is short. *Mesomorphy* refers to bone and muscular development. It is associated with a hard, rectangular body which is strong and tough. A person who is high in this component has an athletic build. *Ectomorphy* refers to physiques that are deficient in both fat and muscular development. This component is associated with a linear, fragile body and a relatively large brain and central nervous system.

Sheldon devised a method called *somatotyping* for measuring the degree of each of the primary components in a person's physique. Each component is rated on a scale of 1 to 7, and each person is described as a three-digit number. For example, a person with a 2-4-6 somatotype is relatively low in endomorphy, about average in mesomorphy, and relatively high in ectomorphy.

Sheldon also identified three components of personality. The adjectives dependent, calm, affable, warm, sociable, soft-tempered, and affectionate describe the component of *viscerotonia*. The adjectives dominant, cheerful, energetic, competitive, assertive, and hot-tempered describe the component of *somatotonia*. The adjectives anxious, shy, introspective, sensitive, withdrawn, and precise describe the component of *cerebrotonia*. Again, the strength of each of these components in a particular person is rated on a scale of 1 to 7, and the person is described using a three-digit number (see Table 4-2).

Sheldon presented a good deal of evidence to indicate that the physique of endomorphy was associated with viscerotonia, mesomorphy with somatotonia, and ectomorphy with cerebrotonia. Although later research has supported his conclusions, the strength of the associations has been found to be quite weak.

Sheldon believed that genetic factors determine both physique and personality. However, other explanations for the association between physique and personality might be equally plausible; for example, social expectations may lead people to make such associations. If members of a society expect fat people to be jovial, then well-socialized fat people may well grow up to be jovial. In addition, it may be that certain environmental influences affect both physique and temperament, such as the type of food parents give their children and the way in which they feed them.

TABLE 4-2. ADJECTIVES THAT DESCRIBE EACH OF SHELDON'S THREE COMPONENTS OF PERSONALITY

VISCEROTONIA	SOMATOTONIA	CEREBROTONIA
_____ dependent	_____ dominant	_____ detached
_____ calm	_____ cheerful	_____ tense
_____ relaxed	_____ confident	_____ anxious
_____ complacent	_____ energetic	_____ reticent
_____ contented	_____ impetuous	_____ self-conscious
_____ sluggish	_____ efficient	_____ meticulous
_____ placid	_____ enthusiastic	_____ reflective
_____ leisurely	_____ competitive	_____ precise
_____ cooperative	_____ determined	_____ thoughtful
_____ affable	_____ outgoing	_____ considerate
_____ tolerant	_____ argumentative	_____ shy
_____ affected	_____ talkative	_____ awkward
_____ warm	_____ active	_____ cool
_____ forgiving	_____ domineering	_____ suspicious
_____ sympathetic	_____ courageous	_____ introspective
_____ soft-hearted	_____ enterprising	_____ serious
_____ generous	_____ adventurous	_____ cautious
_____ affectionate	_____ reckless	_____ tactful
_____ kind	_____ assertive	_____ sensitive
_____ sociable	_____ optimistic	_____ withdrawn
_____ soft-tempered	_____ hot-tempered	_____ gentle-tempered

Source: J. Cortes and F. Gatti, *Delinquency and Crime* (New York: Seminar, 1972), p.55

In his study of male delinquents, Sheldon reported that in almost all cases his subjects had an excess of mesomorphy and a deficit of ectomorphy. Although Sheldon's report has been the target of considerable criticism, subsequent research has confirmed his findings.[29] For example, Glueck and Glueck, in their comparison study of 500 male delinquents and 500 nondelinquents who were matched for age, intelligence, race, and social class, found that delinquents were more mesomorphic and less ectomorphic than nondelinquents.[30] The Gluecks classified the delinquents as predominantly one type or another and obtained the following distribution:

	DELINQUENTS	NONDELINQUENTS
Predominantly endomorphic	59	72
Predominantly mesomorphic	298	148
Predominantly ectomorphic	72	191
Balanced physiques	67	71

Cortes and Gatti criticized these earlier studies on grounds that the methods used to determine physique were not objective. Their primary objection was that these studies focused on adolescents whose physiques had not yet fully developed; moreover, they felt the samples were not necessarily representative of all delinquents since the Gluecks used only institutionalized delinquents in their studies. Cortes and Gatti tried to eliminate these defects in research design and found that male delinquents were more mesomorphic, less endomorphic, and less ectomorphic than nondelinquents.[31] They found these differences to be even greater in adult criminals.

If the relationship between physique and personality holds, then one can postulate that the somatotonic personality is in some way related to deviance. The mesomorph, with an energetic, outgoing, aggressive personality, is more likely to commit delinquent or criminal acts. But what is the rationale for this conclusion? Sheldon does not provide a specific answer to this question, but other theorists have attempted to explain the mechanism by which mesomorphy is associated with deviance.

Hans Eysenck

Eysenck's theory of personality rests on the assumption that all behavior results from an interaction between the genetically determined physical characteristics of the individual (genotype) and the environment in which he or she lives. He presents the formula

$$P_B = P_C \times E$$

where P_B is the behavioral personality, P_C is the genotype, and E is the environment.[32] Thus, if specific behaviors are to be understood, information about both physical characteristics *and* surroundings must be obtained.

According to Eysenck, some behavior tendencies are inherited. This is difficult to prove, but studies of twins have provided some evidence for it. One such study compares the behaviors of people who are monozygotic twins—that is, twins who have identical genetic structures. Monozygotic twins are sometimes called identical twins because they come from a single ovum (fertilized egg) that has split into two. Dizygotic, or fraternal, twins develop from two different ova and have roughly a 50 percent genetic overlap. In many instances dizygotic twins are no more similar than any two siblings; in fact, they may not even look alike. If dizygotic twins differ, the differences can be attributed to either genetic or experiential factors. But if monozygotic twins differ, the differences must result from their experiences after birth. Thus, if monozygotic twins resemble each other in some behavior or personality trait, it is possible to conclude that these similarities are a result of the influence of genetic factors.

The major argument against this view is that because they look alike monozygotic twins may receive more similar treatment during the formative childhood years; thus their great similarity may result from their shared experiences. It could, however, be plausibly argued that because monozygotic twins are identical, parents may make a special effort *not* to treat them alike, but to emphasize their differences in order to create separate identities. Evidence relevant to this issue comes from a study by Scarr, who studied parents who accidentally mislabeled their children; that is, parents who thought their twins were monozygotic when they were actually dizygotic and vice-versa.[33] Scarr found that the degree of similarity between twins was determined more by their actual zygosity than by what the parents believed their zygosity to be.

Research on the relationship between the deviant behavior patterns of twins has indicated a greater concordance rate among monozygotic twins than among dizygotic twins. This means that if one monozygotic twin displays criminal behavior, the other twin might also show this behavior. Many studies have found higher concordance among monozygotic twins. (See Table 4-3.)

TABLE 4-3. CONCORDANCE RATES FOR CRIMINAL BEHAVIOR IN MONOZYGOTIC AND DIZYGOTIC TWINS

	MONOZYGOTIC TWINS		DIZYGOTIC TWINS	
	Concordant	Discordant	Concordant	Discordant
ADULT CRIME				
Lang 1929 Germany	10	3	3	15
Stumpfl 1936 Germany	11	7	7	12
Kranz 1936 Germany	20	11	23	20
Borgstrom 1939 Finland	3	1	2	3
Rosanoff, et al. 1934 USA	25	12	5	23
	67% concordance		35% concordance	
JUVENILE DELINQUENCY				
Rosanoff, et al. USA	39	3	20	5
	93% concordance		80% concordance	

Source: J. Shields, "Personality Differences and Neurotic Traits in Normal Twin School Children," *Eugenics Review* 45 (1954): 213–246.

The twin studies indicate that there is strong evidence for the idea of inherited behavior traits. Eysenck describes two major traits in relation to behavior. These two traits, *extraversion* and *neuroticism,* are thought to be genetically linked characteristics. Physiological processes contribute to these specific, observable characteristics, and the primary trait related to delinquent behavior is *extraversion.*

Extraversion concerns the effect that stimulation has on an individual. Eysenck argues that the extravert has a central nervous system that inhibits the effects of stimulation on the brain. This inhibition builds up quickly and serves to suppress mental activity. In contrast, the central nervous system of the *introvert* facilitates activity within the brain; thus stimulation has a strong effect. Studies of extraverts and introverts have indicated that the more extraverted subjects have higher sensory thresholds for sound and pain (they are less sensitive to it) and find sensory deprivation (being placed in an environment with very few stimuli) more difficult to endure.

Another area in which introverts differ from extraverts is in learning. In classical conditioning, a stimulus elicits an automatic response in the subject—a puff of air to the eye makes him blink. By pairing this stimulus (a puff of air) with a neutral stimulus—say, a bell ringing—one can eventually elicit the same response (an eye blink) using either stimulus (the puff of air or the bell ringing).

US (Unconditioned Stimulus)	UR (Unconditioned Response)
Puff of air	Eye blink
CS (Conditioned Stimulus)	CR (Conditioned Response)
Bell ringing	Eye blink

As one might expect, classical conditioning is easier to set up in introverts than in extraverts.

Eysenck described extraverts as being characterized by a *stimulus hunger* whereas introverts are characterized by a *stimulus aversion*. The inhibitory central nervous system of the extravert reduces the intensity of stimulation, and thus in order to maintain a reasonable level of arousal in his brain, the extravert has to seek out novel and intense stimulation. So we find that extraverts prefer louder music and brighter colors and generally have more friends than introverts. They may smoke more and be more sexually promiscuous. Table 4-4 summarizes some of the major differences between extraverts and introverts.

TABLE 4-4. DIFFERENCES BETWEEN INTROVERTS AND EXTRAVERTS

	INTROVERTS	EXTRAVERTS
Neurotic syndrome	Phobias, obsessions, and compulsions	Hysteria
Body build	Ectomorphy	Mesomorphy and endomorphy
Level of aspiration	High	Low
Conditioning	Quick	Slow
Stress reactions	Overactive	Inert
Sensory deprivation	Tolerant	Intolerant
Social attitude	Tender-minded	Tough-minded
Persistence	High	Low
Speed	Slow	Fast

Source: N. Brady, *Personality* (New York: Academic Press, 1972), p. 45.

Eysenck devised a self-report inventory that attempts to assess the dimensions of extraversion and neuroticism. This test was given to large numbers of people so that the average scores of different groups could be estimated. Prisoners and delinquents alike were found to have high extraversion and neuroticism scores.

Thus, the delinquent is classified by Eysenck as an extravert. This means that all of those traits that were mentioned above as characteristic of extraverts will also characterize delinquents. In particular, delinquents will condition less easily.

According to Eysenck, most people consider committing illegal acts at various times in their lives. Almost everyone is tempted to break society's laws from time to time, but most people choose not to do so because of their conscience. Not only do they feel it would be wrong to break the law but they also fear the consequences—namely, the punishment. Conscience develops, according to Eysenck, as a result of classical conditioning.

When a child was young, for example, he stole some money from his father. When the father found out, he punished the child. The punishment (unconditioned stimulus) hurt the child and frightened him (unconditioned response). Just prior to receiving the punishment, the child had stolen something. The stimulus associated with the theft will now act as a conditioned stimulus. If the child is often punished for stealing, the stimulus associated with stealing will eventually arouse enough fear and pain to prevent the child from stealing. In effect, the child will have undergone classical conditioning.

US (punishment) ————————————→ UR (fear and pain)

CS (stimuli associated ————————→ CR (fear and pain)
with stealing)

Now consider the delinquent as an extravert. Such people do not respond well to classical conditioning and so will learn this stimulus-response sequence more slowly, if at all. As a result they will not develop a strong conscience.

Obviously, other factors are involved in the development of conscience. Do the parents try to condition the child? What do they punish the child for—sexual acts, aggressive behavior? If they never punish him, then he may not be given the chance to develop a conscience. If they teach him criminal behavior, then the introvert will learn better and so become the criminal.

The above analysis touches on only one aspect of the development of conscience. Eysenck would argue that the *subcultural* delinquent has conditioned well and thus will be introverted rather than extraverted. Likewise, people who commit crimes of passion are not necessarily extraverted. A crime of passion is one in which impulses build up to a point where the person is no longer able to control his or her behavior. At this point the impulses break through the control, and the person commits a criminal act. Such people have learned the rules of society but have not learned acceptable ways of releasing their impulses. The problem is one of control and not a deficit in learning.

This, in essence, is Eysenck's theory of delinquency. A review of the research tells us that the overall results support Eysenck's theory. Generally speaking, delinquents and adult criminals *do* obtain high scores on tests of extraversion and neuroticism.[34] Eysenck noted that despite the fact that some studies fail to find a significant difference between delinquents and nondelinquents, no studies have found delinquents to have *lower* scores than nondelinquents.

Criticism of Physiological Theories

The major criticism of physiological-psychological theories of delinquency focuses on the fact that there is insufficient evidence for some of their basic assumptions. Specifically, the link between physical characteristics and personality traits has not been established. The twin studies, which provide perhaps the most supporting evidence, are not without problems. Ideally, a study of monozygotic twins reared in separate households would be the best sample to test, but unfortunately it is very difficult to find subjects who have both of these characteristics.

Another problem with Eysenck's explanation of delinquency is that it fails to explain the role of neuroticism. Delinquents have high extraversion and neuroticism scores but the theory mainly involves extraversion and conditioning. The extraverted delinquent has not been conditioned enough, and the introverted delinquent has either been overconditioned or conditioned to have the wrong values. The role of neuroticism in delinquency, then, is not clear.

Treatment Implications

Eysenck believes that abnormal behavior stems from faulty or impaired learning. Thus he is a firm advocate of therapy techniques that involve relearning—in particular, behavior therapy which uses techniques such as classical conditioning (described above) to teach delinquents socially acceptable behavior.

But as we have shown, Eysenck believes that the delinquent is extraverted with an inhibitory central nervous system that makes it difficult for him to learn the rules of the society and to obey them. Before his behavior can be modified through learning, his central nervous system must be changed, or "uninhibited." Some researchers have experimented with administering drugs to children with behavioral problems in order to release their inhibitions. One drug that accomplishes this is amphetamine.

In the 1940s, a number of studies reported that when children with behavior problems of various kinds (including hyperactivity, aggressiveness, destructiveness, and stealing) were given amphetamine, their behavior improved.[35] These studies found that other drugs did not have such positive effects. Phenobarbital, for example, made the children act worse.

More recently, Eisenberg and his colleagues demonstrated that the behavior of the training school boys improved considerably when they were given amphetamine.[36] The Eisenberg group took twenty-one boys in a cottage at a training school and gave seven of them amphetamine and another seven a placebo (a pill containing only ineffectual substances, such as flour or sugar). The remaining seven boys were given no drugs or pills. The house parents and teachers were then asked to rate the boys on their behavior. The behaviors that were rated included antisocial behaviors such as fighting, lying, and swearing and disturbed behaviors such as bedwetting, nail biting, and anxiety. Neither the parents, the teachers, nor the boys knew who was taking the amphetamine and who was taking the placebo.

The boys were rated on their behavior before the project started (days 0 to 40 in Figure 4-2). Soon after the project started on day 40 the behavior of all of the boys improved, but by day 100 the boys who were taking the amphetamine were behaving significantly better than the other boys. Then the drugs were stopped and by day 140 all of the boys were behaving similarly again.

The behavior of the boys who were taking the amphetamine was markedly less antisocial and less disturbed than that of the other boys. This suggests that perhaps the boys who were taking the amphetamine were behaving in a more introverted fashion, with the result being that they acted-out less, misbehaved less, and thus could learn and obey the rules of the institution.

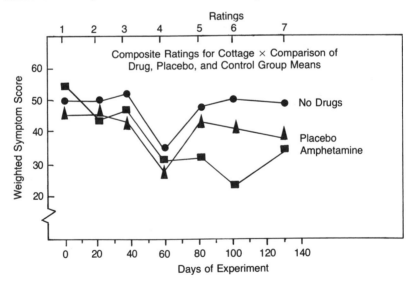

Source: L. Eisenberg et al., "A Psychopharmacologic Experiment in a Training School for Delinquent Boys," *American Journal of Orthopsychiatry* 33 (1963): 436. Reprinted, with permission, from the *American Journal of Orthopsychiatry;* copyright 1963 by the American Orthopsychiatric Association, Inc.

Figure 4-2. Antisocial behavior of training school boys given amphetamines, placebos, and no drugs.

Conclusions

Both Sheldon and Eysenck proposed general theories of personality, which they attempted to apply to delinquent behavior. Eysenck viewed the delinquents as extraverts and Sheldon viewed them as mesomorphs. As we have tried to show, both these theories seem to be focusing on the same basic dimension of personality. Extraverts are mesomorphs, and extraverts and mesomorphs are commonly found in delinquent populations.

Even if it is true that delinquents are generally more extraverted than non-delinquents, it is clear that many delinquents are introverted. Similarly, although delinquents *do* appear to be somewhat more mesomorphic than non-delinquents, some delinquents are endomorphic and some are ectomorphic.

Thus, it appears that what these three theories really provide is a typology of delinquency based on psychological descriptions of personality. These typologies are very similar to Quay's clusters of traits discussed in the previous section.

QUAY	SHELDON	EYSENCK
Unsocialized psychopathic	Mesomorphic	Extraverted, neurotic
Socialized subculture	Endomorphic	Introverted
Disturbed neurotic	Ectomorphic	Introverted, neurotic

We then have to ask, what distinguishes the different kinds of delinquents from one another?[37] For example, we know that the extravert is a poor learner. People of this type fail to learn the rules of the society and never acquire a conscience. They may be the psychopaths or the sociopaths. They will be very difficult to treat since they do not respond well to attempts to teach them the rules of society.

On the other hand, the stable introvert is a good learner and can internalize the rules of society. How then does this person become delinquent? Juveniles of this type become delinquent by belonging to a deviant or delinquent subculture or by having parents or friends who teach them behaviors and rules that are seen as deviant by the larger society. Since delinquents in this category are good learners, they will respond well to treatment and will find it relatively easy to learn a new set of rules for their behavior.

DISCUSSION QUESTIONS

1. If one adopts the Freudian explanations of delinquent behavior, what then would be the primary treatment goals?

2. Discuss the problems inherent in predicting future delinquency in terms of accuracy and individual freedom.

3. At present, what can be said about the general personality characteristics of delinquents?

4. Discuss the interaction between psychology and physiology in Eysenck's theory of delinquency. Under what circumstances might delinquency be related to extraversion? To introversion?

5. Discuss the problems and potential dangers of the treatment strategy for extraverted juveniles suggested by Eysenck.

NOTES

1. W. Toman, *An Introduction to the Psychoanalytic Theory of Motivation* (New York: Pergamon, 1960).

2. Fritz Redl and David Wineman, *Children Who Hate* (New York: Free Press, 1951).

3. Ibid., p. 92.

4. Ibid., p. 176.

5. Albert Cohen, *Deviance and Control* (Englewood Cliffs, N. J.: Prentice-Hall, 1966).

6. Ibid.

7. Edwin I. Megargee, "Undercontrolled and Overcontrolled Personality Types in Extreme Antisocial Aggression," *Psychological Monographs,* 80 (1966).

8. S. Palmer, *A Study of Murder* (New York: Crowell, 1960).

9. S. Glueck and E. Glueck, eds., *Identification of Predelinquents* (New York: Intercontinental Medical Book Corp., 1972).

10. Palmer, *Study of Murder.*

11. L. Robins, *Deviant Children Grown Up* (Baltimore: Williams and Wilkins, 1966).

12. Redl and Wineman, *Children Who Hate.*

13. M. Q. Warren, "The Case of Differential Treatment of Delinquents," *Annals of the American Society of Political and Social Science,* 381(1969): 47–59.

14. N. Caplan, "Intellectual Functioning," in *Juvenile Delinquency,* ed. H. Quay (Princeton: Van Nostrand, 1965), pp. 100–138.

15. H. Goddard, *Juvenile Delinquency* (New York: Dodd, Mead, 1912).

16. L. Siebert, "Otis 12 Scores of Delinquents," *Journal of Clinical Psychology,* 18 (1962): 517.

17. M. Lichtenstein and A. Brown, "Intelligence and Achievement of Children in a Delinquency Area," *Journal of Juvenile Research,* 22 (1938): 1–25.

18. S. Porteus, "Porteus Maze Test," *British Journal of Medical Psychology,* 20 (1945): 267–270.

19. Caplan, "Intellectual Functioning."

20. N. Caplan, "A Comparative Analysis of Average and Superior IQ Delinquents" (Ph.D. diss., Case Western Reserve University, 1961).

21. N. Caplan and A. Gligor, "A Study of the Relationship Between Intelligence and Offense Among Juvenile Delinquents." Unpublished paper (1964).

22. H. Quay, *Juvenile Delinquency* (Princeton: Van Nostrand, 1965).

23. P. Briggs and R. Wirt, "Predictions," in *Juvenile Delinquency,* ed. H. Quay (Princeton: Van Nostrand, 1965), pp. 170–208.

24. S. Glueck and E. Glueck, *Unraveling Juvenile Delinquency* (New York: Commonwealth Fund, 1950).

25. Glueck and Glueck, 1972, *op. cit.,* pp. 36, 49.

26. S. Hathaway and E. Monachesi, *Adolescent Personality and Behavior* (Minneapolis: University of Minnesota Press, 1963).

27. Ibid., p. 89.

28. W. Sheldon, *Varieties of Delinquent Youth* (New York: Harper, 1949).

29. T. Gibbens, *Psychiatric Studies of Borstel Lads* (New York: Oxford University Press, 1963); P. Epps and R. Parnell, "Physique and Temperament of Women Delinquents Compared with Women Undergraduates," *British Journal of Medical Psychology,* 29 (1952): 249–255.

30. S. Glueck and E. Glueck, *Physique and Delinquency* (New York: Harper, 1956).

31. J. Cortes and F. Gatti, *Delinquency and Crime* (New York: Seminar, 1972).

32. H. Eysenck, *Crime and Personality* (London: Paladin, 1970), p. 100.

33. S. Scarr, "Genetic Factors in Activity Motivation," *Child Development,* 37 (1966): 663–673.

34. Eysenck, *Crime and Personality.*

35. D. Lindsley and C. Henry, "The Effects of Drugs on Behavior and the Electroencephalogram of Children with Behavior Disorders," *Psychosomatic Medicine,* 4 (1942): 140–149.

36. L. Eisenberg et al., "A Psychopharmacologic Experiment in a Training School for Delinquent Boys," *American Journal of Orthopsychiatry,* 33 (1963): 431–447.

37. C. Franks, "Recidivism, Psychopathy and Personality," *British Journal of Delinquency,* 6 (1956): 192–201.

5 Patterns of Delinquent Involvement

In this chapter we will discuss specific topics in juvenile delinquency that are important in order to obtain an accurate view of this behavior. Delinquency among lower-class males has been the major focal point of researchers and theorists. The study of middle-class, upper-class, and female delinquency represents a relatively recent shift in focus. In the past, affluent juveniles and females were considered unlikely to be involved in delinquent activities. We will consider some of the popular assumptions about the nature of middle-class and female delinquency and will examine research results that refute these assumptions.

In the minds of many people the term delinquent conjures up the image of the juvenile gang. Here we will review the structure of juvenile gangs and their activities, from the descriptions contained in the early works of the 1930s up to the present. Hopefully some misinformation and incorrect stereotypes about the gang will be countered.

Violence by juveniles is an issue that is of great concern to many people in our society. But what is the true extent of violence committed by juveniles and what are the causes of this behavior? This chapter will attempt to answer these questions by examining the characteristics and backgrounds of the violent offender. Although we will not discuss treatment strategies used with violent offenders, the reader is encouraged to review the treatment projects and techniques described in earlier chapters.

Middle-Class Delinquency

Although delinquency theory and research have concentrated primarily on lower-class juveniles, the higher-status youngster has been the subject of inquiry for some writers.[1] Although the existence of middle- and upper-class delinquents in the United States has been acknowledged by traditional theorists, it has always been viewed as a much less serious problem than the lower-class delinquent.[2] The working-class gang delinquent was a more frequent and dangerous offender and was often arrested and processed through the juvenile justice system. Thus official records were thought to provide a vivid reflection of the social-status distribution of deviant behavior, which singled out lower-class youngsters as the most prevalent offenders.

With the advent of self-report techniques, which enabled researchers to investigate the incidence of delinquency at all levels of society, the old assumptions about social class and delinquency were cast into doubt since middle- and upper-class youngsters reported great numbers of offenses. It became clear that much deviant behavior was undetected and that children from higher-status backgrounds were simply more likely to escape official attention than their lower-status counterparts. (See Table 5–1.)

TABLE 5-1. AVERAGE NUMBER OF SELF-REPORTED AND OFFICIAL DELINQUENT ACTS BY FATHER'S OCCUPATION

FATHER'S OCCUPATION	SELF-REPORTED ACTS	OFFICIAL OFFENSES	NUMBER OF BOYS
Lower	.81	.32	124
Upper-Lower	.68	.28	112
Lower-Middle	.83	.27	300
Middle	.88	.24	128
Upper-Middle	.61	.22	241
Total Sample	.76	.26	905

Source: Travis Hirschi, *Causes of Delinquency* (Berkeley, Calif.: University of California Press, 1972), p. 74

Other research similar to this study indicated little or no relationship between social status and juvenile offenses.[3]

The use of frequency of offenses as the measure of delinquent involvement was criticized by some writers who suggested that the type of offense may vary considerably according to social status. Indeed other researchers have found that lower-status juveniles report more serious offenses.[4] The types of behavior found among middle- and upper-class juveniles include drinking alcohol, traffic violations, and "joyriding."[5] Other activities, such as gambling, shoplifting, minor vandalism, and petty larceny, have also been found among higher-status juveniles.[6]

Thus the child from a middle-socioeconomic status is not immune to delinquent behavior. The type of offense he or she commits may be of a less serious nature than that committed by a poor juvenile, but even "less serious" offenses can be both dangerous and costly to society. Drunken driving and drag racing, for example, though seen as milder forms of delinquency than armed robbery and other offenses, are potentially destructive to both the participants and other citizens. It is interesting to note that the middle-class delinquent is often described in terms that obscure this fact; the middle-class delinquent has been described as "mischievous" or "amusing" by observers of a middle-class gang.[7] There is some evidence that serious offenses among affluent juveniles are simply undetected by officials. Karacki and Toby described a middle-class gang that committed acts ranging from armed robbery to serious larcenies.[8] Although such offenses appear to be rare among more privileged juveniles, they do sometimes occur.[9]

Although children from more privileged homes *do* commit delinquent offenses, they are often treated differently by adults who are more tolerant of a well-dressed youngster's pranks. The police may choose to divert a contrite, well-mannered youngster who comes from a good home; likewise, a teacher may react to a "good student" who cuts classes with merely an informal reprimand.

Because social class has long been considered a major etiological factor in delinquency, the middle-class delinquent presents a problem for theorists. The effects of social disorganization, lower-class values, and lack of opportunity cannot explain deviance among youngsters who occupy advantaged positions in society. Other factors must be involved in producing delinquency among these adolescents.

Theories of Middle-Class Delinquency

Theories of middle-class delinquency have focused on changes in the structure of industrialized, modernized, and urbanized societies. Industrialization increases the wealth of society, social mobility, and the amount of leisure time available to its members. Family structures become less important as agents of socialization, and other institutions such as the school are given a more important role in the training and control of the young. Children remain dependent on their parents for longer periods of time and enter the work force at a later age. These social structure changes are linked in a variety of ways to the phenomenon of delinquency among the privileged.

Family Structure   The changing role of the family is considered by many to be a key factor in the etiology of middle-class delinquency. The responsibility for socialization of the young, once in the realm of kinship groups, now belongs to the nuclear family. Today parents perform a task that was once shared by aunts, uncles, cousins, and grandparents. The increased employment of women outside of the home and the amount of time children spend in educational institutions have expanded the role of the school in socialization, thus shifting the training of the young away from the domain of the family.

Albert Cohen suggested that the school now serves primarily as a means of social control since it must keep a larger population of young people off the streets and out of the labor market.[10] The 16-year-old dropout has nowhere to go because unskilled workers are no longer in demand. For the uninterested or unmotivated child, school is a holding tank. The emphasis on hard work and achievement has given way to the idea that school should be a "pleasurable experience," and the values and opinions of peers have replaced those of authority figures in importance. The relationship between success in school, acceptance to college, and occupational security is no longer seen as viable, so what one does in school (and outside of it) is not perceived as dangerous to one's future. The result of these changes is "a weakening of one of the principal insulators against juvenile delinquency."[11] The school and traditional middle-class values have been superseded by a "youth culture" that encourages delinquency.

The family structure has also been related to middle-class delinquency through its failure in socialization for sex-role identification and self-control. Parsons noted that it is often difficult for the male child to learn sex-role-appropriate behavior in the nuclear family due to the minimal interaction with the father.[12] When male role models are not available for the young boy, frustration results. The female child has exposure to the mother as a female role model, but the male child must learn to reject this model. This may lead to "compulsive masculinity" among male children.[13] Jackson Toby has suggested that this compulsive masculinity may be expressed in a symbolic form by some juveniles, especially those from affluent backgrounds.[14] Instead of overt aggression, "playboy" delinquency of a less serious nature may result.

Hirschi's control theory also dealt with the role of the family in middle-class delinquency.[15] According to this theory, the child with the weakest attachments to parents (and school) was most likely to engage in delinquent acts regardless of social class. The child's relationship to the parent then would be important in the causation of delinquency. As we noted in our discussion of control theory in Chapter 2, specific child-rearing techniques are associated with child-parent attachments. Inconsistency, unfair punishment, or parental rejection engender weak ties. Bandura and Walters, in a study of aggressive middle-class youngsters, emphasized similar factors in the interactions between the subjects and their parents.[16] Inconsistency in parental warmth, fulfillment of dependency needs, and punishment were found to be present in the backgrounds of all these children.

Another factor that has been related to delinquency among the affluent is increased democracy within the family, with each family member having a more equal position in family decision making. Cohen and Short pointed to the lack of a strong authority figure within the family and greater permissiveness as key contributors to delinquency.[17] Concern about what the "experts" say about child rearing and the inclusion of children in decision making have weakened the socialization powers of parents. According to Vaz, relaxed parental control and the encouragement of children to engage in peer-related activities have also served to increase delinquency.[18]

Social Structure   Society's value systems have also been related to misconduct among middle-class juveniles. Much has been made of the influence of the "youth culture" on children in industrialized nations, which is thought to encourage hedonistic behavior.[19] The young, who are wealthy, without responsibility, and with much free time, develop their own norms, attitudes, values, and modes of dress. The emphasis on sociability (being popular in school) and peer-related activity among juveniles further strengthens the youth culture and in effect produces delinquency. Delinquency is often non-utilitarian for these juveniles; it is a way of having fun and passing the time. It is also possible that rather than standing in opposition to middle-class values, the youth culture actually represents a distortion or a reordering of conventional values. Ralph England noted that adult leisure values may be adopted by juveniles.[20] Alcohol use, sexual activity, and the importance of the automobile are all part of the system of adult norms and behaviors. When young people attempt to act out these values, engaging in "adult" behaviors, the result is what some label "middle-class delinquency."

The final perspective on affluent delinquency that will be discussed here is interesting in that it views delinquency as a by-product of the diffusion of lower-class values throughout society. Miller and Kvaraceus suggested that the lower-class "focal concerns" have moved upward in the social structure.[21] As a result, middle-class values such as responsibility, deferred gratification, and education have been challenged by the focal concerns of toughness, smartness, and fate. They suggest that an upward diffusion was caused by the acceptance of lower-class music forms, such as jazz and rock and roll, and the glorification of toughness and violence in the media.

Robert Bohlke offered a different perspective on the role of values in middle-class delinquency.[22] The social mobility experienced by some people meant upward or downward movement in the social hierarchy, or stratification system, without an accompanying change in values. The *nouvelle bourgeoisie,* or new middle-class, adolescent may have a middle-class income but may be rejected by other middle-class juveniles because of his or her unaltered working-class values. Thus delinquency would result from hostility toward one's rejectors. Downwardly mobile middle-class families may experience delinquency among their children when their middle-class values fail to bring the desired rewards, at which point rebellion may occur. Movement within the social order causes dislocation or "status disequilibria" because the old value systems do not transfer well to the new social status environment.[23]

Theories of middle-class delinquency concentrate on the effects of changing social structures. Generally, industrialized nations have higher rates of delinquent behavior, which suggests that the changes associated with an industrialized economic system are surely related to both middle- and lower-class deviance. Lack of control from family and school and the development of a youth culture encourage stronger peer influence. A lag in value acquisition by the upwardly mobile or in some cases the failure of middle-class values encourage a distrust of conventional norms, attitudes, and behaviors. Problems in masculine identification for male children may lead to undue aggressive behavior.

Criticisms of the Theories

The major problem with most theories of middle-class delinquency is that they fail to explain why social structure changes affect some affluent juveniles and not others. Hirschi's research indicates that family relationships are an important determinant in delinquency and thus offers a possible explanation for such differences. Other theories do not broach this issue.

Another problem with theories regarding middle-class delinquency is the dearth of empirical data on the causes of the behavior. Theories remain untested, and much of the research that has been conducted focuses on the amount and types of hidden delinquency among middle-class juveniles rather than on the causes. We also have little information on female delinquency and on changing trends in middle-class offense patterns. At present, we know that affluent youngsters *do* engage in delinquent behavior but that their acts are often undetected and are usually of a less serious nature than those committed by poorer youngsters.

Female Delinquency

From a review of the literature on delinquency one could easily assume that females are seldom involved in delinquency.[24] Theorists rarely include female offenders in their explanations of delinquency, and much of the empirical work has been conducted using samples consisting only of male juveniles. This lack of interest in females no doubt resulted from official records of delinquent acts which indicate that females commit many fewer offenses than males.

Delinquency came to be seen as a male phenomenon. Indeed, Lombroso explained female criminality as occurring among women who possessed masculine characteristics in appearance and personality.[25] Official statistics sometimes place the ratio of male to female delinquents at 50 to 1, thus lending support to the assumption that most delinquents are males.[26]

The gap between male and female offense rates has closed considerably since the 1900s, with the present ratio of males to females at approximately 5 to 1. Adler has explained these changes as a result of the industrialization of society and the greater emancipation of women.[27] With more women having jobs, schools and other social institutions have assumed additional responsibility for socialization of the young. The female sex role has expanded to include behaviors that were once considered "masculine," such as aggressiveness and achievement orientation. As a result, the female juvenile has more freedom and more opportunities for involvement in delinquency.

The types of offenses that females commit, according to police and juvenile court records, are very different from those committed by males. Official female delinquency most often consists of sexual offenses, running away from home, incorrigibility, and truancy whereas males are more likely to commit property offenses.[28] These differences are not surprising since they coincide with sex-role expectations for females and males. Women are encouraged to be expressive and to establish status in terms of sexual atttractiveness.[29] Men are encouraged to be success oriented and to engage in instrumental behaviors. Thus the female who experiments with sex is seen as expressing rebellion or a desire for status whereas sexual activity among males is considered acceptable. A male is more likely to be arrested for property offenses or violence.

An example of official female offense patterns is shown in Table 5-2, which lists the first arrests of 500 delinquent women studied by Sheldon and Eleanor Glueck in 1934.[30] Their sample consisted of women who had been paroled from a state institution. When the histories of these women were examined, a high percentage of sexual offenses was found. Over 37 percent of first offenses were offenses against chastity; another 20 percent were the classic status offenses of runaway, truancy, and waywardness. A small percent, 12.4, had initially been involved in property offenses, and only 1.8 percent had engaged in acts against the person. The information in this table, which was obtained from official arrest records, provides a good example of the types of arrest patterns found among females. Only 14.2 percent of the women studied by the Gluecks had committed first offenses that were similar to those committed by males. The majority of the women had been involved in status offenses or sexual offenses.

These offense patterns must be critically evaluated since they are not found when self-report questionnaires are used to gather data from juveniles. Studies have indicated that female juveniles report participation in many forms of delinquent behavior in addition to those found in the official records. Barton and Wise compared the responses of middle-class males and females and found that similar types of offenses were reported, but generally the overall incidence of delinquency was found to be higher among males. The difference between males and females, however, was not as large as that found in the juvenile court records.[31]

Other researchers have had similar results when utilizing self-report techniques to gather data. For example, Gold found that the females in his sample reported running away, incorrigibility, and fornication as comprising 8 percent of their total delinquent acts. These acts represented 6 percent of the offenses reported by males. Interestingly, the official records for this sample indicated that these types of offenses accounted for over 43 percent of female offenses and 8 percent of male offenses.[32]

TABLE 5-2. CAUSE OF FIRST KNOWN ARREST

OFFENSE	PERCENT
1. Offense against person	1.8
2. Offense against chastity—adultery, polygamy	7.6
3. Offense against chastity—common nightwalking or frequenting a house of ill fame	5.8
4. Offense against chastity—fornication	5.2
5. Offense against chastity—keeping house of ill fame or sharing proceeds of prostitution	1.0
6. Offense against chastity—lewd and lascivious behavior	18.0
7. Stubborn children (runaway, truancy, waywardness, breaking glass, unnatural act)	20.2
8. Against family and children	2.4
9. Against public health, safety, and policy (except drink and drug)	16.2
10. Drink	9.0
11. Drugs	0.4
12. Offense against property	12.4

N = 500

Source: Reprinted by permission of the publisher, from *Women and Crime* by Rita James Simon (Lexington, Mass.: Lexington Books, D. C. Heath and Company. Copyright 1975, D. C. Heath and Company).

Although females do not report the same degree of involvement in delinquency as males, the difference does not appear to be as large as it was once thought to be. Granted, offense patterns are similar among males and females but females (especially lower-status females) are more likely to become official delinquents as a result of status and sex offenses. Self-report studies provide little evidence to support the contention that girls commit more sexual offenses; indeed, one researcher found that males report five times as many sexual offenses as girls.[33]

Obviously the type of data available to researchers can lead to many conflicting conclusions. Official female delinquents are reportedly involved in sexual misconduct and "incorrigibility" whereas unofficial reports indicate very different patterns. Because neither of the two data sources is infallible, it is difficult to draw a completely accurate picture of the female delinquent. The fact that discretion is used by police officers, school officials, social workers, probation officers, and juvenile court judges in deciding who will be labeled and for what types of offenses must be considered when interpreting official records. The end result of this process—official records— indicates as much about the values and biases of the people in power, those who make the decisions about whom to arrest, as they do about the frequency and nature of delinquent behavior. Despite the fact that self-report studies do

offer opportunities to exaggerate or minimize one's involvement in misconduct, the considerable discrepancies between the two sources of data suggest
that official records alone are at best only marginally useful in describing
delinquency among girls.

TABLE 5-3. SEX DIFFERENCES IN DELINQUENT INVOLVEMENT

STUDY	SOURCE OF DATA	FREQUENCY RATIO BY SEX: FEMALES TO MALES
Wattenberg and Saunders	Complaints to police	1 to 3
Gibbons and Griswold	Referrals to juvenile court	1 to 3.5
Barker and Adams	Training school records	1 to 4
Hindelang	Self-report	1 to 2.56
Barton; Wise	Self-report	1 to 1.7

Sources: W. Wattenberg and F. Saunders, "Sex Differences Among Juvenile Offenders," Sociology and Social Research 39 (1954): 24–31; D. Gibbons and M. Griswold, "Sex Differences Among Juvenile Court Referrals," Sociology
and Social Research 42 (1957): 106–110; G. Barker and W. Adams, "Comparisons of the Delinquencies of Boys and
Girls," Journal of Criminal Law, Criminology, and Police Science 53 (1962): 470–476; Michael Hindelang, "Age, Sex,
and the Versatility of Delinquent Involvement," Social Problems 18 (1971): 522–533; Nancy B. Wise, "Juvenile Delinquency Among Middle-Class Girls," in Middle Class Juvenile Delinquency, ed. Edmund W. Vaz (New York: Harper
and Row, 1967), p. 179–188.

Table 5–3 summarizes findings from five major studies of female delinquency. The ratio between female and male involvement increases in official
records as one moves further into the juvenile justice system. This may actually reflect the selective factors used in decision making within the system.
As we discussed earlier, self-reported delinquency studies indicate a smaller
gap between male and female offense patterns.

Theories of Female Delinquency

One of the earliest explanations of female criminality emphasized the role of
biological differences between women and men. Cesare Lombroso described
women as more "primitive" than men in brain development and anatomy.
In his book, *The Female Offender,* he noted that women were less variable
in their anatomical, physiological, and sensory traits and as a result of this
lack of variation were less likely to be involved in crime.[34] Those women
who did commit offenses, according to Lombroso, tended to be more "masculine" in their characteristics. Born criminals were rare among females but
prostitutes were described as congenital criminals. Most women criminals
were occasional offenders who responded primarily to situational temptation.

Lombroso's ideas are interesting only in that they underscore some of the
basic assumptions and misconceptions about women that theorists have traditionally adopted. First, theorists have assumed that women are different
creatures from men and are naturally less inclined toward criminality. Sec-

ond, women are thought to commit sexual offenses when they do become involved in illegitimate activity. Subsequent research has refuted Lombroso's notion that criminal behavior could be explained in terms of biological differences between males and females, yet some of the basic ideas set forth in *The Female Offender* are still discussed by criminologists.[35]

The sexually delinquent girl was the topic of another theoretical work on female offenders published in 1923. W. I. Thomas emphasized the importance of socialization in female delinquent behavior.[36] He described four basic wishes that he believed people sought to satisfy. These were desires for new experience, security, response, and recognition. According to his theory, the female delinquent attempted to fulfill these needs through inappropriate and often illegal means. Lack of adequate socialization, especially among the poor, resulted in an inability on the part of females to deal with these desires in a socially acceptable manner, and as a result the young girl utilized her body as a means of gaining new experiences, security, response, and recognition. Thus sexual delinquency was to be expected from undersocialized girls. Thomas underscored the fact that poor girls, who were not privy to alternative means of realizing these desires, were the most likely to exhibit this behavior.

Otto Pollak questioned some of these assumptions about female offenders in his book, *The Criminality of Women*.[37] Pollak believed that the low official crime rates for women were incorrect because large numbers of offenses committed by women were hidden. The reasons for these hidden crimes were that: 1) females commit offenses that are underreported such as shoplifting, domestic thefts, abortions; 2) women are not detected as often as men because they are more deceitful; and 3) law enforcement officials are more lenient with women.[38] The possibility that female offenders might exhibit different offense patterns was an important one, but it was not until the use of self-report techniques that an empirical test of Pollak's suggestions was made. The offenses he cited as more common among women were not supported by official research on female juveniles. Evidence has been presented to support the idea of leniency by law enforcement officials, but this appears to be the case in only some instances. Offenses such as incorrigibility, truancy, or running away from home appear to be considered more serious when the offender is female.

More recently, the female sex role has received much attention as a determinant of delinquency among girls. Some writers have explained both male and female delinquency as an attempt to obtain status. Males seek status through achievement, and females seek to fulfill these needs through interpersonal relationships. Failure to attain these goals through legitimate channels results in property offenses among males (to impress peers) and sexual delinquency among females (in an attempt to establish ties with members of the opposite sex).[39] Female delinquency then is a manifestation of maladjustment or failure in the traditional female sex role. Girls may seek security

and emotional support but fail to fulfill these needs through legitimate channels.[40] The expressive role of the female adolescent, if not supported by family and friends in appropriate ways, prompts the girl to seek other sources of
gratification. Thus delinquency among girls is encouraged by an inability to
succeed as a female. That offense patterns in official records look the way
they do is not surprising according to this explanation because sex-role related
offenses are to be expected. The development of interpersonal relationships
outside of the family is enhanced by promiscuity, truancy, and running away.

A recent book by Freda Adler, *Sisters in Crime*, considers female delinquency in light of recent research.[41] Adler notes that the traditional conception of the delinquent girl describes her as unadjusted, intropunitive, and as
utilizing her sexuality as a coping mechanism. Adler criticizes this perspective on grounds that it is based on the records of the juvenile court. She points
out that the courts judge girls on the basis of social expectations of the female
sex role. Girls are to be "sexy" (but not sexual), passive, and cooperative.
Sexual activity is seen as pathological in girls yet the same behavior is considered normal in a boy. The chivalry factor, or the leniency toward females
described by Pollak, operates to decrease the number of girls who are officially labeled, but it also serves to treat those girls who do appear in court
more harshly. Female juveniles are more frequently institutionalized, which
reflects the assumption that females need more care and protection.

Adler explains female delinquency as originating from basically the same
sources as male delinquency. Problems in transition from child to adult in
society, the effects of societal changes, and opportunity structures push both
sexes toward delinquent involvement. She notes the changes in crime rates
and the concomitant change in the female role in our society.

> The era when girls sewed dresses and boys sowed wild oats has yielded to a
> period when both are expected to achieve a degree of self-sufficiency. Passivity
> is no longer a self-evident feminine virtue, and status is not automatically con-
> ferred on the girl who is docile and chaste.[42]

Girls are involved in more typically masculine offenses—stealing, gang activity, and fighting. The move away from traditional sex roles to a conver-
gence of male and female roles may explain the changes in frequency of
offense by sex. Between 1960 and 1972 the national arrest statistics show an
increase for juvenile males of 82 percent and for juvenile females of 306
percent.[43] Indeed Adler predicts even more delinquent involvement for females because today there is so much confusion about the female role. Identity problems are more severe for female adolescents because

> they are discarding the ways of their mothers and are not yet quite certain about
> how much of the ways of their fathers they will wish to or be allowed to adopt.
> More and more girls are hanging around the corner in psychosocial limbo with

little to do, no place to go vocationally, or domestically, and protected by few structural restraints from delinquency.[44]

Lack of legitimate opportunities for females and the contrasting models of the traditional domestic role and the new, more liberated woman make adolescence a very difficult period for girls. That their involvement in delinquency has increased and is of a more "masculine" nature results from the greater freedom and opportunity for illegal activities available to women.

Criticisms of the Theories

Theories of female delinquency suffer from many of the same shortcomings as those found in theories of middle-class delinquency. The source of information on delinquency rates and offense patterns greatly affects the conclusions researchers draw about the behavior. Official records indicate a higher incidence of delinquency among lower-class females and the offenses are often of a sexual nature. Self-report techniques, on the other hand, indicate offense patterns that are more similar to those of males, a greater frequency of female offenses in general, and little difference in offense frequency by social class among female delinquents.[45] Depending on the data used by the theorist, very different explanations of delinquency can be drawn.

Theories that rely on differences between males and females—from Lombroso's biological explanations to the later sex-role theories—have been undermined considerably by studies indicating similarities between the offenses committed by males and females. Those theories that utilize the traditional sex-role expectations and strivings have been outdated by the changes in the status and roles of women in society. The causes of female deviance may be as similar to those of male delinquency as are the offenses they commit.

The Delinquent Gang

The delinquent gang has received much attention from social scientists, the media, police, and concerned citizens. Not a new phenomenon in the United States, delinquent and adult gangs were found in urban areas early in our history. Neighborhood gangs controlled illegal activities in their territories, and some of the more prosperous ones went on to develop an organized crime syndicate.[46] Herbert Asbury reported on adult gangs called the "Dead Rabbits," the "Plug Uglies," and the "Dusters" in his book titled *Gangs of New York*.[47] These gangs inhabited the Bowery in New York City in the late nineteenth century and frequently resorted to violence in order to maintain their "control." Other writers of the early 1900s described youth gangs that engaged in activities ranging from playing games to stealing and fighting with other gangs.[48] Thrasher provided a detailed look at juvenile gangs in Chicago in the 1930s and noted that 1,313 such gangs were located during his study.

Gangs have flourished in urban areas for a long time, and they have been studied, analyzed, and described by many writers. Often delinquency has been treated as if it were primarily a gang-related behavior. For example, the theories of Miller, Cohen, and Cloward and Ohlin focus on lower-class gang members rather than on delinquency in general. The assumption has been made by many people that delinquent acts are most often committed by members of gangs. The solitary or nongang member who committed such acts was thought to be an exceptional case.

Little evidence was mustered to defend these assumptions about the prevalence of gang-related delinquency. The greater visibility of juvenile gangs and the fact that they made more interesting newspaper copy served to reinforce the idea that delinquents were usually gang members. The youngster who vandalized a building or took a car for a "joyride" was not likely to create the concern that intergang fights did.

Recent studies which utilize self-report questionnaires have provided information on juvenile behavior that undermines these previous ideas about gangs. One researcher found that a large percentage of the delinquent acts reported by youngsters were committed without stable gang support. Some subjects reported delinquent involvement even though they were not members of an organized group or gang.[49] Another study indicated that much delinquency occurs in the absence of accomplices.[50] Because many offenses are not gang related, the importance of the gang in relation to the frequency of delinquent acts appears to have been greatly overstated.

Although gang delinquency does not appear to account for the largest proportion of delinquent acts, gang violence does present a danger to many neighborhoods in urban areas. It has also been a popular topic in the field of delinquency for researchers and many delinquency prevention projects.

It is important to emphasize that adolescent groupings or gangs are not always delinquency producing. Indeed such peer groups may perform an important social function in aiding the transition of their members from childhood to adult roles. Athletic and social clubs, for example, provide opportunities for a child to develop feelings of independence and social competence. Rehearsals of adult behaviors can take place in such settings and to a large extent, this is seen as positive by adults. It is only when these groups concentrate on antisocial or illegal activities that their role is seen as dysfunctional for society.

The Nature of the Gang

One of the first studies of the delinquent gang was conducted by Frederic Thrasher in the early 1900s.[51] From his examination of a large number of gangs in Chicago, Thrasher concluded that gangs originated from spontaneous play groups that became increasingly integrated through conflict with persons *outside* the group. The gang that developed from this play group was attached to a local territory, maintained *esprit de corps,* solidarity, morale, group awareness, and informal internal structure. Roles evolved within the gang, and a leadership position was filled by a member with a strong personality and physical prowess.

Thrasher and other members of the Chicago School explored the nature of the gang and the neighborhoods in which they were found. Their ideas were widely accepted. Yablonsky has summarized the Chicago School's conception of the gang as follows:

1. The juvenile begins his involvement in play which may be mischievous, and then becomes more involved in the delinquency of the gang.
2. Community reaction to this behavior (disapproval) serves to drive the child further into the gang.
3. Gangs result primarily from the failure of the family in some neighborhoods to integrate children into conforming behavior.
4. The gang becomes cohesive through its emphasis on loyalty and *esprit de corps*.
5. Gangs may become a "street-corner family" for youngsters who are alienated from other attachments.
6. The gang may provide opportunities and training for a criminal career.
7. Societal institutions that deal with gang members encourage greater gang involvement.
8. By associations and training in the gang, the delinquent becomes a hardened adult offender.[52]

The gang developed in communities or neighborhoods that were characterized by poverty and disorganization. Delinquent patterns continued even after changes in the composition of the population in these areas had occurred, mainly because the gang offered the children of immigrants opportunities to become integrated into a new culture.

The influx of immigrant populations and the replacement of one ethnic group by another in slum neighborhoods has subsided in urban areas, leaving a "stable slum."[53] Since populations have remained fairly constant, traditions and neighborhood patterns have evolved. The stable slum areas of the eastern United States consist of black and Puerto Rican populations, and the western cities have Mexican-American *barrios*. These stable areas give rise to gang structures that are somewhat different from those found in a transitional, changing neighborhood. The gang described by the Chicago School, with its spontaneous, informal nature, is replaced by a large, vertically structured gang.[54]

Malcolm Klein has called these two gang types *spontaneous* and *traditional*. The spontaneous gang includes 10 to 30 members who are close in age. This type of gang is transient and often survives less than a year. The traditional gang includes two to five age-graded subgroups within the overall gang. These subgroups often have their own names and their own identity, yet they maintain allegiance to the superordinate "cluster."[55] The traditional gang structure is typically found in stable slum areas.

Figure 5-1 shows the structure of a traditional gang from a California city. Note the name differences and age groups; the members of this particular gang range in age from 11 to 23. The traditional gang may have as many as 100 or 200 members over a period of time, and may have a tradition going back as far as 50 years.[56]

Other types of gang structures have been described, but these tend to be less extensive than the two major categories. *Specialty cliques* have been found by some gang researchers. A few members become heavily involved in specific types of activities. These occur within larger gang structures.[57] Another type of structure, the "near group," has been described in relation to the violent gang and middle-class gangs.[58] The near group is quite similar in structure to the spontaneous gang. It is impermanent, has limited cohesion, and shifting membership.

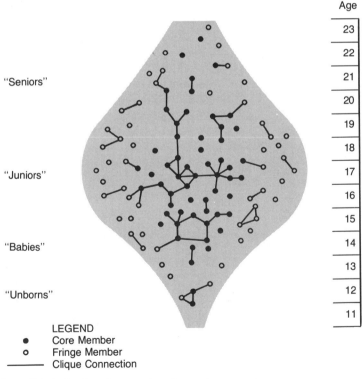

LEGEND
● Core Member
○ Fringe Member
── Clique Connection

Source: Malcolm Klein, *Street Gangs and Street Workers*, © 1971, p. 66. Reprinted by permission of Prentice-Hall, Inc., Englewood Cliffs, New Jersey.

Figure 5-1. The Latins: a traditional gang cluster.

The roles of the members of the gang differ in terms of frequency of involvement and types of activities. The concept of "core" and "fringe" members has been utilized by many gang researchers. Figure 5-1 differentiates between these two types of youngsters who make up the structure of the traditional Latin gang. The core members are the most frequent participants in gang activities, and often direct the actions of the gang. Klein's data on street gangs indicated that core members were charged with 70 percent more offenses than were the fringe members and with 35 percent more assaultive offenses.[59] The core member appears to be more aggressive and more delinquent than the fringe members, who may associate with the gang sporadically and drift in and out of membership.

The leadership role in the gang is another important dimension of gang structure. Some writers have characterized the leadership position as a more or less permanent one, often with an official title of "president."[60] Yablonsky[61] has characterized the leaders of violent juvenile gangs as psychopathic individuals who impose their twisted fantasies on the other youngsters in the group, but there is little evidence to support his contention.[62] A more common description of the gang leader includes such characteristics as an active imagination, organizing skills, reputation, and strong leadership abilities.

Other gang studies have offered a different picture of leadership in the gang.[63] Instead of a fixed position or role filled by one youngster, leadership shifts according to personal ability and the specific situation. This can be seen when a leader is arrested by police and the gang remains active because other members move into the leadership role. Even without removal of a leader, certain circumstances may require talents that the fighter may not have. One member may be the leader in intergang conflict; another may be successful with members of the opposite sex; still another may be noted for athletic prowess. The mentally disturbed member is rarely followed by other members. Indeed, those individuals who wield the most influence in the traditional gang structure are within the subgroup rather than the overall cluster.

A final characteristic of leadership in the gang is a lack of willingness to assume this role, which Klein refers to as "hesitant leadership." He notes that this reluctance to be a group spokesman or a leader results from a fear of loss of status, since one's position of power is unclear and there is a possibility of conflict with another rival leader within the gang.[64] It is, of course, very difficult for a gang worker to determine which members are leaders under these conditions.

Gang cohesion refers to the degree of solidarity within the group. The greater the cohesion, the longer the life span of the particular gang. Where does this cohesion come from? One might assume that the relationships or ties among members create it, which to an extent is true, but there have been many writers who have noted the important contribution of factors *external* to the gang. Thrasher described the evolution of a play group into a gang as resulting from conflict with persons outside of the group, and others have observed the greater cohesion brought on in a gang conflict situation. External threats drive members closer together. Short and Strodtbeck described gang leaders who initiated aggression against some out-group (often another gang) when their own status was threatened.[65] The greater cohesion that resulted from the conflict reinforced their leadership role.

Unfortunately there is some evidence that gang workers assigned to specific gangs may also increase cohesion and, in effect, encourage higher amounts of group-related delinquent acts.[66] The greater the gang cohesion, the higher the rates of offenses committed. The worker may serve to encourage stronger gang identification and increased interaction among members.

Characteristics of Gang Members   Who becomes a gang member? Gang members tend to be males from lower socioeconomic backgrounds who are minority group members. Sometimes females are affiliated with the gang, and there are accounts of all-female gangs in some urban areas.[67] We might expect a change in the sex composition of gangs in the future due to the changing sex roles in society, but at this point the female gang is an unusual phenomenon. The members range in age from 10 to the early 20s, but the majority of the members are teenagers.[68] The backgrounds of these youngsters are extremely disadvantaged. Broken homes, poor school performance, and the many other problems associated with poverty and slum neighborhoods are frequently found.

Although the violent acts of gangs have received much attention, there is evidence that the major types of offenses gangs commit are property offenses.[69] Gang members do not specialize in offenses, but engage in a wide variety of behaviors, many of which are nondelinquent. Newspaper accounts encourage both the belief that the gang is mainly involved in violence and the fear that victims are chosen at random. In reality, the victims of gangs are most often other gang members, and the next most likely group of victims consists of people who live in the gang neighborhood.[70] In any case, violent offenses make up a small proportion of the delinquent behaviors of gang members, as is illustrated in Table 5-4. Klein found these official charges against gang members in a Los Angeles project during a four-year period.

Theories of Gang Delinquency

The major theories of gang delinquency have been considered in Chapter 2, so they will not be repeated here. In general the theories focus on the needs of the poor youngster, which delinquent involvement fulfills. The gang offers adventure and relief from boredom as well as a means of achieving status among one's peers. The importance of peer influence may account for delinquent behaviors within the gang since the dynamics of the group may en-

TABLE 5-4. OFFENSES BY GANG MEMBERS

OFFENSE	BOYS (PERCENT)	GIRLS (PERCENT)
Thefts	26	14
Status offenses	17	47
Auto theft	14	5
Assaultive	13	9
Drugs and alcohol	10	4
Disturbing the peace, Malicious mischief	7	6
Traffic	3	1
Sex	2	5
Other	7	10
Total	99	101

Source: Malcolm Klein, *Street Gangs and Street Workers,* © 1971, p. 17. Reprinted by permission of Prentice-Hall, Inc., Englewood Cliffs, New Jersey.

courage actions which the youngster would not pursue independently. An example of peer-group influence is provided by Yablonsky in the following interview with members of a gang called the "Egyptian Kings." The Kings had attacked and killed a fifteen-year-old polio victim in a New York City park.

> *First Egyptian King:* I was scared. I knew they were gonna jump them an' everythin' and I was scared. When they were comin' up, they all were separatin' and everything like that.
>
> *McShane:* I saw the main body of the gang slowly walk out of the bushes, on my right. I turned around fast, to see what Michael was going to do, and this kid came runnin' at me with the belts. Then I ran, myself, and told Michael to run.
>
> *Second Egyptian King:* He couldn't run anyway, 'cause we were all around him. So then I said, "You're a Jester," and he said, "Yeah," and I punched him in the face. And then somebody hit him with a bat over the head. And then I kept punchin' him. Some of them were too scared to do anything. They were just standin' there, lookin'.
>
> *Third Egyptian King:* I was watchin' him. I didn't wanna hit him, at first. Then I kicked him twice. He was layin' on the ground, lookin' up at us. I kicked him on the jaw, or some place; then I kicked him in the stomach. That was the least I could do, was kick 'im.
>
> *Fourth Egyptian King:* I was aimin' to hit him, but didn't get a chance to hit him. There were so many guys on him—I got scared when I saw the knife go into the guy, and I ran right there. After somebody ran, this guy stayed, and started hittin' him with a machete.
>
> *First Egyptian King:* Somebody yelled out, "Grab him. He's a Jester." So then they grabbed him. Magician grabbed him, he turned around and stabbed him in the back. I was . . . I was stunned. I couldn't do nothin'. And then Magician—he went like that and he pulled . . . he had a switchblade and he said, "You're gonna hit him with that bat or I'll stab you." So I just hit him lightly with the bat.[71]

Although this example of group influence is an extreme one, it does illustrate the strong pressure placed on individual gang members to conform to gang norms, values, and behaviors. There is some evidence that the more cohesive a group is, the greater such pressures will be. Conflict situations increase cohesion, which in turn may increase conformity by members.[72] Since the gang fulfills many of the needs of the youngsters, the possible threat of exclusion serves as a strong means of social control. Derision and ridicule are often used to control the actions of members, and if this fails stronger sanctions can be applied. The strong dependency of some juveniles on the gang and the pressures exerted by the other boys may encourage more deviant behavior. The age-old notion of parents, who blame their children's behavior on their friends, may have some validity.

The Violent Offender

The crimes that inspire the most concern and fear among members of the general public are those involving violence. Crimes such as murder, assault, rape, and kidnapping make people fear for their own safety, regardless of the actual likelihood that they will be victimized. Violence among youths typically has been associated with delinquent gangs, whose members are reputed to be attackers of anyone who is unfortunate enough to cross their path. Media coverage of sniping incidents or multiple murders committed by deranged but armed juveniles serves to confirm the fears and beliefs of many citizens about youth and violence.

The incidence of violent crime is actually somewhat low in the United States when compared to the number of property offenses committed. In 1975 the rate for murder was 10 per 100,000 per year, the rate for forcible rape was 26, and the rate for aggravated assault was 227. In contrast, the rate for burglary was 1,526, the rate for larceny and theft was 2,805, and the rate for auto theft was 469.[73] Thus violent crime is comparatively rare.

If crime rates in the United States are compared to those in other countries, violence rates look somewhat different. A comparison of homicide statistics by Wolfgang and Ferracuti indicated that the rate of homicides varied greatly by country.[74] At the time of this study, the United States had a rate of 4.5 per 100,000, England and Wales had a rate of 0.6, and France had a rate of 1.7. Although the highest rate of 34.0 was found in Colombia, the homicide rate in the United States was much higher than those of other industrialized nations.

Violence is a more frequent occurrence in the United States than in other, comparable nations, but within the United States property offenses are more common than violent crimes. It would seem that although violent acts are cause for concern, other offenses such as burglary, larceny, and theft are actually greater problems. Still, public fear has typically focused on the violent offenders and recent crime statistics show that violence among young offenders is increasing. (See Table 5-5.)

TABLE 5-5. TREND IN ARREST RATES FOR PERSONS BY AGE GROUPS: 1970–1975

	UNDER 18 YEARS OF AGE			18 YEARS OF AGE AND OVER		
	1970	1975	Percent Change	1970	1975	Percent Change
Violent crime*	47,311	72,867	+54.0	162,069	224,068	+38.3
Property crime†	476,165	590,334	+24.0	434,600	623,954	+43.6

*Violent crimes include murder, forcible rape, robbery, and aggravated assault.
†Property crimes include burglary, larceny-theft, and motor vehicle theft.
Source: Adapted from FBI, Uniform Crime Reports, 1976, pp. 184–185.

There are many problems in using official crime statistics to prove or disprove increasing crime rates; thus caution is urged in interpreting the data presented in Table 5-5. There is always a possibility that these increases could be a result of changing police policies that affect reporting and law enforcement practices. Changes in the population structure may also be a factor. Police departments may have concentrated on arrests of younger offenders or may have begun reporting these arrests more accurately to the FBI. Changes in the population structure may have caused an increase in the number of people under the age 18 in society and thus higher rates could be linked to these shifts rather than to new crime trends.[75] One must conclude that violence by the young has become more common, but the size of the increase is still not known.

Although gang delinquents are often credited with the majority of these violent crimes, there is little evidence to support this conclusion. Klein noted that the offenses committed by gang members in one California city consisted primarily of property offenses,[76] and Miller has recently found that when gang violence does occur it is most often directed at other gang members.[77] Random victimization of passersby is infrequent, although this type of incident receives substantial media coverage when it does occur. Gang delinquents alone cannot be held responsible for increasing violent crime rates, for other juvenile offenders contribute their share to the prevalence of aggression.

Characteristics of the Violent Offender

Violent crime occurs most frequently in large cities, in neighborhoods characterized by low incomes, broken homes, low levels of education, high unemployment, overcrowded and substandard housing, and high-population density. The offenders are primarily male, black, poor, and young (15 to 24 years of age). The victims are similar to their attackers, and in the crimes of homicide, assault, and rape, they often know the offender as an intimate or an acquaintance.[78]

As for types of violent offenders, there appear to be two major categories. First, there are those who lead relatively crime-free lives until, apparently without warning, they commit some brutal and seriously violent crime. A significant proportion of violent offenders are committing their first offense when they resort to aggression. Pittman and Handy found that 37 percent of their sample of violent offenders were first offenders.[79] These offenders do not have criminal careers, they do not consider themselves to be real criminals, and crime does not play a significant part in their lives.

The second category consists of the career offender. Wolfgang carried out a study of boys who were born in 1945 and who resided in Philadelphia while they were between the ages of 10 and 18.[80] About 6 percent of these boys were chronic delinquents; that is, they had committed five or more offenses. Of some 815 personal attacks (homicide, assault and rape), 53 percent were committed by these chronic delinquents. The chronic delinquents also committed 62 percent of the property offenses.

Thus violent crime is committed to a large extent by career delinquents, but these youths do not restrict themselves to only violent crimes. Their criminal careers encompass all kinds of crimes. Wolfgang and his colleagues found that the type of crime committed by these delinquents was not accurately predictable on the basis of their past offenses. The youths frequently switched offense categories.

These types of violent offenders match a theoretical proposal made by Megargee in his discussion of violent offenders and murderers.[81] Megargee proposed that there are two kinds of violent offenders—the overcontrolled and the undercontrolled. The *undercontrolled* aggressive person has weak inhibitions against aggression. Whenever he is frustrated or provoked, he aggresses. He is not completely without control, though, for he may refrain from attacking some people, such as his parents or the judge before whom he is brought. The anger may be displaced in these cases and aimed at other persons or things, but typically he aggresses against his frustrator. He does not aggress wildly, gouging eyes or wielding an axe, but he does aggress. Because he is constantly engaged in violent behavior, he may occasionally kill his victim. He is often diagnosed as a psychopath or sociopath because of his minimal inhibitions against aggression and his chronic pattern of violence. This fits the category of the chronic violent offenders.

The *overcontrolled* person has abnormally rigid controls against aggression. No matter what the provocation, he will rarely aggress. His controls are so great that he rarely displaces his aggression or substitutes a less drastic behavior, such as verbally reprimanding his frustrator. His aggression, therefore, builds up until his controls can no longer contain it. Then, some trivial frustration brings about a release of all of his pent-up anger. The model citizen becomes a murderer, and his murder is often a violent one. The victim may be shot thirty times, or the body knifed repeatedly and dismembered. After his aggression has been released, his controls can be reinstated, and the murderer becomes once again a model citizen. This resembles the category of the one-time, first-offense violent offender. The National Commission on the Causes and Prevention of Violence also noted that the more serious the initial offense, the less likely was the crime to be repeated, which fits in with Megargee's ideas.

Theories of Violence

Most explanations of violent behavior are similar to other theories of delinquency and criminality. Some investigators focus on the social or cultural influences that encourage aggression whereas others point to psychological or biological causes. All of these attempts to explain the etiology of violent behavior are based on evidence that supports their contentions, but some theories are more strongly supported than others.

The sociological explanations of violent behavior point to the social-class distribution of violent acts and conclude that these class differences result from differing values, family structures, and patterns of social interaction. Wolfgang and Ferracuti hypothesized the existence of a subculture of violence that condones and even requires aggressive behavior in certain social encounters.[82] For example, an insult in a bar may require a violent response if the recipient of the insult is to maintain his status and reputation. This subculture of violence is found in poor neighborhoods where residential segregation has enforced a barrier that excludes these people from the major society.

Family structures in these communities are unstable and often consist of a single parent with many children. In this type of structure the amount of supervision given the young is reduced. In female-headed homes, males have difficulty adopting the male sex role owing to the absence of a consistent male role model, and as Walter Miller has noted this may produce anxiety, which in turn encourages a great concern over appearing tough and masculine.[83]

Patterns of social interactions in these communities may enhance violence since aggressive responses are seen as appropriate. The use of alcohol is frequently found in the victims and perpetrators of violent acts. Of course, alcohol does not cause violence, but it may reduce inhibitions or controls over aggressive impulses. The victim may also play an important role in the onset of violence. Wolfgang described a type of homicide in which the victim helped to escalate the hostilities and termed it "victim precipitated."[84] In this type of situation the victims react in such a way as to actually encourage their own victimization. An example of this is the wife who is told by her husband that if she speaks another word, he will strike her. She speaks again and he attacks.

Psychological theories of violent behavior often emphasize the early events of a child's life, which may contribute to their violence as teenagers and adults. Henry and Short argued that child-rearing techniques were crucial in determining whether a child would later become violent.[85] They noted that children who are physically punished are more likely to become violent than children who are punished with threats of love withdrawal. If a child is punished physically, anger results, but to lash out at the parents merely means another blow from them. If one is punished with threats from one's parents that they will withdraw their love, then to be angry with them further threatens the supply of love. Such children learn to inhibit their anger and aggression. Similarly, Henry and Short argued that if the father punishes the child (while the mother nurtures him) he will be less likely to inhibit aggression than if the mother both punishes and nurtures.

There is evidence that physical punishment facilitates the development of aggressive behavior. Studies of delinquents in Boston conducted by the Gluecks found that the delinquents were more likely to have been physically punished than the nondelinquents.[86] Bandura has also emphasized the modeling effects of parents. Parents who use physical punishment raise children who naturally model themselves on their parents and consequently they too will resort to violence when frustrated.[87]

Palmer compared the childhoods of a group of murderers with those of their brothers.[88] He found that the murderers had experienced more frustrations of all kinds. These included difficult births, forceps injuries, serious illnesses, accidents, and operations, beatings by people other than their parents, negative attitudes on the part of their mothers toward their birth, rigid treatment from their mothers, severe toilet training, negative experiences at school, behavior disorders (such as bedwetting, nightmares, stammering, and phobias), and temper tantrums.

Palmer provided an example of a teenager, Mike, who at the age of 18 murdered a middle-aged prostitute with whom he had just had intercourse and whom he was trying to rob. Mike had been constantly beaten as a child. When he was five, his uncle had become angry with him and thrown him across the room so that he hit the stove. His two older brothers once beat him with branches until he was covered with welts and bleeding, after which he was unconscious for two days. On several occasions his uncle put him under the hood of a car and started the engine. His uncle and brothers once gave him an electric shock for fun. His brothers had thrown him in a stream on the pretext of teaching him to swim and he had nearly drowned. They had also tied a snake around his neck once causing him to "go out of his mind" with fear.

Although the case of Mike is an extreme example of childhood frustration and violence, it does provide an illustration of how early experiences can affect subsequent behavior. Recent interest in the problem of child abuse has pointed to similar background factors in the lives of abusive parents. Children who are abused often grow up to become abusive parents themselves.[89] Palmer's study indicates that there is empirical evidence for this type of relationship in the case of other violent offenders.

Another approach to understanding the origins of violence involves genetic or biological influences. Studies have shown that identical twins tend to behave more similarly than nonidentical twins in their law-abiding or law-breaking behavior.[90] In relation to violent behavior, there has been a recent surge of interest in genetically abnormal males (the so-called XYY syndrome) in which a male has three sex chromosomes instead of the usual two, XY. It was argued that XYY males commit a high proportion of violent crimes. More detailed research, however, has produced little evidence to support this conclusion.[91] Furthermore, XYY males are extremely rare and account for only a minute fraction of all criminals.

Other investigators have focused on the possibility of brain damage in violent offenders. There is an area of the brain called the limbic system that appears to control violence. Mark and Ervin have found that damage to parts of the limbic system can lead to epileptic-like electrical activity in that region of the brain, with accompanying violence.[92] They described the case of Julia, whose brain damage resulted from encephalitis at the age of two. By the age of 21, she had shown epileptic seizures, had made serious suicide attempts, and had seriously assaulted other people without provocation. When she was 18, she knifed a girl in a theater during a mild seizure.

When Mark and Ervin sank electrodes into one part of her brain, they observed spontaneous, seizure-like electrical activity, with Julia baring her teeth and clenching her fists as if she were on the verge of an attack. Mark and Ervin argued that many violent criminals may be suffering from mild brain damage to these areas of the brain. The damage may be so mild that it is undetectable by current neurological methods, but it may still be present.

Criticism of the Theories

Theories of violent behavior have many of the same shortcomings as the delinquency theories discussed in previous chapters. Sociologists fail to explain why *all* of those people who grow up in lower-class surroundings with a subculture that condones violence do not become violent offenders. Psychological perspectives fail to account for the uneven distribution of violence throughout the social structure and for the child who suffers abuse and rejection but does not commit crimes of aggression. The biological ideas about violence require much more research before they can be accepted. Unfortunately, in the past research evidence has been nonexistent or very sketchy for explanations that became widely publicized and popular, as with the XYY chromosome.

Eventually a theory of violence may be developed that will be free of the flaws of those that presently exist. Perhaps a combination of perspectives is required. Eysenck has postulated that all behavior results from an interaction between biological and environmental influences.[93] This may be a starting point for a comprehensive explanation of violence.

DISCUSSION QUESTIONS

1. What are some of the reasons that traditionally middle-class delinquency has been of so little interest to those who study delinquency?

2. How does sex-role stereotyping affect theories of female delinquency? What are some of the common assumptions that many theorists make about females?

3. According to Klein, the nature of juvenile gangs has changed in recent years. In what ways have they changed and why?

4. Why are delinquent gangs best known for the violent crimes they commit? What are some of the positive functions of gangs?

5. Studies have shown that violent offenders often have particular types of childhood experiences. Describe these experiences and discuss how they can influence later behavior.

NOTES

1. The authors would like to thank Renee Lewin for the opportunity to read her unpublished manuscript, "Theories of Affluent Delinquency: Review and Critique of the Literature" (March 1975).

2. See for example: Albert Cohen, *Delinquent Boys* (New York: Free Press, 1955); and Richard Cloward and Lloyd Ohlin, *Delinquency and Opportunity* (New York: Free Press, 1960).

3. F. Ivan Nye, *Family Relationships and Delinquent Behavior* (Westport, Conn.: Greenwood Press, 1958); Martin Gold, *Delinquent Behavior in an American City* (Monterey, Calif.: Brooks/Cole, 1970); Travis Hirschi, *Causes of Delinquency* (Berkeley, Calif.: University of California Press, 1972); Roger Hood and Richard Sparks, *Key Issues in Criminology,* (New York: McGraw-Hill, 1970), pp. 53–87.

4. Hood and Sparks, *Key Issues in Criminology,* pp. 55–59.

5. Roland Chilton, "Middle-Class Delinquency and Specific Offense Analysis," in *Middle Class Juvenile Delinquency,* ed. Edmund W. Vaz (New York: Harper & Row, 1967), pp. 91–104.

6. Arthur L. Paddock, "Incidence and Types of Delinquency of Middle-Class Youth: The Effect of Selected Sociocultural, Socialization, and Personality Factors" (Ph.D. diss., Southern Illinois University, 1975).

7. Howard L. Myerhoff and Barbara Myerhoff, "Field Observations of Middle Class 'Gangs'," in *Middle Class Juvenile Delinquency*, pp. 117–130.

8. Larry Karacki and Jackson Toby, "The Uncommitted Adolescent: Candidate for Gang Socialization," *Sociological Inquiry,* 32 (Spring 1962): 203–215.

9. Marvin Wolfgang, Robert Figlio, and Thorsten Sellin, *Delinquency in a Birth Cohort* (Chicago: University of Chicago Press, 1972), pp. 53–87.

10. Albert Cohen, "Middle Class Delinquency and the Social Structure," in *Middle Class Juvenile Delinquency,* pp. 20–207.

11. Ibid., p. 206.

12. Talcott Parsons, "Certain Primary Sources and Patterns of Aggression in the Social Structure of the Western World," *Psychiatry* 10 (1947): 167–181.

13. Ibid., p. 171.

14. Jackson Toby, "Violence and the Masculine Ideal: Some Qualitative Data, *The Annals of the American Academy of Political and Social Science* (March 1966): 19–27.

15. Hirschi, *Causes of Delinquency.*

16. Albert Bandura and Richard Walters, *Adolescent Aggression* (New York: Ronald Press, 1959) p. 00.

17. Albert K. Cohen and James Short, "Research in Delinquent Subcultures," *Journal of Social Issues* 14, no. 3 (1958): 20–37.

18. Edmund Vaz, "Juvenile Delinquency in the Middle-Class Youth Culture," in *Middle Class Juvenile Delinquency,* pp. 131–147.

19. Ibid.

20. Ralph W. England, "A Theory of Middle Class Juvenile Delinquency," in *Middle Class Juvenile Delinquency,* pp. 242–251.

21. William Kvaraceus and Walter Miller, "Norm Violating Behavior in Middle Class Culture," in *Middle Class Juvenile Delinquency,* pp. 233–241.

22. Robert H. Bohlke, "Social Mobility, Stratification Inconsistency, and Middle Class Delinquency," in *Middle Class Juvenile Delinquency,* pp. 222–232.

23. Ibid., p. 231.

24. The authors would like to thank Carol Facella for the opportunity to read her unpublished manuscript, "A Critical Review of Female Delinquency: Its Extent, Nature, and Causes," (Spring 1975).

25. C. Lombroso and W. Ferrero, *The Female Offender* (New York: Appleton, 1897), p. 288.

26. Freda Adler, *Sisters in Crime* (New York: McGraw-Hill, 1975), p. 87.

27. Ibid., p. 88.

28. W. Wattenberg and F. Saunders, "Sex Differences Among Juvenile Offenders," *Sociology and Social Research* 39 (1954): 24–31; D. Gibbons and M. Griswold, "Sex Differences Among Juvenile Court Referrals," *Sociology and Social Research,* 42 (1957): 106–110; G. Barker and W. Adams, "Comparison of the Delinquencies of Boys and Girls," *Journal of Criminal Law, Criminology, and Police Science,* 53 (1962): 470–476.

29. Talcott Parsons, "Age and Sex in the Social Structure of the United States," *American Sociological Review,* 7 (October 1942): 604–616.

30. Sheldon Glueck and Eleanor Glueck, *Five Hundred Delinquent Women* (New York: Knopf, 1934).

31. Nancy Barton Wise, "Juvenile Delinquency Among Middle-Class Girls," in *Middle Class Juvenile Delinquency,* pp. 179–188.

32. Gold, *Delinquent Behavior in an American City,* pp. 60, 64.

33. Michael Hindelang, ''Age, Sex, and the Versatility of Delinquent Involvement,'' *Social Problems,* 18 (1971): 522–533.

34. Lombroso and Ferrero, *The Female Offender*, p. 107.

35. See Don C. Gibbons, *Society, Crime, and Criminal Careers,* (Englewood Cliffs, N.J.: Prentice-Hall, 1973), pp. 136–149.

36. W. I. Thomas, *The Unadjusted Girl* (1923; reprint ed., New York: Harper & Row, 1967).

37. Otto Pollak, *The Criminality of Women* (Philadelphia: University of Pennsylvania Press, 1950).

38. Ibid., p. 1.

39. R. Morris, ''Female Delinquency and Relational Problems,'' *Social Forces,* 43 (1964): 82–89.

40. G. Konopka, *The Adolescent Girl in Conflict* (Englewood Cliffs, N.J.: Prentice-Hall, 1966) p. 40.

41. Adler, *Sisters in Crime,* p. 87.

42. Ibid., p. 94.

43. Ibid., p. 95.

44. Ibid., p. 107.

45. Gold, *Delinquent Behavior in an American City*.

46. Marshall Clinard and Richard Quinney, *Criminal Behavior Systems: A Typology* (New York: Holt, Rinehart & Winston, 1967), p. 383.

47. Herbert Asbury, *Gangs of New York* (New York: Garden City, 1927).

48. Lewis Yablonsky, *The Violent Gang* (Baltimore: Penguin Books, 1966), pp. 154–156.

49. Gold, *Delinquent Behavior in an American City,* pp. 82–99.

50. Michael Hindelang, ''The Social Versus Solitary Nature of Delinquent Involvements,'' *British Journal of Criminology* (April 1971): 167–175.

51. Frederic Thrasher, *The Gang* (Chicago: University of Chicago Press, 1936).

52. Yablonsky, *Violent Gang* (Pengiun Books edition), p. 164. Originally published by Macmillan Publishing Co., Inc., New York. © Lewis Yablonsky 1962.

53. Malcolm Klein, *Street Gangs and Street Workers* (Englewood Cliffs, N. J.: Prentice-Hall, 1971), p. 59.

54. Ibid.

55. Ibid., pp. 64–78.

56. Ibid., p. 66.

57. James Short and Fred Strodtbeck, *Group Process and Gang Delinquency* (Chicago: University of Chicago Press, 1965), p. 98.

58. Yablonsky, *Violent Gang*.

59. Klein, *Street Gangs,* p. 74.

60. New York City Youth Board, *Reaching the Fighting Gang* (1960), pp. 51–53.

61. Yablonsky, *Violent Gang*.

62. Klein, *Street Gangs,* p. 70.

63. Ibid., pp. 91–99.

64. Ibid.

65. Short and Strodtbeck, *Group Processes.*

66. Klein, *Street Gangs,* p. 118.

67. Adler, *Sisters in Crime,* p. 22.

68. Klein, *Street Gangs,* p. 77.

69. Ibid., p. 17.

70. Ibid., 134–135.

71. Yablonsky, *Violent Gang* (Pengiun Books edition), p. 51. Originally published by Macmillan Publishing Co., Inc. © Lewis Yablonsky 1962.

72. Louis Tognacci, "Pressures Toward Uniformity in Delinquent Gangs," in *Gang Delinquency,* eds. D. Cartwright, B. Tomson, and H. Schwartz (Monterey, Calif.: Brooks/Cole, 1975), pp. 102–110.

73. FBI, *Uniform Crime Reports,* 1975, p. 49.

74. Marvin Wolfgang, *Studies in Homicide* (New York: Harper & Row, 1967), pp. 299–303.

75. Marvin Wolfgang, *Youth and Violence* (Washington, D.C.: Dept. of Health, Education, and Welfare, 1970), pp. 27–39.

76. Klein, *Street Gangs,* p. 77.

77. Walter B. Miller, *Violence by Youth Gangs and Youth Groups as a Crime Problem in Major American Cities* (Washington, D.C.: Government Printing Office, Dec. 1975), pp. 39, 40.

78. National Commission on the Causes and Prevention of Violence, *To Establish Justice, To Insure Domestic Tranquility* (Washington, D.C.: Government Printing Office, 1969).

79. D. Pittman and W. Handy, "Patterns in criminal aggravated assault," *Journal of Criminal Law, Criminology and Police Science,* 55, no. 4 (1964): 462–470.

80. Wolfgang, et al., *Delinquency in a Birth Cohort,* pp. 88–105.

81. E. Megargee, "Uncontrolled and Overcontrolled Personality Types in Extreme Antisocial Aggression," *Psychological Monographs* 80 (1966).

82. Marvin Wolfgang and F. Ferracuti, *The Subculture of Violence* (New York: Tavistock, 1969).

83. Walter Miller, "Lower Class Culture as a Generating Milieu of Gang Delinquency," *Journal of Social Issues* 14, no. 3 (1958): 5–19.

84. Marvin Wolfgang, "Victim-Precipitated Criminal Homicide," *Journal of Criminal Law, Criminology, and Police Science,* 48. no. 1 (1957): 1–11.

85. A. Henry and J. Short, *Suicide and Homicide* (Glencoe, Ill.: Free Press, 1954).

86. Sheldon Glueck and Eleanor Glueck, *Unraveling Juvenile Delinquency* (New York: Commonwealth Fund, 1950).

87. A. Bandura and R. Walters, *Adolescent Aggression* (New York: Ronald Press, 1959).

88. Stuart Palmer, *A Study of Murder,* (New York: Crowell, 1960).

89. R. J. Gelles, "Child Abuse as Psychopathology: A Sociological Critique and Reformulation," in *Violence in the Family,* eds. S. K. Steinmetz and M. A. Straus (New York: Dodd, Mead, 1974), pp. 190–204.

90. Hans Eysenck, *Crime and Personality* (London: Paladin, 1970).

91. E. Hook, "Behavioral Implications of the Human XYY Genotype," *Science* 179 (1973): 139–150.

92. V. Mark and R. Ervin, *Violence and the Brain* (New York: Harper & Row, 1970).

93. Eysenck, *Crime and Personality,* p. 100.

6 Case Study: An Interview with Terry

This chapter presents an interview with a young man, Terry, who was tried and convicted for murder. Terry was sentenced to a prison term and served his sentence. At the time of the interview Terry was a senior in college, pursuing a course of study that would prepare him for a career in penal reform. His goal is to become actively involved in expanding educational opportunities for prison inmates.

In the previous chapters we have presented a number of theories that attempt to explain why certain people develop delinquent behavior patterns. As you read the case study below, attempt to answer the following questions:

1. Considering each of the theoretical positions that have been described earlier, what kinds of questions would you ask Terry if you were the interviewer? What areas of his experience and what aspects of his personality would you want to explore?

2. How would you relate Terry's answers to each of the theories that have been described in previous chapters?

Interview

INTERVIEWER: *How old were you when you first got in trouble with the police?*

TERRY: Well, I got in trouble when I was about ten years old. Bike thefts and stuff like that. But I was never fully detained overnight until I was about 13 years old.

I: *What had you done?*

T: I started a fire in school. Then I was sent to Menlo Park for diagnostic treatment to determine if there was anything psychologically wrong with me. I spent 90 days there. Menlo Park suggested to the court that I not be sent home, but sent to a private school. And I was. That was in Philadelphia. I went to Philadelphia to a private school.

I: *When you did these things, like setting fire to the school, were you alone or were you in a group?*

T: I was alone.

I: *Did you commit most of your offenses alone? Were you ever in a gang?*

T: I was in a gang, but the gang members didn't do the things I did. I was the wild one of the gang, even though I was the youngest one of the gang. That's probably why I did a lot of the things I did. I was always trying to prove myself to the gang. And they encouraged me to do these crazy things. But they never did it themselves. It was always me.

I: *How long were you in the private school?*

T: I was there about six months and I ran away. I was going with a young girl in Trenton at the time. We were both 13 years old, and she had got locked up for something or other, I don't remember now, and I ran away to go see her. I stole a car and the judge thought that Jamesburg was the best place for me after that. That's why I went to Jamesburg.

I: *And how long were you there?*

T: I did about two years in Jamesburg. I would say that out of those two years I spent maybe six months in jail in Jamesburg itself. The rest of the time I was on the run, going to Trenton. I stayed out two or three months at a time.

I: *Why did you run away from these institutions?*

T: I didn't want to be there. It started like a pattern, I guess. When I was in a school in Philadelphia, this friend I had there, said, "Let's just run." That was the first time I ran, and I liked the freedom. I just kept it up.

I: *Was it exciting to be on the run?*

T: Yes, it was. I felt free, like I could really do what I wanted to do. Just roam the streets and take clothes off people's clotheslines. Things like that.

I: *That sounds like it would be exciting. What other kinds of offenses did you commit?*

T: After Jamesburg, when I was 16 years old, they sent me to Anandale. I was too old for Jamesburg, so they just transferred me to another institution. I didn't know where I was at in Anandale. Anandale is up in North Jersey. That's one of the reasons why I didn't run away. I stayed in Anandale for 11 months. When I came out of Anandale I was about 17 years old, and I had a new kind of crowd I was hanging out with. I had moved out of the old neighborhood I was in, and moved into a new part of Trenton. I started to do B and E's—gas stations, laundromat machines, milk machines, soda machines, and things like that. And I was doing these every night for about a year. Good money for the most part, and I was very active in B and E's at that time.

I: *What's B and E?*

T: Breaking and entering. I got arrested in '58, and I was sentenced to Bordentown for five years. I guess I did about two years in Bordentown. I got out, got back involved in B and E's, and was arrested. In a matter of six months I was back in Bordentown. I got in some trouble in Bordentown and was sent to prison for five years, and then I got out of prison in '65 and got back in for my last charge, which was a homicide and armed robbery. I got 10 to 15 years for that, and did about eight years and then got out. I was very easily influenced, very easy to talk into doing all kinds of things, even with the homicide.

I: *Well, now, that last crime seemed to be more serious than the ones that you had committed before.*

T: Yes. I think that if you looked through my records it would show some kind of a pattern. I know in my heart that I'm not a violent person, and I never really resorted to violence at all. I never did any muggings, or robbed pocketbooks, or any of that. I was always a sweet kind of a person. It was because of the social pressures that I was under, the group that I was hanging out with. They were all very aggressive physically, and I just had to stay with them. I was just caught up in it.

I: *That later group you were with, after you came out of Anandale, was a different kind of gang than the early one?*

T: Right. When I was 17 or 18 years old, we used to go out and drink and do B and E's and stuff like that. We were just wild kids. But when I got to prison, I met a much different kind of person. We were thinking about robberies and just shooting people to show manhood, stuff like that. I did five years in Trenton, and it was very dramatic on my personality and how I thought and did things. I was only out of prison three months and I was busted for homicide.

I: *What happened in the armed robbery?*

T: It was a fellow that I had worked for. We stuck him up and he recognized me, I thought. Anyway, we went back with the intention of, first of all, talking to him and telling him not to press charges. I knew the guy. He knew my family. But he was drunk when we got there. We got to fighting, and the guy got stabbed. Then, once we went that far, we burned the house down, and then we tried to hide it. But like I said, I know that really I wouldn't do that on my own. I wouldn't go out and try to hurt somebody on my own. It's just not me. It's just that you can get involved in those kinds of activities very easily, and not really want to.

I: *Who actually did the stabbing?*

T: My partner did.

I: *Your partner.*

T: Yes. But I don't say that he's guilty or not, because I helped burn the place down. I helped hide the car, and I had the gun on the guy while we were fighting. So I was right there doing it.

I: *Do you think you would have been capable of actually stabbing him?*

T: I think if it came to my life or his life, it would have been more of a reaction type of thing than maliciously trying to hurt him. Yes, I think that I could have done it under a reaction type of situation.

I: *Did that offense have a stronger effect on you because it seemed to be more serious than the others you had committed?*

T: After we were arrested and in the county jail awaiting trial, and I realized that the state was going to ask for the death penalty and that there was a very good case building against us, I realized that I could very easily wind up in the electric chair. I was only 23 years old at the time. It was then that I started really questioning some of the influences on me. It wasn't that I was questioning wanting to do them, but I wanted to know *why* I wanted to do them, and why I was willing to keep on doing them. I wanted to know why in my own mind. I wanted to feel at peace with myself. Because of that I started to get closer to my family. I started to ask myself some serious questions. I started to grow up. I was in the county jail two years and I think those two years were very meaningful in terms of why I am where I am today.

I: *It sounds as if you'd committed the offense, but it didn't upset you.*

T: No, it didn't. It didn't upset me until much later, two or three years later. Then I really realized that the guy is not alive now because of me. Before that, I was more worried about myself. What was going to happen to me? What were my friends going to do to me? All these kinds of ideas just kept popping into my head. I wasn't at all concerned about the person who died until much later.

I: *You never did anything else that was serious?*

T: No, that was the most.

I: *Did you ever carry a gun before?*

T: No, just on that one night.

I: *Why did you have a gun that night?*

T: Because the crowd that I was there with was into armed robberies, and we were going to go at it all the way. We went out and bought shotguns and sawed them off. I had two sawed-off shotguns in my car, which is really out of character for me, you know. It was all because these people that I was hanging out with were doing it, and they were the only friends I had. I was really sucked into criminal code, if you know what I mean by that. I lived by that, and it was my life. What they thought was much more important to me than what I or anybody else thought. I would do anything to win their approval.

I: *Did you also find it enjoyable?*

T: What's that?

I: *Well, riding around in a car with a shotgun on the seat. Did that give you a good feeling?*

T: I think having a gun in your possession makes you feel bigger. Because I'm a small person, I've always known how to take care of myself physically. But I know that I have to really be conscious of my size, and get myself in and out of situations depending on my physical capabilities. As I grew up, I learned how to do these kinds of things. How to see a situation developing before it got to a point where I would get physical, and get out of it. So I compensated for that. But carrying a gun alleviated all those anxieties. I knew that I could just pull a gun out and stop any situation I wanted to stop. So it made me feel a little bit more secure, for awhile anyway.

I: *Well, it seems to be different. When you started at 9 or 13, then it was exciting and fun. And you were kind of a leader, maybe the showoff in the group?*

T: I was never the leader. I'm more of a leader type now, and it's really surprising me because in the last five or six years I've somehow just taken up a leader role. But all my life I've always been a follower, always been the one to be influenced. If somebody wanted to go to see something, well let 'em go get Terry to do it, you know, and I would go do it.

I: *When you think about the offenses you committed, what was really enjoyable about them? Was it the actual commission of the act, or was it the peer support, the reactions of your friends?*

T: I don't think it was either. I think it was doing what I shouldn't be doing. There's a sense of freedom in that. As a youngster, I was just trying out my guardian. I lived with a guardian, and I would just see how much I could get away with. And it becomes a pattern. Some of them were enjoyable, but I think it was just being out there running. And being loose, and not worrying about restrictions and order, and all that kind of stuff. Just doing whatever came in your mind. And that was what felt good.

I: *What was your childhood like?*

T: I came from a broken home. My father was from the West Coast and he came here in '41, when war broke out, Fort Dix, and I had diabetes and rickets. I was very sick, and they took me to a doctor. The doctor's nurse took me in, and she became my guardian. My father went overseas when he and mother split up. So I've lived with her since I was about six months old till now. Till I got married. Except when the state had me, which was most of the time. I think that she did a good job on me considering. She took care of me. I was healthy physically, but she used to beat the hell out of me. I think that when I got to be about 12 years old, I realized that her name was different than my name and a lot of guys in the neighborhood used to tell me that she wasn't my real mother. I think that really bothered me. I felt rejected.

I: *When did you first find out for certain that she wasn't your real mother?*

T: I think when I was about 12 years old. Right about the time I started the fire. There's a very close correlation there and I really can't believe in my own mind that that developed that quick from just that understanding. I think it was a very slow process, but there is a very strong correlation between when I found out that she wasn't my parent and when I started the fire. And I thought about it quite a bit, and I know now that I did have a lot of hurt feelings from my childhood. Through therapy and things like this, a lot of this came out. It was a very slow process. Not because I found out that she wasn't my mother, for I was doing various types of things before I knew this.

I: *Your offenses seem to have become more serious once you found out that you were adopted?*

T: Well, I think that it had more to do with me getting incarcerated than finding out I was adopted. When I finally was incarcerated, I almost immediately drew a very quick attachment to the guys that were in jail with me, especially in Jamesburg. I met a lot of guys in Trenton I had been running streets with who were there also, and we were all losers in one sense. We just sort of formed a common bond. It was because of the acceptance I experienced, I realize now, that I kept going back to that situation so often. I would go through four or five years of being locked up, telling myself every day that it's four or five years, that I wanted to get outside, I wanted to see the world, I wanted to go back to school, I wanted to lead a normal life. As soon as I got back outside, in about a month or so, I got back into the same thing I was doing before, to get back to jail, because I couldn't handle being on the outside for some reason. I wasn't willing to try to handle it. I was happy in jail for a long time. And it's not only me, because I observed a lot of people coming back for the third and fourth time to jail, in quarantine, big smiles on their faces, carrying five and ten years. They're happy to see you. I think that jail is a haven that helps people feel happy about themselves, because they're with other people they like. It's just a rut that's very hard to get out of.

I: *You mentioned that your adopted mother was brutal.*

T: Well, she wasn't really brutal. She used to beat me up pretty good though. I used to get the ''cat o' nine tails,'' as she called it.

I: *She used to whip you?*

T: Oh, yeah, and it got to the point where, even though I knew I was going to get a whipping, that she was going to beat me, I used to go and do what I wanted to do anyway, and then come home and take the beatings. They were very ineffective, because she would just whip me harder and harder. It would hurt, and I would dread them, but I would still go and do what I wanted to do.

I: *How about emotionally? Was she warm, loving?*

T: I really don't remember. I don't remember any real affection in my home environment at all. I don't remember any warmth at all. She also took care of old age pensioners, and she had about four or five people at the house all the time. I guess she had too many demands on her to take care of these people. To make beds and to cook food and to do this and do that. She just didn't have time to give me what I really needed. But now I don't hold anything against her for it. Because I love her very dearly for what she did for me. I was very sick when she got hold of me. But I don't think that she was a strong enough person to give me the kinds of things I really needed. I was a weak person myself. We were both weak people in the same boat, and she didn't give me what I needed.

I: *Did anyone else abuse you as a child?*

T: Not really. Like I said, very early in life I developed this ability to detect danger. And I learned how to sidestep it very quickly. I became a manipulator. I would be very passive just to avoid a conflict. But I might get into a situation where I would get beat up. She has a son who used to try to be like a father to me, and I manipulated him very well, in terms of getting whippings off him and stuff like that. He belted me a few times, but I used to avoid it pretty good.

I: *He was much older than you?*

T: Well, he's in his 50s now. He's about 20 years older than I am.

I: *But he didn't beat you up much?*

T: I got a few off him, but not many. I got around him pretty good.

I: *How would you describe yourself as a kid? What kind of kid were you?*

T: Very immature, very easily influenced. I think that I can understand why people thought that there was something psychologically wrong with me. I went to all kinds of counselors. I went to Menlo Park for treatments, and I can understand, looking back on some of the things I did, why they thought there was something wrong with me.

I: *Do you feel angry?*

T: I feel angry towards myself because I cheated myself out of so much in my life. Because I didn't get hold of myself until many years went by. I missed a lot of my teenage life, a lot of teenage experiences, a lot of foundational things that I'll never be able to gain now.

I: *But you didn't feel angry then? Were some of the things you did acts of rebellion?*

T: Oh, sure they were.

I: *Who were you angry at?*

T: Probably my parents, myself, my guardian. Probably a combination of all those things. Probably more at myself than anyone else, because of the weak character I was.

I: *You mentioned that you set fire to your school once. What made you do that?*

T: Well, I was going to a Catholic school, and I was kicked out of the Catholic school, and about two weeks after I was kicked out of the Catholic school, the Catholic school burnt down. And my cousin was still going to the Catholic school, and they had the day off from school. Well, I wanted a day off from school too, so I set fire to the school.

I: *It wasn't that you were angry at the school?*

T: I know now that my reasons for doing things were all rationalizations. Things I knew in my conscious mind. But I think that there were other reasons in my subconscious. I know there were because I have felt them. I'm not able to tag a lot of the things, but I felt them. I felt the hurt of them through therapy.

I: *But at the time, it was just that you felt like having a week off from school.*

T: Right. That's what was in my mind when I set the fire.

I: *You mentioned that it was good to be in the early institutions you were in. It was a community.*

T: Right.

I: *Were there any negative things about being in jail that you didn't like?*

T: Oh yeah. I got locked up at night. There were no girls, a lot of authority around me. Although that's a tricky thing too, because I think I needed the authority at the time, even though I outwardly rejected it. I think that it was good for me. That I wanted it. But I remember lying in a cell and really feeling a burning in my stomach, a longing for a female companion. You learn to suppress that and to fight those things. You learn a lot of negative things in jail. A lot of negative things. When you get out, and you're out for a little while, you forget all about those negative things, all those hassles, and all those petty things that go on inside the jail. And you remember all the card playing, TV, and playing out in the big yard. You remember all the good things. And that happens very quick when you're out. So jail doesn't seem so bad in comparison to the struggles of getting a job, having responsibility, supporting yourself, and things like that out here. It's very hard to come out here and do all those things.

I: *After you'd been convicted for the armed robbery and murder, you said your attitude toward your life changed, and you wanted to try and understand yourself better. Did you find it easy to use the prison facilities to change?*

T: Well, not at first. First, I was looking for something that I couldn't get. I was looking for the institution to give me something. They call it rehabilitation. But it took me about a year or so to realize that the change had to come from within. It had to be some kind of thing inside that said, "Okay, you want to change, Terry. Now you can go out and use the facilities that are there." You just don't go into a program and go through a program and come out at the other end cleaned. It takes a lot of desire in your own self, a lot of will, and a gamble. That's what it takes. To be willing to sacrifice or to give up something that you've been living with all your life and try something new.

I: *Was there peer pressure against it?*

T: Yes, there was. Not necessarily for therapy. I never had therapy until I went to Bordentown my last time, and the therapy did help me a lot. There was no peer pressure against that. But I started to go to college, and initially there was a lot of peer pressure. Not only peer pressure, but there was a lot of pressure from the guards. In Bordentown a lot of people thought that the inmates were getting free education and they really didn't deserve it. But, I think that education and the kind of insights I got from education, the kind of things I got from the teachers who taught me, were more valuable than any therapy sessions I ever had. Therapy was good for introspection. To go into yourself and to hear other people talk and say, "Well, damn, I feel that way too" or "I've experienced something like that, too." But education, getting in social science programs, and psychology programs, and learning the real dynamics of what makes people think, how they think, problem solving, things like that, were of great value to me.

I: *Were those opportunities always there and it's just that you decided to make use of them at this time?*

T: No. When I was at Bordentown in 1965, there was no college program at all. GED was the highest they had in the terms of education. The County College had just opened up in 1969, so a few of us who had our GED's already and could go no further educationally inside the institution put pressure on the administration to let the college come in. And the college program just developed. But it was primarily because of our desire to do something about getting out of jail and we saw education as a means of making that happen.

I: *So there was a small group of you who formed and pushed for the program?*

T: Right.

I: *And that gave you the peer support, too?*

T: Right. And that's when I started becoming a leader. When I started pushing for college, I started going around recruiting and selling the guys on the college program and getting involved in what courses would come in and funding sources and things like that. And I just kept going from there. So the college experience has been the catalyst for all my growth.

I: *Since you've been out, have you found there's much stigma attached to your being an ex-convict?*

T: Well, I let people know that I'm an ex-offender. It's my livelihood now. I'm very much involved in penal reform, in penal education. I let people know this. This is a strong point. I don't see being in jail as a negative factor in my life anymore. I see it as a positive factor. I've had experiences. I've gone through certain kinds of things that were very bad for me. But I've gone through them, and I survived. And I think that they're experiences that I can benefit from now. And I can relate to people and help society come to grips with the problem of crime. Because it is a problem, and I don't think jail is the answer to crime. I think we have to find some other means of dealing with criminals.

I: *So now that you're secure and more self-confident, what society thinks doesn't really matter to you so much?*

T: It really doesn't. I'm really happy with myself. I've grown a lot in the last couple of years. Maturity is the key to the whole thing. I'm married now. I have a little baby. I have a fairly decent job. I've been working for two and a half years now. I'm just a different person, a completely different person.

I: *What happened to those needs that you used to have when you were younger, that you used to satisfy by breaking and entering and so on? Do you still have them?*

T: Yeah. I still have those longings. Like I remember when I was talking about my father when I was in therapy. We started talking about my relationship with my father, and I admitted that I had a longing to have a father-son relationship, a little boy and a man relationship. But I was 24 or 25 years old at the time. I had to come to grips with it. I couldn't have that kind of relationship. I had to settle for an adult relationship with my father, if anything. And those frustrations that I had as a child, I've learned to deal with in a realistic way. To recognize who I am now and what kinds of relationships I can have now, and to develop those kinds of relationships. Not to keep looking for something that was lacking in my past.

I: *What about the excitement?*

T: When I came home this time, I did an awful lot of hitchhiking the first month. I went to Trenton and back to Stockton. Just did a lot of hitch-hiking. I think that was an expression of those feelings. I think I've given up the excitement of running and being loose and free for the joy of ex-periencing another person and caring for another person. Having another person care for you. My child means an awful lot to me. My wife means an awful lot to me. And these are the kinds of relationships I never had in my life before. And they're very important to me because they replaced the freedom and the wildness that was in me before. I've substituted some-thing else.

I: *Do you have any resentment or anger toward society and its institutions?*

T: I think I've benefited from society. Even though I spent some 16 years behind bars, I think I came out a much better person than I would have ever been had I just remained in society. Because I was hidden from so-ciety for so long, I was allowed to become mature very rapidly and I was allowed to establish values as an adult. Not have values imposed on me as a child and develop the values and attitudes as I grow old. I laid dor-mant for so many years that when I did start growing, I did it very rapidly. I think I have a much better grasp on reality than people who have lived outside all their lives.

I: *How do you think that society could have facilitated that?*

T: I don't think it can at all. I think maturity has to come from within. I think the only way society can intervene into a rehabilitative process is to identify the problem at a very early stage and rectify it then. I think that once a person sets up peripheral types of desires you loose track of what the real problem is and you start saying, "Well, it's because I want money . . . or it's because I'm frustrated with my girlfriend . . . or it's because of my job," or whatever. You start blaming your actions on things that are not related to what the cause really is. And the further you get away from that the harder it is to get back to it. And society can't do anything about it at all. It's you. You have to realize that you're not going out and stealing cars and money because of frustrations for a girl or whatever. You're doing it because of some problem in you that started when you were five years old. I don't think it's really important to find what the problem is. I think that what you have to come to grips with is that that is the situation. And start building from there.

I: *And for you it seems to have been that last crime, and then thinking about it afterward.*

T: It's very easy to say that. It appeared to be that that was the case. But I was 24 or 25 years old, and I think I was just beginning to become a man, to mature, and to think for myself. I think that sparked some kind of drive in me to find out who I was. But all the things that happened to me after that were very important, maybe more important than the crime itself, even though the crime did spark that. Taking on responsibility and accepting myself for my faults as well as my good things, and realizing that it was me. I had to live with it. You know? I could wear a mask all my life. I could've stayed behind bars all my life. It was a choice I had to make.

I: *To go back a little bit, have you ever met your real parents?*

T: Yes. I met my father when I was in county jail waiting trial for this last charge. I met him. He's dead now. We talked a little. We had a conversation, and I learned a lot about him and he learned a lot about me. But we never even got close to a father-son type of relationship.

I: *What about your mother?*

T: Not at all.

I: *You've never seen her?*

T: No. She came when I was about 12 years old. Right about the time I found out that I was adopted, and that's the last I've seen of her.

I: *Why did she come?*

T: She came for my birthday. I think it was my 12th birthday. She just popped in.

I: *How did you get to see your father when you were in the county jail?*

T: My father was in the service, and I wanted to get hold of him. I tracked him down through the service. I wrote letters to different kinds of people.

I: *And you had never tried to contact him before that?*

T: No. But I feel good about my relationship with my father. At least I got to know my father a little bit, and I got to know what kind of person he was, and I can see myself doing the same kind of things he did. I can see myself getting into frustrations with my wife, having hassles, not wanting to live with her, and maybe even leaving. I can see that happening to me; it's a possibility. But I'm going to do everything in my power not to let it happen.

An Analysis of Terry's Delinquency

Terry's delinquency can be analyzed from both the sociological and the psychological perspectives. Although the information contained in the interview with Terry is perhaps not as detailed as one might like, we do know enough about his childhood, his interactions with his peers, and his general feelings about his past to be able to conduct a reasonable analysis of his delinquency using many of the theories we have discussed in previous chapters.

From the sociological perspective, it is easy to see that the most important factors in Terry's delinquency were his family environment and the influence of his peers. During his earliest years, Terry was exposed to a disorganized family structure, which began to dissolve when his mother deserted him while he was still an infant. Eventually, his father abandoned him as well, and he was left in the care of a nurse who became his foster mother. Because Terry makes no mention of a foster father, we can assume that he grew up in a female-centered household in which there was no male role model. Walter Miller has pointed to this type of family structure as contributing to the focal concern of "toughness" found among lower-class males. In order to prove that he is truly masculine, the delinquent boy develops a style of exaggerated masculinity that includes fighting and using weapons. Terry tells us that he wanted to be seen as tough and strong by others, and describes how he felt most secure when he carried a gun.

Affiliation with a delinquent peer group was also an influential factor in Terry's deviant life-style. Terry belonged to a delinquent subculture for much of his life. Many of his antisocial acts were committed while he was under the influence of other delinquent children. By his own admission he was a follower; thus going along with the crowd necessitated engaging in delinquent behavior. Peer-group influence continued to be an important factor for Terry even after his incarceration. Although he longed for freedom while he was in prison, he missed his inmate friends once he was on the outside. Because he missed the social environment of the prison and the support and acceptance he felt from his fellow inmates, he committed new crimes in order to be able to return to the "safety" of the institution. Thus, from the time he was very young, his attachments to his antisocial peers were stronger than his attachments to authority figures, such as parents.

Nothing is mentioned in the interview about the financial situation in which Terry lived as a child, but the fact that his "mother" took boarders into the home would suggest that her income level was low. This would be consistent with the sociological perspective, which contends that socioeconomic status is a key factor in the etiology of delinquency.

Interestingly, Terry claims that the formal education he received while he was in prison played a major role in bringing about his reform. We might interpret this information in terms of "opportunity theory." Because Terry was eventually given an opportunity to pursue a college education, which provided him with a legitimate means of achievement, he was able to reject his former deviant life-style and begin planning a socially acceptable future for himself after his release.

From the psychological point of view, the major influences on Terry's behavior would be the relationships he experienced during his early childhood. Soon after Terry was born, his mother left him with his father and disappeared. His father gave him to a nurse to raise at the age of six months, so Terry did not have a stable and constant mother figure during his first year of life. Because the mother is a crucial figure in the development of the young child, this early experience may have contributed to Terry's later problems.

After he was placed in a foster home, Terry was disciplined in a brutal manner. Although he professes love for his guardian and gratitude, the fact remains that she regularly beat him with a whip. His elder foster brother also beat him. This harsh physical punishment was carried out in a home in which there was a minimum of emotional support. In addition, because his guardian had to attend to other lodgers in the home she had little time for Terry, and he has no memory of affection. We know from Chapter 4 that the rejecting and brutal parent is often found in the backgrounds of violent offenders. This finding has led psychologists to speculate that children who are exposed to cold, aggressive role models in the home are more likely to display similar behavior patterns in their own lives.

It is also important to note that Terry grew up in an environment in which there was no appropriate male role model. Thus two features that are essential for healthy psychological development—a stable mother figure during the first few years of life and a strong, socially appropriate father figure—were both absent. The importance of parental support is clearly illustrated by the fact that Terry's antisocial behavior took a dramatic turn for the worse at exactly the same time that he discovered he was adopted. This traumatic discovery at the age of 12 may well have influenced the decision to set fire to his school. Then, to make matters worse, his biological mother dropped by for his birthday, only to disappear again. Terry now recognizes that all these events hurt and angered him. He felt unloved, unwanted, and abandoned.

Other explanations of Terry's behavior would take into account the physical traumas and psychological frustrations he endured as a young child. Terry tells us that he was sick with diabetes and rickets. Unlike adults, who can relate physical pain to illness, children do not understand the origins of their pain and are frightened and frustrated by it. Palmer found, in his comparison of murderers and their brothers, that the murderers had suffered more severe physical illness and traumas as children. Thus it is possible to speculate that

Terry's poor health as a child may have contributed in some way to his final offense. Of course, there were also the frustrations of losing his parents when he was very young, the harsh punishments meted out by his guardian, and the general lack of attention and supervision he experienced in his foster home.

If one examines Terry's childhood from Eysenck's point of view, the lack of appropriate conditioning would emerge as an important factor in his delinquency. The absence of a stable family structure and the minimal amount of attention given Terry by his guardian may have resulted in little conditioning or training for acceptable behavior. Eventually Terry submitted to beatings but claims they had no effect on his behavior; thus the conditioning process did not work. It is not clear whether Terry is an extravert or an introvert. It may be that he is an extravert who does not condition easily *and* that the amount of attention he did receive was not sufficient to condition him to appropriate behaviors.

Terry's Reform

In discussing his reform and how the changes in his attitude and behavior came about, Terry mentioned three experiences as being most important in helping him decide to change his life. First, the knowledge he gained as a result of the college courses he took as an inmate provided him with insights into his own behavior and motivations. Second, the therapy he received while in prison helped him to understand, express, and come to terms with his feelings about his parents, his foster mother, and his past. Third, the major change in his own attitudes occurred when he finally was able to accept full responsibility for his actions.

After his final offense, Terry had a lot of time to think about the consequences of his actions, yet many months passed before he finally came to accept the fact that because of his actions, a man was dead. This acceptance of responsibility for one's actions is what Glasser seeks to achieve with his patients through Reality Therapy. In Glasser's view, deviant behavior occurs when people are irresponsible, when they satisfy their needs in an irresponsible manner. The key to changing deviant behavior then is to encourage people to take full responsibility for their actions. Once this is accomplished, people can begin to fulfill their needs in a socially and interpersonally responsible manner.

Once Terry accepted responsibility for his crimes, prison became aversive. It was a place to get out of so that he could begin to live a responsible life (which now includes a wife, child, and helping other prisoners rehabilitate themselves). Terry refuses to blame society or to criticize the institutions in which he spent so many years of his life. In fact, he claims to have learned some valuable lessons while in prison and has no animosity toward the system. Any anger he feels is toward himself for having made so many mistakes.

PART II

The Juvenile Justice Process

Introduction

The first part of this book presented definitions of delinquency, a consideration of its nature and frequency of occurrence, and a review of some of the theoretical explanations of the causes of juvenile delinquency. It was pointed out that the value placed on children in our society has contributed to public concern about youthful offenders. Such concern has been reflected in the changes in law as it affects children who are delinquent or in need of care.

During the late nineteenth century, a specialized court was established that would handle cases of juvenile delinquency and neglect or abuse of children and orphans. The concept of the juvenile court, or family court, became popular and today is a common part of state court systems throughout the United States.

It is this court that officially labels a child as a delinquent or a status offender. But the juvenile court is not the only official organization with which children have contact. In fact, there are many organizations that may exert power over a child. It is this network of organizations and their decision-making powers that are known as the juvenile justice process.

The juvenile justice process begins with a complaint made by the police; citizens; officials of schools, welfare departments, or hospitals; or parents (see diagram). Most complaints are filed by police officers, who may arrest the child or divert the child by use of a reprimand rather than a formal complaint. Decision-making practices of the police are important determinants of those children who come to the attention of the juvenile court. The police may make the initial detention decision, which means that the child may be held in a facility overnight or longer.

The next decisions are made by the juvenile court intake staff, usually comprised of probation officers. Cases that are recommended for further court action are held for an intake hearing. The others are diverted or dropped from the entire process. At intake, a further decision whether or not to detain the youth while awaiting a court hearing is made. At adjudication, or the court hearing on the facts of the case, the child may be found to be delinquent or a status offender, or the case may be dropped.

The final stage in the juvenile justice process involves a decision on the disposition of those cases where the juvenile was found to be delinquent or in need of some type of care. The court once again determines the future of the juvenile. The child may be placed on probation, in an institution, or released. Finally, the child will be released from probation or an institution. This decision may be made by a judge or by those persons who run the correctional facility.

As will be seen in the following chapters, the juvenile justice process is much more complex than it appears in this brief overview. It involves a variety of organizations such as the police, probation officers, the juvenile court, and correctional institutions. At each decision point the child may be diverted out of the process; or, conversely, sent deeper into it. Not only are these decisions important to the children involved, but they determine the number of children going on to subsequent stages of the process. In a sense, the decision network of the juvenile justice process acts as a screen that keeps some children out and permits others to pass through.

The functioning of the entire process is directly affected by the actions of each component part, such as the police or the court. But it is also affected by the environment in which the process exists. For example, the number of delinquent acts committed may decrease, new laws concerning juveniles may be enacted by a state government, or economic trends may encourage the development of less expensive treatment programs for juveniles. The importance of the components of the process and the importance of the environment in which they exist will be examined in the following chapters.

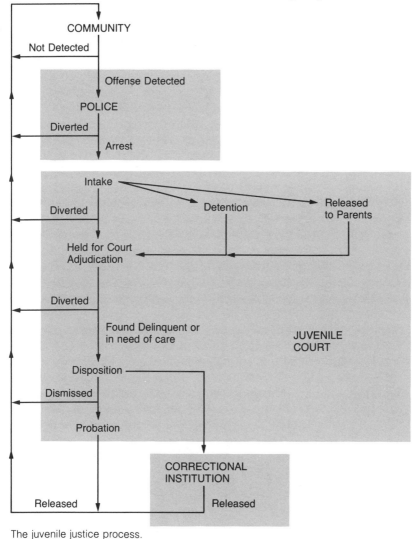

The juvenile justice process.

7 Children and the Juvenile Court

The first juvenile court in the United States was officially established with the passage of the Juvenile Court Act of 1899 in Illinois.[1] This court was designed to handle a variety of problem children ranging from delinquents to deprived children and orphans. In contrast to criminal courts, which imposed punishment for legally proscribed behaviors, the juvenile court would pursue the humane goals of care and rehabilitation for children found to be in need of such services.

To understand how the concept of a juvenile court developed, it is necessary to examine the factors that contributed to its philosophy of treatment. This changing approach to delinquency resulted in part from new beliefs about the nature and causes of delinquent behavior which had been formulated by criminologists. A shift away from classical criminology—which had emphasized the responsibility of the offender for his or her behavior—toward the later positivist approach influenced the idea that delinquency could not only be treated but could be eventually eradicated. A modified version of positivism, which acknowledged the role of biological and social factors in the causes of delinquency, was adopted in the United States.[2] A force known as the child-saving movement developed in the late 1800s. This movement employed these new ideas of criminology and advocated specialized rehabilitative programs for children who were delinquent, neglected, or deprived.

Changing Perspectives on Crime and Delinquency

Under the philosophy outlined by the classical school of criminology, children were considered responsible for their criminal acts and could be convicted and sentenced as adults. The classical school was led by Cesare Beccaria of Italy and Jeremy Bentham of England in the late eighteenth and early nineteenth centuries. These men were concerned about the arbitrary and often excessive punishments that were meted out to child offenders and wished to eliminate such inhumane practices through a system of new laws that would protect the individual from the state. The classical school believed that laws must be specific, well known, and applied equally to all persons.[3] To attain this equality, mitigating circumstances could not be used as excuses for behavior. Punishments should be devised so that they would be appropriate for the crime since it was believed that people exercised free will in order to maximize pleasure and to minimize pain. It was thought that when enough pain was attached to a criminal act, it would deter the offender from committing further acts.[4] Although the classical school encouraged reforms that insured due process in trial procedures and limited judicial discretion, individual differences among offenders were still ignored. Thus the French Penal Code of 1791, which grew out of the classical reforms, treated minors, mental defectives, psychotics, and normal adults as equally competent to stand trial.[5]

The classical school contributed to the protection of the rights of the individual and to the application of equal punishment for offenses, but presented problems in the day-to-day administration of the law. A lack of flexibility in considering the specific circumstances of a case created a new harshness for some offenders. Subsequent revisions of the classical position granted some discretionary power to judges in certain situations. Occasionally exceptions were made for minors, the elderly, and incompetents.[6] The neoclassical reformists encouraged punishments that would contribute to the rehabilitation of the offender.[7]

In the beginning of the twentieth century, Enrico Ferri presented a new perspective on crime and human nature. This new school of criminology, positivism, refuted the "free will" ideas of the classical school. Instead of focusing on the *choice* to commit offenses, the positivists proposed a science of society. Using scientific techniques, the "true" causes of crime could be discovered, and appropriate treatments could be made available to the criminal. Unlike the classical school, the positivists advocated the protection of society over the rights of the individual. The criminal law was to be used to protect society and reform the criminal. Indefinite sentences were needed to individualize justice in each case and to treat those who were pathologically disturbed.

One of the explanations of criminality that resulted from the scientific approach of the positivist school was the biological positivist school. Cesare Lombroso, its founding father, first presented his ideas in 1876.[8] His theory rested on the notion that some people were atavistic criminals; that is, reversions back to an earlier evolutionary period. The born criminal's behavior was determined by biological factors that were responsible for certain physical stigmata or atavistic traits found among many criminals. These stigmata, or physical characteristics, included abnormal teeth, toes, fingers, large ears, asymmetrical faces, and eye defects. Lombroso's research, in which he compared convicted criminals with control groups of soldiers, uncovered significant differences between the two groups in the number of stigmata.[9]

Lombroso did not postulate that all offenders were evolutionary throwbacks. Indeed, two other types of criminals were considered in addition to the *born criminal—insane criminals* and *criminaloid*.[10] The criminaloid was physically and psychologically normal but committed crimes in response to circumstantial pressures. Here environmental influences as well as biological traits were thought to contribute to crime.[11]

Although Lombroso's research was subsequently refuted by other researchers, the impact of his ideas was great.[12] In the United States the idea of social Darwinism meshed easily with biological positivism. Social Darwinism suggested that only the strongest, or "fittest," members of a society survive in the competitive struggle for life and in so doing improve the quality of society. These beliefs discouraged the concept of rehabilitation and also helped to explain the failure of criminal law to effectively deter crime. The early positivist criminology in the United States stressed the irreversible character of criminal behavior, but this position was modified to emphasize the importance of environmental factors in the origins of crime. By 1890, a modified version of biological determinism had become more popular, especially among penologists. The existence of "degenerate classes" was acknowledged but there was also a belief in the possibility that offenders could be reformed.[13]

The Child-Saving Movement

The popularity of positivist criminology paved the way for the implementation of special treatment programs for children in the United States, but a modification in criminological beliefs was not enough to bring about the development of the juvenile court. Other social and political forces were at work during the late nineteenth and early twentieth centuries which contributed to the child-saving movement. The "child savers" were reformers who were concerned with "rescuing those who were less fortunately placed in the social order."[14] How did these child savers become powerful enough to influence legislatures to begin juvenile courts?

Three important factors helped precipitate child-saving and juvenile court legislation. These were: 1) increased concern about the treatment of children under the criminal law; 2) increased concern about the effects of urban life and the threat it posed to middle-class rural American values; and 3) the rise of the feminist movement.[15] Although we will see that the harsh treatment of children and the evils of urban life were exaggerated, these issues became a rallying point for women who were concerned about the welfare of the young.

According to the tenets of classical criminology, all citizens could be treated in the same manner under the law. Children could be held responsible for criminal actions and could be tried, convicted, and punished for offenses as if they were adults. It has long been assumed that children were regularly subjected to harsh punishments, but there is much evidence to suggest that in fact they were shown great leniency.[16] Sentences, if given, were not always carried out, and frequently juries acquitted children from charges due to the child's "lack of knowledge" or inability to understand the import of the offense.[17] The common law of England had long presumed that felonious intent was impossible for a child of seven or under, and a child between the ages of 7 and 14 was also incapable unless it could be shown that there was an understanding of the consequences of the actions.[18] Nevertheless, the inhumane treatment of children was a popular concern during the 1800s.

There were some children who were found guilty and were incarcerated alongside adults, but others escaped punishment by appealing to the sympathy of the jury. These problems prompted the establishment of special institutions for children in the United States. In order to circumvent issues of due process in criminal court, the power of *parens patriae* was used. The *parens patriae* doctrine had been established in English Chancery court to insure the protective jurisdiction of the king over all of the children of the realm.[19] In American courts, *parens patriae* acknowledged the right of the state to intervene on the behalf of children and to place them in apprenticeships or institutions.[20]

Under *parens patriae* children could be placed in special institutions which had been designed for their welfare and reform. These institutions had become popular in the United States in the 1830s with the establishment of private orphan asylums, and within a short period of time another type of caretaker institution was set up—the reformatory or refuge.[21] The refuge took in delinquents, orphans, and disobedient children and maintained a flexible admission policy that allowed commitment of a child to the institution by the "decisions of a judicial body, the less formal recommendations of overseers of the poor, or the personal inclination of the head of a household."[22]

The refuge or reformatory was designed to transform the character of children so that they could survive within a disordered community. At the core of the treatment programs set up in these institutions was the belief that strict discipline and complete obedience by children was required to train the young for appropriate social behavior. As a result, the authority of the institution replaced that of the parent, and strict regimentation of children was employed. Each day would be scheduled to include work, some schooling, and religious instruction. Punishment for infractions of rules could be severe and included the use of the whip, solitary confinement, and the ball and chain.[23]

Such institutions, though originally privately owned and operated, were also established by the states and claimed to offer industrial training and educational opportunities for children. Their structures often consisted of cottages in which the children lived in what was thought to be a more homelike setting, but many of these refuges were in fact large structures that resembled prisons. A congregate system, or one in which large numbers of juveniles could be housed together, was common in institutions built in urban areas.

Urban environments were described as the most dangerous settings for children; thus it is not surprising that institutions for the care of children were built in rural areas. The city was thought to serve as a breeding ground for criminals, and the poorly educated, unskilled immigrants who had come in increasing numbers to urban areas were thought to be particularly vulnerable to this influence. Attitudes toward immigrants ranged from empathy to condemnation, but there was agreement that city life was hardest on these citizens and that intervention to save their children from such environments was beneficial and necessary.[24]

The child savers mobilized to rescue children from the harsh treatment they received under the criminal law and from the ill effects of the city slums. Women were often among the reformers who sought such change, and their qualifications for saving children were widely accepted. Women were seen as better teachers and child rearers than men and so they knew what was appropriate for children. Although middle-class women had leisure time and were well-educated in the nineteenth century, there were very few career opportunities open to them. Child saving provided "a reputable task for any woman who wanted to extend her housekeeping functions into the community without denying anti-feminist stereotypes of woman's nature and place."[25] Child saving did not encourage competition for jobs usually held by men and was less threatening to those who opposed changes in the female role. Ultimately this led to a new professional role for women—the role of social worker.[26]

The Early Juvenile Court

The efforts of the child savers culminated in a juvenile court system that differed drastically from that of other courts. The goals of this new court were prevention of future delinquency and treatment of those juveniles who had already committed delinquent acts. Prevention required early intervention in the life of a youngster who might become delinquent in the future; thus dependent, truant, and neglected children were included under the jurisdiction of the court.[27] These children could be taken from their parents and placed in institutions or given other treatment, a practice that resembled the more informal procedures existing prior to the establishment of the juvenile court. The enactment of juvenile court legislation did not create a totally new institutional mechanism for the control of juveniles, but instead expedited policies set up prior to 1899.[28]

The procedures of the juvenile court were civil rather than criminal in nature. The informality of civil proceedings was necessary since the constitutional constraints placed on criminal courts were thought to impede efforts to help the child. Moreover the formality of criminal proceedings would stigmatize the juvenile as a "criminal." Attorneys were rarely present, and the proceedings were nonadversary in nature. The use of hearsay evidence was acceptable because it was thought to provide a clearer insight into the child's background and past experiences. Because the act that had been committed was not considered to be as important as the child's condition, a "preponderance of evidence" was required to establish the child's condition rather than "proof beyond a reasonable doubt" that the specific act had been committed.[29]

Efforts were made to protect and help individual juveniles processed through the court. Proceedings and records were private, and different terminology was used with juveniles. The arraignment procedure was called *intake,* the trial was called a *hearing,* and sentencing was called the *disposition* of the case. Many of the roles filled by lawyers in criminal court were performed by social workers or probation officers in juvenile courts. For example, the decision to bring a child into court was often made by a social worker at the intake stage. If the child was referred for a court hearing, a presentence investigation on the youngster was presented to the judge. This report which was completed by a probation officer, included information on school performance, home environment, and other contacts the child may have had with the court. A recommendation on appropriate treatment was also included. The judge in juvenile court was to make decisions concerning the child on the basis of need for treatment rather than punishment for offenses. One writer described the requirements of juvenile court judge as not only knowledge of law but also deep interest "in the problems of philanthropy and child life, as well as a lover of children."[30]

Judges could have children incarcerated for periods of time to be terminated when an improvement in the child's attitude and behavior was detected. Thus, the success of treatment would be used as the criterion for release; this indeterminate sentence structure was thought to enhance rehabilitation.[31] Other forms of treatment, such as probation, were also used. The probation officer was to assist and train parents in dealing with their children through supervision of the child in the community. The New York Probation Commission in an annual report published in 1908 described effective probation as follows.

> The probation officers obtaining the best results enter into intimate friendly relations with their probationers, and bring into play as many factors as possible, such as, for instance, securing employment for their probationers, readjusting family difficulties, securing medical treatment or charity if necessary, interesting helpful friends and relatives, getting the cooperation of churches, social settlements and various other organizations, encouraging probationers to

start bank accounts, to keep better hours, to associate with better companions, and so forth.[32]

As for the rights of the child, procedural and due process provisions for adults were not applicable. The rights that concerned the juvenile court were the child's right "to shelter, protection, and proper guardianship."[33] Assuming that the welfare of the child was foremost in decision making and that efforts at treatment were effective, the power of the court could perhaps be justified. But the failure of the court to protect or rehabilitate juveniles became increasingly apparent as did the danger of unbridled discretion, and after a long period of criticism the juvenile court came under evaluation by the United States Supreme Court.

Constitutional Positions

The informality of the juvenile court prevailed for over 60 years. Its flaws were apparent to many writers, jurists, and criminologists during this period, but major changes in court procedures did not come about.[34] Many people held to the treatment-oriented philosophy of the original court and justified its practices on grounds that actions were taken only for the benefit of the child.

During the 1950s and 1960s, the U.S. Supreme Court enlarged and upheld the procedural rights of adult defendants.[35] This prompted renewed attacks on the juvenile court and ultimately culminated in a series of Supreme Court decisions which provided specific procedural rights for children. The position of the court rested on the failure of the juvenile justice system to obtain its goals of treatment and rehabilitation and the proposition that constitutional rights should apply to children as well as adults.

The first Supreme Court case to deal directly with the rights of juveniles was *Kent* v. *U. S.* in 1966.[36] Although this decision concerns the interpretation of a District of Columbia statute rather than Constitutional issues, the court discusses the failures of the juvenile court and indicates a concern for the rights of children. Morris Kent, a sixteen-year-old male, was charged with housebreaking, robbery, and rape. Jurisdiction was waived by the juvenile court and Kent was tried as an adult. Maximum confinement by the juvenile court was five years, but the maximum sentence when charged as an adult was death. According to statutory provisions, a hearing on waiver of jurisdiction was to have been held. Kent did not receive a hearing, and it was on this error that the United States Supreme Court reversed Kent's conviction. Criticisms of the practices of the juvenile court made by the justices focused on the lack of personnel, inadequate facilities, and ineffective treatment techniques. In addition, critics pointed out that some children received neither the protections given adults nor the care and treatment they were supposed to receive. The court concluded that the hearing must "measure up to the essentials of due process and fair treatment."[37]

The Kent decision was followed the next year by the case of *In re Gault*.[38] It is this decision that truly marks the beginning of constitutionalist revisions of the juvenile court. Gerald Gault, a fifteen-year-old male, was adjudicated as a delinquent for having made obscene telephone calls. He was to be incarcerated in a state training school until he reached the age of 21 or for a period of 6 years. If Gerald had been over 18 years of age, the maximum sentence for this particular offense would have been a fine of $5 to $50 or imprisonment in jail for not more than two months.

The specific provisions of the Gault decision concern notice, counsel, and proof. Gerald Gault's parents were not notified that he had been taken into custody, and they were not notified of the date of the hearings and the specific charges. The court stated that written notice must be given of the charges and date of hearing, and given sufficiently in advance so preparations can be made.

Counsel was not provided for Gault, and he was not notified of his right to legal representation. The court rejected the claim that a probation officer fulfills this function for the child and stated that the child and his parents must be notified of this right and must have counsel appointed if they are unable to afford a privately retained lawyer.

The issues of proof concerned confrontation, self-incrimination, and cross-examination. The complainant against Gerald Gault did not appear at his hearing. The court held that without a valid confession by the child, confrontation and an opportunity for cross-examination of witnesses must be provided. The confession made by Gerald Gault was not considered a valid one because it was made to a police officer "out of the presence of Gerald's parents, without counsel, and without advising him of his right to silence."[39]

The impact of the Gault decision on the juvenile court was great. Although this decision provides for counsel only at the hearing stage, it has encouraged the presence of attorneys at other stages in the process. It also has encouraged increased formality in court proceedings in the use of witnesses and cross-examination of them. This decision did not require that juvenile hearings conform to *all* of the requirements of a criminal trial, but rather held that the constitution requires "the essentials of due process and fair treatment."[40]

The Gault decision established the relevance of due process considerations in juvenile justice, and in 1970 the Supreme Court broadened the scope of such rights. In the case of *In re Winship,* the court held that a determination of delinquency may only be made upon the same evidentiary standard as used in criminal proceedings.[41] *Proof beyond a reasonable doubt* replaced the standard of a *preponderance of the evidence* in juvenile proceedings. The preponderance standard had been adopted from civil proceedings and required less evidence for a finding of delinquency than did the standard used in criminal trials. It had been justified because the goal of the juvenile court was not punishment but treatment, but the Supreme court noted that delinquency proceedings can result in significant loss of freedom, and are comparable to felony prosecution. Thus the more demanding standard of proof must be used in delinquency hearings, since it is an essential of due process and fair treatment.

The Gault and Winship decisions served to establish the due process rights of juveniles, but did not include the right to jury trial. In *McKeiver* v. *Pennsylvania,* the right of juveniles to jury trials was considered, but was not granted.[42] The court noted that jury trials were provided in some states, but emphasized the detrimental effects of making the juvenile court exactly like criminal courts. If jury trials became a fundamental right for juveniles, the justices felt there would be no need for a separate court system for children. The negative aspects of trial by jury were also cited, such as the length of *voir dire* proceedings. The Supreme Court was unwilling to completely abridge the informality and treatment orientation of the juvenile court and in this decision drew limitations on the applicability of Fifth and Sixth Amendment rights for children.

In 1975 the Supreme Court considered the issue of double jeopardy for juveniles. In *Breed* v. *Jones,* the court considered the case of a juvenile who had been adjudicated a delinquent in juvenile court and then was transferred to adult court and convicted of robbery.[43] The court held that such transfer after adjudication in juvenile court constituted double jeopardy and that juveniles are protected against this by the Fifth Amendment. The importance of this protection for children is great since prior to this decision a child could be institutionalized in a juvenile institution, retried as an adult, and then incarcerated in an adult institution.[44]

Between the time of the Kent decision in 1966 and the Breed decision in 1975, the constitutional position in juvenile justice was introduced, expanded, and then curtailed. The due process rights afforded youngsters ultimately included right to counsel, notice of charges, freedom from self-incrimination and double jeopardy, right to confrontation and cross-examination of witnesses, and adjudication only upon proof beyond a reasonable doubt. The right to a jury trial or a public trial have not been granted and perhaps will be unlikely provisions since they have been described as those aspects which serve to differentiate the juvenile court from criminal court.

These Supreme Court decisions have checked some of the discretion and power of the juvenile justice system and have developed more formality in procedures. It must be emphasized that these court rulings set up minimum requirements that juvenile courts must follow across the United States. In some states, these procedural safeguards were operative before the Supreme Court decisions, and there are states today which legally require more extensive rights for juveniles than those set down so far by the Supreme Court.

The belief in the nonpunitive nature of the juvenile court and the desire to maintain flexibility and an emphasis on treatment can be seen in the evolution of the constitutionalist position. Although critical of the lack of success by the juvenile court, the Supreme Court is also wary of making the proceedings comparable to those used in criminal trials. Instead of rejecting the juvenile court, the U.S. Supreme Court has sought to interject procedural standards and increased orderliness into the already-existing structure. The end result has been a court that is less formal than criminal proceedings but that, at least in theory, can provide rehabilitative care.

Although this has been the position of the Supreme Court, there is ample evidence that from the days of the early institutions known as refuges up to the present time the rehabilitative goals of the juvenile court have seldom been met. The abuses and lack of care children may experience in both state and private institutions have been well documented.[45] Often these institutions merely serve as holding facilities where the goal of rehabilitation is replaced with the goals of discipline, secure custody, and efficient institutional operation.

The question of whether juveniles committed to institutions have a right to treatment has been confronted in federal cases in several parts of the United States.[46] In 1974 a decision in the U.S. Court of Appeals for the Seventh Circuit upheld a constitutional right to treatment for juveniles under the Fourteenth Amendment, which makes constitutional rights applicable to the states. In this case, *Nelson* v. *Heyne,* the court considered a lower court decision that juveniles have a right to treatment under the concept of due process.[47] The appellate court pointed out that the *parens patriae* powers of the juvenile court can only be justified if treatment is available for those committed to institutions. If such treatment is not available, the constitutional rights of the incarcerated juveniles are violated. The court stated that

> . . . the "right to treatment" includes the right to minimum acceptable standards of care and treatment for juveniles and the right to *individualized* care and treatment. Because children differ in their need for rehabilitation, individual need for treatment will differ. When a state assumes the place of a juvenile's parents, it assumes as well the parental duties, and its treatment of its juveniles should, so far as can be reasonably required, be what proper parental care would provide. Without a program of individual treatment the result may be that the juveniles will not be rehabilitated, but warehoused.[48]

The conditions of confinement that existed at the institution which was under scrutiny in this case included the use of corporal punishment in the form of beatings with a wooden paddle, the use of tranquilizing drugs to control behavior, and a staff-to-juvenile ratio of one to thirty in the treatment program. Of the twenty staff members, three held undergraduate degrees and there was only one part-time psychiatrist. It is easy to understand why the court is concerned about the conditions of confinement and the lack of rehabilitation services.

How representative this institution is of juvenile institutions in general is difficult to determine, but similar conditions have been cited in other court decisions.[49] The effect that court decisions such as that upheld in *Nelson* v.

Heyne will have on juvenile institutions is still unclear, but there is some reason to believe that stricter standards for institutional care will result. In those juvenile facilities where only warehousing occurs, the child does have the right to be released.

The Juvenile Court Today: Divergent Goals

The evolution of the juvenile court has been marked by a conflict between divergent objectives. The welfare and care of children have consistently been a primary concern, but throughout the history of the court other goals have been proposed and supported. For example, protection of the community from dangerous offenders and deterrence of future offenses have been seen as functions of the juvenile court. Indeed, much of the criticism of the original juvenile court was based on the belief that the moral force of the law was weakened by the leniency of the juvenile system.[50] Some writers have encouraged either a return to punishment in lieu of treatment or a lowering of the age at which a child can be legally tried as an adult.

Part of this conflict arises from the wide variety of juvenile offenses that the court handles. Children who have committed serious offenses, children who are themselves victims of abuse or neglect, and juveniles who have engaged in status offenses may all come under the jurisdiction of the court although each case is quite different and thus may require a different type of response.

Another factor that produces problems for the juvenile court is popular concern among the citizenry, which in recent years has tended to focus on one of two groups of offenders—dangerous juveniles or status offenders. These two types of offenders represent extreme examples of the juvenile court's responsibility, often obscuring those juveniles who fall somewhere in between these two types. The following articles, which appeared in *The New York Times,* are examples of the kind of publicity given to juveniles and the juvenile court and illustrate some of the perspectives on juvenile delinquency that are presented to the American public.

Tale of Two Young Muggers Who Prey on the Elderly
By Joseph B. Treaster

When William Harper was 14 years old, the police say he dropped out of school and began working as a mugger, preying on old men and women in the Coney Island section of Brooklyn.

He was arrested twice for mugging and sent home both times with a warning. Then he was arrested for sexual abuse of a 10-year-old boy and put on probation. While on probation he was caught mugging another old person and, for the first time, was sent to a reform school.

He was released in March after nine months in the institution and in less than two weeks, young Harper, now 16, and Roy Collins, 14, were caught moments after beating and robbing a 72-year-old woman of $3 in the elevator of her building.

The 14-year-old had been arrested nine times previously for burglary and mugging, beginning at the age of 9. Until his latest encounter with the police he had never spent a day in detention.

The Harper and Collins youths, whose names have been changed in this article because of their ages, are typical of an increasingly large number of youths prowling the city's streets, the police say, and their stories illustrate what virtually every expert describes as the failure of the juvenile-justice system in New York.

The system has been bound by a philosophy of rehabilitation rather than punishment. But rehabilitation has not worked—either because, as some experts say, it has never been given a chance, or, as one specialist said, "We really don't know what would help these kids."

Many authorities feel a complete overhaul of the system is needed, but so far the reaction by state legislators has been piecemeal and has responded mainly to public cries to "get tough."

A number of those in the field of social services feel that harsh treatment of juveniles might exacerbate, rather than improve the crime picture in the long run, but Louis Telano, a plainclothes housing detective who, along with his partner, John Sepe, arrested the youths last month, scoffs at that notion.

"The whole thing's a joke to these kids," he said with no effort to conceal his bitterness.

"As soon as you grab them they say, 'I'm only 14' or 15 or whatever, and 'there's nothing you can do to me,'" Detective Telano said. "They know nothing's going to happen."

After their latest arrest, the two boys told Detectives Telano and Sepe, a police team that calls themselves Tonto and the Lone Ranger, that they had mugged a total of seven elderly persons—five women and two men—in the less than two weeks that young Harper had been back on the street.

And Detective Sepe said the boys, both of medium build and weighing about 140 pounds, fitted the descriptions of the assailants in at least 20 other attacks on elderly men and women in Coney Island in the same period.

Crossing the Line

When the detectives arrested young Harper, he had passed his 16th birthday, the demarcation line for juveniles in New York state, and was taken to Criminal Court, the first level in the adult system that can issue sentences of up to life imprisonment.

The Collins boy went to the Family Court for his 10th appearance.

By its own accounting, the Family Court functions like a sieve. Last year, for example, more than 25,000 juvenile cases were taken to the Family Court in New York City, including 54 for murder, 232 for rape, 5,276 for robbery and 1,230 for felonious assault. By the beginning of this year, however, there were fewer than 1,000 juvenile delinquents in detention in state and private institutions.

More than half of the cases had been dismissed by a probation officer after a cursory review and a brief conversation with the youth, his parents, the victim and the arresting officer.

Young Harper's first two arrests for mugging were discarded in this manner as were the younger boy's first arrest, for burglary, and his second for robbery of a bicycle at knifepoint.

Retaliation Feared

Many other cases were thrown out of court later for lack of evidence or the failure of witnesses or victims to appear in court. Five robbery charges against the younger boy were dropped because elderly victims refused to testify against him.

"Most of them are afraid of retaliation," said Detective Telano. "In over 10 years I've never seen any retaliation on any mugging victim. But you can't convince an old person of that."

Some of the cases were not prosecuted, as with two mugging charges against the younger boy, because the accused youths did not return to court after having been released in the custody of their parents.

Following is the arrest record of the 14-year-old boy who law-enforcement officials say is typical of the repetitious offenders who come before the Family Court. He was first arrested at the age of nine.

Offense	*Disposition*
Burglary	Sent home with warning
Robbery (took bicycle at knife point)	Sent home with warning
Robbery (mugging)	Dismissed (no complainant)
Robbery (mugging)	Dismissed (no complainant)
Robbery (mugging)	Dismissed (no complainant)
Robbery (mugging)	Dismissed (no complainant)
Robbery (mugging)	Dismissed (no complainant)
Burglary, possession of stolen property	Pending, youth failed to appear in court; reminder mailed, but no warrant issued
Robbery (mugging)	Pending; youth failed to appear in court; warrant issued
Robbery (mugging), assault, burglary, possession of stolen property	Found guilty on all but burglary charge; awaiting sentence

Arrest warrants were issued in these cases, and in the majority of them the police say, the youths were returned to court. But sometimes, as in the case of the 14-year-old they did not return before they had committed another crime—and then usually only the most recent charges were considered.

Still other cases crept through the full court process only to end, as with young Harper, in meaningless probation.

With sometimes as many as 100 cases each, probation officers have almost completely stopped making home visits and usually have youths come into their offices. Sometimes the only contact is by telephone, and if a youth drifts off altogether no one goes looking for him.

The few young criminals who do not slip through the sieve end up in the training schools where the maximum term for murder or any other crime is 18 months.

There is no minimum stay, and officials of the state's Division for Youth, which runs the training schools, may release youths without conferring with the court. At present, those who have committed the most serious crimes are being released after a year of good behavior while others are generally freed in nine to 10 months.

Among the juvenile justice experts who urge a restructuring of the system, many feel the first step should be a shift in the guiding philosophy to provide for a blend of rehabilitation and punishment. They would completely revise the Family Court and also create a central agency to coordinate and direct efforts to deal with juvenile delinquents.

At present, however, government leaders appear to favor simpler, more direct measures.

For example, one of the most popular themes for reform these days is for longer sentences. Some advocates would like to see youths who commit serious crimes spend up to five or six years in the training schools. Others believe the youths should be turned over to the Criminal Court at 14 or 15 instead of 16 and be sent to prisons on the same terms as adults.

"If they can reduce the voting age because they feel the kids are more mature, then the same should go for 14-year-olds committing serious crimes," Detective Telano said.

Those with backgrounds in social services argue against lowering age standards and longer incarceration. They point out that in most states a youth is considered a juvenile until his 18th birthday. They argue also that years in jail are not likely to change a youth for the better.

The Prosecutor's View

Maybe so, said Detective Sepe. But he added that sending young criminals away for a few years would at least give neighborhoods some respite from their violence.

Larry K. Schwartzstein, the supervisor in charge of the Corporation Counsel's staff in Family Court in Manhattan—in effect, the chief prosecutor—said he believed longer detention would "teach youngsters discipline and respect for human life and the court."

Many traditionalists in juvenile delinquency feel that rehabilitation has never been given the amounts of money and manpower that might enable it to succeed.

In recent interviews, they said they were primarily for reorganizing the old system and having another go. They don't see juvenile delinquents as miniature criminals, but as misguided, only partially developed individuals who can be redirected toward useful lives.

"They're talking about sending 14- and 15-year-olds away for 20 years or more," said Sheridan Faber, a senior research analyst in juvenile delinquency and a former probation officer. "I'm very reluctant to write them all off this way. I don't think you can deal with a 15-year-old the way you do an adult."[51]

Eddie G., Status Offender

At age 15 Eddie G. was jailed for truancy. . . . His father told the Family Court that he wanted Eddie to be assigned to the State Training School because, "He never goes to school . . . he hangs around the house all day . . . and stays out all night raising hell."

The judge took exactly seven minutes to dispose of the case. He was apologetic when he signed the order. "What else can I do," he said. "The mother has vanished, the father doesn't want him, the social worker couldn't arrange a suitable placement."

Eddie's father thought a few months in the training school would be "for his own good . . . to teach the boy a lesson."

Eddie learned his lesson well.

Over the next four years he would return to court a half dozen times—most recently, in 1975, for armed robbery.

Only two years before his first run-in with the American juvenile justice system, Eddie was earning good grades in all his subjects and was a star quartermiler on the junior high school track team. Why did Eddie end up in that courtroom? What changes did he undergo at the State School?

The answers to these questions provide a disturbing portrait of the way we handle children who have committed no actual crimes—the so-called status offenders, who are in trouble with the law, solely because of their status as juveniles.

There were problems in Eddie's family before his parents split up. But it was after the divorce that Eddie's teachers first noticed that there was something wrong. The quality of his work was seriously deteriorating. He was acting sullen and withdrawn.

Some days he didn't show up in school at all.

At first, there was no reason to suspect that the neatly typed and signed excuses weren't genuine.

Then Eddie's father—a welder in a boiler factory—was laid off. Coming so soon after the disintegration of his marriage, it was difficult for the father to accept.

Now he was home when Eddie left for school in the morning, home all day, and home when Eddie returned from track practice at 5 o'clock. One evening, when Eddie asked to borrow $10, they argued. His father hit him across the face with the open palm of his muscular hand.

The next time they quarreled, Eddie, who is lean but athletic, hit him back.

After that, Eddie went his own way at nights—hanging out in the park with friends, playing basketball till midnight by the dim light of streetlamps, killing time in a local bar that never asked for ID's.

The records show that habitual truancy was the main complaint against him. But Eddie was also picked up twice for curfew violations and once for panhandling . . . offenses for which no adult would ever be prosecuted. He was detained in the city jail for 3 days before appearing in Family Court. On November 17, 1973, he was remanded to the State Training School for an indefinite term.

At first Eddie was terrified in the school. As part of a very unofficial orientation, the "old boys" told him stories about knifings and homosexual rapes.

(Actually, the latter was not a problem at the institution Eddie attended, although it does occur with terrifying frequency in many juvenile facilities.) Soon, however, he adjusted to life in the fenced-in complex of grim brick buildings.

It's an oft-repeated oversimplification to say that training schools are a breeding ground for young criminals. Eddie didn't learn from his peers how to shoplift, commit a mugging, or burglarize a home. (About the only thing he did learn in 14 months of incarceration was how to smoke cigarettes.) But he did undergo a disturbing change in his attitude and values.

When he emerged from Elgin Training School he was placed in a series of foster homes. And, for the first time, became involved in serious trouble. Before his appearance in Family Court Eddie had never been arrested for a single misdemeanor or felony. Now his name was all too familiar at the local precinct station:

July 1973: Arrested for shoplifting; charges dropped.

September 1973: Gets into fight with his teacher. Not reported.

October 1973: School reported chronic truancy to parole officer.

October 1973: Suspended from school for fighting and carrying a weapon.

November 1973: Arrested again for shoplifting.

November 1973: Returned to Elgin State Training School for an indeterminate sentence.

June 1974: Released from Elgin Training School, assigned to a new foster home.

August 1974: Has violent argument with foster parents.

October 1974: Arrested on suspicion of robbery; released on account of insufficient evidence.

November 1974: Arrested for possession of a firearm; charges dropped.

February 1975: Arrested for robbery of an all-night grocery and possession of a firearm; committed to maximum 18 months term in the state training school.

Eddie's story is by no means complete. He shouldn't be written off as a lost cause. But his future is very much in jeopardy. He is angrier and more unapproachable these days. And the same institutions where he acquired his rage and disrespect for law are the ones that are assigned the task of rehabilitating him. The recidivism rate of Elgin graduates is over 58 percent. But Eddie won't come back to Elgin again. He will be sixteen this fall. From then on he is under the jurisdiction of the adult justice system.[52]

New Trends in Juvenile Justice

The preceding cases illustrate two of the major concerns of juvenile justice today—treatment of serious offenders and handling of status offenders and neglected and deprived children. The violent juvenile may receive little, if any, formal contact with the courts and correctional facilities, but the child who has not committed a crime is often more likely to go to court and to be incarcerated. The efforts that some states have made to change these patterns consist of moves to place status offenders and delinquents in separate facilities and to increase the severity of disposition for violent youngsters.

In response to increased public concern over 14- and 15-year-old children who were committing violent offenses, the state of New York enacted the New York Juvenile Justice Reform Act in 1976.[53] This act is designed to require restrictive placement for dangerously violent youth. It provides for a mandated minimum placement with the state correctional agency for such juveniles in a secure facility. The first year of incarceration must be in a secure facility, and only after three years of custody may the child be discharged through a court order. Informal adjustment of these cases by intake staff is allowed only with the approval of a judge. This act provides much longer periods of confinement for young children who have committed felonies, and curtails the discretionary power of intake personnel.

Efforts aimed at the treatment of status offenders have called for separate correctional facilities for these juveniles, so that they are not placed with children who have been found by the court to be juvenile delinquents.[54] Hopefully, this practice will decrease some of the stigma of institutions for these children and minimize the learning of new deviant behaviors from more seasoned offenders.

Another means of decreasing the harshness of treatment of status offenders—as well as other juveniles who have not committed serious crimes—is the use of diversion programs. Diversion programs utilize techniques to divert children away from or out of the juvenile justice system. They encourage the use of community agencies and facilities for these children, rather than formal contact with the juvenile court. Parents, schools, police, probation officers, and the courts can all refer children who are in trouble to local counseling centers, remedial education programs, foster homes, and group homes. Since exposure to the juvenile justice system is thought to provide many stigmatizing and traumatizing experiences for children, keeping them out of the system has been advocated as a more positive alternative for many youngsters.

DISCUSSION QUESTIONS

1. Popular explanations of criminality in the United States during the 1800s made certain assumptions about deviants. What were these assumptions and in what ways did the law reflect them?

2. The child savers wanted to rescue children from harsh punishment. What steps did they actually take to improve conditions and bring about reform?

3. What was the reasoning behind the informality of the juvenile court?

4. Discuss the development of Constitutional rights for children in the juvenile court.

5. Discuss current issues related to the handling of status offenders and seriously delinquent children by the juvenile court.

NOTES

1. Anthony Platt, *The Child Savers* (Chicago: University of Chicago Press, 1969), p. 9.

2. Ibid., p. 32.

3. C. Ray Jeffrey, "Theoretical Structure of Crime Control," in F. Faust and P. Brantingham, eds., *Juvenile Justice Philosophy* (St. Paul, Minn.: West, 1974), pp. 5–6.

4. Ibid.

5. Ibid.

6. G. Vold, *Theoretical Criminology* (New York: Oxford University Press, 1958), pp. 24–26.

7. I. Taylor, P. Walton, and J. Young, *The New Criminology* (New York: Harper & Row, 1973), p. 9.

8. Cesare Lombroso, *L'Uomo Delinquente* (Milan: Hoepl, 1876).

9. Taylor, et al., *New Criminology*.

10. Don Gibbons, *Society, Crime, and Criminal Careers,* 2nd ed. (Englewood Cliffs, New Jersey: Prentice-Hall, 1973), p. 137.

11. Ibid.

12. Charles Goring, *The English Convict: A Statistical Study,* (London: His Majesty's Stationery Office, 1913).

13. Platt, *Child Savers,* p. 32.

14. Ibid., p. 3.

15. F. Faust and P. Brantingham, eds., *Juvenile Justice Philosophy,* (St. Paul, Minn.: West, 1974), p. 36.

16. Wiley B. Sanders, "Some Early Beginnings of the Children's Court Movement," in *Juvenile Justice Philosophy.*

17. Robert M. Mennel, "Origins of the Juvenile Court: Changing Perspectives on the Legal Rights of Juvenile Delinquents," in *Juvenile Justice Philosophy,* pp. 52–64.

18. President's Commission on Law Enforcement and Administration of Justice, *Task Force Report: Juvenile Delinquency and Youth Crime* (Washington, D.C.: Government Printing Office, 1967), p. 2.

19. Ibid.

20. Douglas R. Rendleman, "Parens Patriae: From Chancery to the Juvenile Court," in *Juvenile Justice Philosophy.*

21. David J. Rothman, *The Discovery of the Asylum* (Boston: Little, Brown, 1971), p. 207.

22. Ibid., p. 209.

23. Ibid., p. 231.

24. Platt, *Child Savers,* pp. 36–43.

25. Ibid., p. 76.

26. Anthony Platt, "The Rise of the Child-Saving Movement: A Study in Social Policy and Correctional Reform," in *Juvenile Justice Philosophy*, p. 176.

27. Julian W. Mack, "The Juvenile Court," in *Juvenile Justice Philosophy*, p. 152.

28. Platt, "Rise of the Child-Saving Movement," p. 176.

29. Faust and Brantingham, *Juvenile Justice Philosophy*, p. 146.

30. Mack, "Juvenile Court," p. 165.

31. Gustav Schramm, "The Juvenile Court Idea," in *Juvenile Justice Philosophy*, p. 205.

32. Mack, "Juvenile Court," p. 163.

33. Miriam Van Waters, "The Socialization of the Juvenile Court Procedure," in *Juvenile Justice Philosophy*, p. 191.

34. Faust and Brantingham, *Juvenile Justice Philosophy*, pp. 206–209.

35. *Mapp* v. *Ohio*, 367 U. S. 643 (1961); *Escobedo* v. *Illinois*, 378 U. S. 478 (1964); *Miranda* v. *Arizona*, 384 U. S. 436 (1966); *Gideon* v. *Wainwright*, 372 U. S. 335 (1963).

36. *Kent* v. *U. S.*, 383 U. S. 541 (1966).

37. Ibid.

38. *In re Gault*, 387 U. S. 1 (1967).

39. Ibid.

40. Ibid.

41. *In re Winship*, 397 U. S. 358 (1970).

42. *McKeiver* v. *Pennsylvania*, 403 U. S. 528 (1971).

43. *Breed* v. *Jones*, 421 U. S. 519 (1975).

44. Nicholas Kittrie, *The Right to Be Different* (Baltimore: Penguin, 1973), pp. 102–168.

45. Ibid.

46. *Matarella* v. *Kelley*, 349 F. Supp. 575 (S.D.N.Y. 1972); *Inmates* v. *Affleck*, 346 F. Supp. 1354 (D.R.I. 1972); *Morales* v. *Turman*, 364 F. Supp. 166 (E.D. Tex. 1973).

47. *Nelson* v. *Heyne*, 491 F. 2d 352 (7th Cir., 1974).

48. Ibid, at p. 360.

49. *Inmates* v. *Affleck*, 346 F. Supp. 1354 (D.R.I. 1972).

50. Faust and Brantingham, *Juvenile Justice Philosophy,* p. 206.

51. *The New York Times* (April 11, 1976), pp. 1, 42. ©1976 by The New York Times Company. Reprinted by permission.

52. National Council on Crime and Delinquency, *The New York Times* (September 12, 1976), Supplement. Reprinted with permission of the National Council on Crime and Delinquency, 411 Hackensack Ave., Hackensack, N.J. 07601 and its agent Glen Tarn Associates, Inc.

53. "The New York Juvenile Justice Reform Act of 1976: Restrictive Placement— An Answer to the Problem of the Seriously Violent Youth?'', *Fordham Law Review,* XLV, no. 2 (November 1976): 408–426.

54. This has occurred in some states in response to the federal Juvenile Justice and Delinquency Prevention Act, Public Law 93–415, 93rd Congress, S. 821, September 7, 1974.

8 Referral, Detection, and Intake

The initial stages of the juvenile justice process include: 1) detection of an offense or a need for intervention in order to protect the child's welfare; 2) referral of the case to juvenile court; and 3) the decision by court personnel to recommend the case for court action. A juvenile may be diverted or sent out of the juvenile justice process by the police or by court personnel. In other cases the juvenile may be placed in a detention facility, which is a place where children are held prior to their court hearing.

Self-report studies have clearly shown that many juveniles in our society commit acts that could lead to involvement with the juvenile court. But the fact is that a large number of these acts go undetected by authorities, and even of those that are known, only a small portion result in formal handling of the juvenile's case. The decisions that are made at the initial stages of the juvenile justice process are important ones since they can have a profound effect on the child's future. The choice of whether to handle a case informally or formally is particularly important because it can mean the difference between a verbal reprimand from a juvenile officer and possible incarceration. The process is set into motion by those who initially refer the child to the juvenile court—school officials, neighbors, parents, hospital personnel, and police officers.

Referral

Although most children come into contact with the juvenile court through police handling, other avenues are operative in bringing juveniles into court.

The child's parents, for example, may initiate proceedings by signing a petition stating that the child is out of their control. In New York these petitions are called PINS, which stands for *persons in need of supervision*. Some states use other, similar acronyms, including CHINS (*children in need of supervision*) and MINS (*minors in need of supervision*).[1] Often in these cases the court has become a last resort for parents who find themselves unable to deal with the behavior problems of their offspring. These families may simply lack the resources to utilize alternative means of treatment—such as child psychologists or private schools—and thus are forced to turn to the most available agency.

Public schools also refer children to the juvenile court for problems ranging from overt violence to unruly classroom behavior and chronic truancy. Much delinquency is committed on school property and during school hours. In recent years many school systems have developed alternative classrooms or special schools for problem students, which in some areas have helped relieve the courts of responsibility for such children. Remedial education programs and schools for "predelinquent" youngsters have also been organized in many of the larger school systems.[2]

The relationship between school and delinquency has been examined by many writers and has been included in many theories of delinquency.[3] Often criticized as a middle-class institution, the school has been seen as a major source of frustration for many children, particularly those from lower-class backgrounds. As many of the sociological theories of delinquency point out, the lower-class child may be ill prepared to compete in a middle-class world. Lower-class youngsters may become easily discouraged in their efforts to compete for grades or popularity and thus resort to deviant behavior as a means of attaining status. Unfortunately, the end result of this process is often delinquency. The lower-class child's lack of success has been described as a result of discrimination on the part of teachers who expect students to exhibit middle-class manners and values as well as educational programs that stress college-oriented career goals.[4] But there is little evidence to support these contentions. In fact, recent investigations indicate that school success is mainly a function of family attitudes and the amount of emphasis placed on educational achievement.[5] Nevertheless, the school always has the option of either referring a "problem" student to the court or using available structures within the school system.

Other institutions and agencies within the community also refer children who are delinquent, neglected, deprived, or abused to family or juvenile court. Social workers report children who are in need of placement in foster homes. Hospital emergency rooms and private physicians report cases of suspected child neglect and abuse. Because the jurisdiction, or authority, of the court encompasses children who are victims as well as children who are offenders, a wide variety of agencies may refer cases.

The final avenue for referral, and the one most frequently utilized, is the police. Police officers are sometimes notified by neighbors who have witnessed offenses or by people who have been victims of delinquent acts. However, complainants vary in their willingness to become involved in the process and many refuse to appear in court. In addition, some neighborhoods are more tolerant of youthful misbehaviors; in such neighborhoods, offenses often go unreported or in some instances receive informal handling.[6] In other situations, the police themselves detect children in the act of committing an offense or find children who are suspected runaways or truants.

Obviously the police cannot be expected to detect every delinquent act for the simple reason that so many are committed. Thus police officers must rely on citizen cooperation to obtain information about offenders. There is, however, much evidence that victims do not always report incidents when they occur. Victimization surveys have shown that the police are informed of only a fraction of all offenses committed.[7] Reasons for not reporting offenses range from a fear of becoming ''involved'' to a desire to protect the child from the courts. Some victims fear retaliation from the offenders, and many feel that nothing would be accomplished by reporting the situation.[8]

Police Handling of Juveniles

If the police have detected an offense or have been notified by a complainant, there is still a discretionary judgment to be made. At this point the juvenile may either be diverted out of the juvenile justice process or taken into custody. Many youngsters are diverted at this point; in some police departments two-thirds of the children who come into contact with the police are handled informally.[9] Informal handling may consist of a verbal reprimand, a conversation with the child and his parents, or referral to a community agency for some type of treatment.[10] Formal handling involves official arrest and the possibility of detention and a court appearance.

Diversion has become a commonly used method of dealing with juveniles, partly because there has been little evidence that the juvenile court experience has beneficial effects. Some police departments have implemented policies of diversion of all children, with the exception of those who have committed serious crimes and those who have no parent or guardian to whom they can be released. Diversion usually consists of an agreement between the child, the parents, and the officer; referral to a community agency (such as a family counseling center); and informal probation in which the child reports to a probation officer.

The initial contact with a police officer is a crucial one for many adolescents in that it affects their attitudes toward law enforcement authorities and legal institutions and may influence the extent of their future involvement in delinquency. It is also believed that special techniques should be used in handling youngsters. These two concerns have prompted many police departments to develop specialized units of officers whose task is to deal with juveniles.

Juvenile units were first established in some police departments during the early 1900s and since that time have continued to grow in number.[11] Today large police departments are likely to have specialized units but the average ratio of juvenile officers per 100 officers is 2.7.[12] When one considers the high juvenile offense rate, this is a relatively small allocation of officers. Qualifications for juvenile officers vary from one state to another; in some states officers are required to pass written and oral examinations; in other states, the only qualifications are prior police experience and a high-school diploma. Many police departments require that juvenile officers have specialized training; such departments typically emphasize diversion and rehabilitation goals.[13]

The two main goals of the juvenile specialist are prevention of delinquency and proficiency in handling children. The procedures required for handling juveniles differ from those used with adults, and juvenile officers are trained to develop expertise in working in the juvenile justice system. The advantages of juvenile officers are described below:

> A good juvenile officer, whether [working] alone or as a part of a juvenile bureau, is a great asset to any police operation. He develops and profitably pursues streamlined procedures with the juvenile court and the receiving or detention facilities. He becomes adept in the psychology and problems of children and youth. He cultivates useful contacts which not only serve as sources of needed intelligence, but also act as resources for promoting rehabilitation.[14]

The specialization of juvenile officers is thought to enhance the positive aspects of juvenile police contacts, and also to improve efficiency in crime investigation and future treatment of the offender.

Arrest   Whether the arresting officer is a juvenile officer or not, a decision must always be made concerning whether to take the child into custody. Generally, the legal standards for juveniles are broader than those for the arrest of adults. The standard for arrest of an adult is *probable cause,* which has been defined for police officers in the following manner:

> Probable cause requires a reasonable belief, based on reliable evidence, that the suspect has committed a crime. It must go beyond mere suspicion or a policeman's educated hunch. On the other hand, it is less than absolute certainty.[15]

Instead of the *probable cause* standard used with adults, juvenile law often uses a broader standard as evidenced in the fact that the officer can decide that the child falls under the jurisdiction of the court.[16] Many states do not distinguish between the arrest of children and that of adults and use the single standard of probable cause for both. Nevertheless, police still have more discretionary power in juvenile cases than in adult cases.[17]

As in any stage of the juvenile justice process, discretion has both positive and negative features. The flexibility given the police in decision making can be beneficial, but this flexibility can be misused and applied differentially to individual children. Studies of police arrest patterns indicate that several factors are important in determining whether to handle a juvenile informally or formally.

1. *Offense Severity* is perhaps the most influential variable in the arrest decision process. Serious felonies are generally handled formally; it is in the handling of less serious acts that discretion is broadest. Studies of police handling of juveniles have indicated that serious offenses tend to be handled uniformly whereas other offenses tend to be judged on a wide range of other criteria.[18] Juveniles who commit serious offenses make up a relatively small percentage of the offenders who come into contact with the police though, which suggests that the use of discretion affects a large number of children.[19]

2. The number of *prior contacts* with the juvenile justice system also influences whether the child will be treated formally or diverted by the police. Recidivists are more likely to be brought back into the system.[20] An officer may feel that the youngster who has been warned on previous occasions has been given enough ''breaks'' and needs a more serious response from authorities.

3. The *social status* of the child also appears to be related to police decisions, but it is difficult to separate the role of social status from other variables. Many of the children who go through the juvenile court are poor; thus poor children are more frequently arrested by the police. Self-report studies have indicated that differences in the frequency of delinquent acts by social class are not as significant as they appear to be in official records, which lends support to the idea that police decisions about who to arrest are to some extent based on the child's social status. There is some additional evidence, however, to suggest that if social class does play a role in arrest decisions it is partly a result of the fact that the most serious offenses are often committed by lower-class juveniles.[21]

4. The variable of *race* has been examined by many researchers and similar findings have been presented. Racial discrimination in law enforcement has been a major criticism of the adult criminal justice system as well as the juvenile system. Generally, studies have indicated that police decisions are affected by the racial characteristics of the child; black

children are more frequently referred to court.[22] The harshness toward black juveniles is undoubtedly a result of racial prejudice and stereotyping, and may also indicate a reaction by police to the hostility many black adolescents express toward them.

5. The *age* of the child is another factor that has been related to referral to court; older juveniles are less likely to be diverted than younger ones.[23] The older child is probably seen as more responsible for his or her actions, whereas an 11- or 12-year-old may be seen as possibly less aware of the consequences of delinquent behavior.

6. Another characteristic, *demeanor,* has been found to influence police decisions. The behavior the child displays to the officer may gain leniency, if he or she is mannerly and contrite. The juvenile who is surly, defiant, flippant, or appears to be a gang member is more likely to be referred to court.[24]

Although all of these variables may influence police decision making, they do not explain the wide variation in arrest patterns. Another factor that must be taken into account is the nature of the law enforcement agency itself. Departmental structure and policy guide much of the action of police personnel. Departments that delegate decision-making power to specialized juvenile units have different arrest practices than departments that have no such units. Departmental policy concerning the handling of juveniles is also important because a belief in the rehabilitative effects of diversion may cause a decrease in the number of children referred to court.[25]

Efforts have been made to curb the use of discretion by officers in some departments through the implementation of departmental guidelines regarding the handling of juveniles. Policy guidelines clearly describe how certain situations and offenders should be handled. They do not completely limit discretion since it would be impossible to include every type of situation in a manual of guidelines. Thus a degree of flexibility is needed in order for the officer to respond to special circumstances. Below is an example of such department policy guidelines taken from the Chicago Police Department's *Manual of Procedure, Youth Division*.

GUIDELINES FOR DETERMINING THE DISPOSITION OF JUVENILE OFFENDERS

A. An integral part of the processing of juveniles taken into custody for criminal acts is the consideration of certain factors which will aid the youth officer in arriving at the appropriate disposition. The youth officer and/or policewoman will follow the below listed guidelines in making the appropriate disposition.

B. Cases to be brought to the attention of the Juvenile Court.

1. All felonies will be brought to the attention (referred or detained) of the court with the exception that a Community Adjustment may be made

when the circumstances mitigate the offense and the approval of a Youth Division Supervisor is obtained.

2. All firearms offenses including unlawful possession and unlawful use or threatened use against another will be brought to the attention (referred or detained) of the court.

. . .

4. All serious gang related activity in which the offender is engaged in gang violence, recruiting, intimidation, etc., will be brought to the attention (referred or detained) of the court.

. . .

8. All offenders whose three most recent police actions (within the preceding twelve month period) were disposed of as Community Adjustment for the fourth (4th) offense may be made when the circumstances so justify and the approval of a Youth Division Supervisor is obtained.[26]

The Child in Police Custody　　　　Once the juvenile has been taken into police custody, his or her parents (or guardian) are notified. Legally, a child should only be questioned in the presence of an adult who is concerned with the child's welfare. This was suggested in the Supreme Court decision of *In re Gault.*[27]

The Miranda warning may be given to juveniles before interrogation, but has not been guaranteed to juveniles by the United States Supreme Court. At present some states provide for this warning in their statutes.[28] The Miranda warning consists of notice that: 1) they have the right to remain silent; 2) their statements can and will be used against them; 3) they have the right to counsel; and 4) if they cannot afford counsel it will be provided.

These protections against self-incrimination may be waived, but with minors there has been considerable concern over whether they can waive these without a parent or an attorney present. Often it is up to the court to decide if such waiver was intelligent and voluntary, or if it resulted from coercion and lack of knowledge.[29] A child might be more easily intimidated than an adult and would perhaps confess to offenses in the hope of being allowed to return home. In some states, waiver of these rights can only occur in the presence of an adult or an attorney.[30]

Other procedures, such as search and seizure and lineup, are governed by constitutional rights. Illegally seized evidence is not admissible in a juvenile trial, and exclusion of this incriminating evidence may be requested by the child's attorney. A pretrial motion to suppress evidence could result in the exclusion of illegally obtained evidence from the trial.[31] Information from lineup procedures and other attempts to identify an offender is also inadmissible if an attorney is not present, unless it is obtained before the juvenile is charged with a delinquent act.[32]

The use of photographs and fingerprints is often controlled by statute and restricts the manner in which these records are kept. Some states prohibit the sending of fingerprints and photographs to the Federal Bureau of Investigation's central files, or limit fingerprints to those children involved in felonies.[33] This is an extension of the efforts to protect the identities of juveniles and to make their contact with the police and the court less like that experienced by adult offenders.

Police handling of juveniles has followed practices similar to those set up for adults, especially after the *Gault* decision established due process for juveniles. Limitations on police actions have been established by court decisions and statutes; however, it must be noted that this does not mean that the actual practice always follows these standards. Interrogation of juveniles may take place while they are en route to the station house, and Miranda rights are often waived by children. Departmental policy affects police practices to a large degree, and departments that do emphasize the importance of following legal standards probably have much closer compliance than those departments that adopt a more laissez-faire approach.

Detention

The next stage in the process for the juvenile who has been taken into custody is the detention decision. Detention means incarceration of the child while he or she is awaiting further court action. Unlike adults, juveniles do not have the constitutional right to bail. Some states provide for bail for adolescents, but the United States Supreme Court has declined to rule on whether minors have a constitutional right to bail.[34]

The purpose of detention is often described as an attempt to protect and help the child. Detention also serves to protect the community from additional offenses committed by the child as well as to insure that the child will appear at the hearing.[35] Detention is also used as a punitive measure since the actual detention experience is never very pleasant for the juvenile. A child who does not reach court may be given a powerful shock by being held overnight in detention.

The decision to detain the child is initially made by a police or probation officer. Other options are available at this point. A juvenile may be released to the custody of his or her parents, be released upon the signature of the arresting officer, have the charges dropped, or in some states post bail.[36] Thirty-five states now require some type of judicial review of the initial detention decision within a specified period of time, which ranges from 24 hours in the District of Columbia to a requirement in Maryland and South Dakota that the hearing be held "promptly."[37] This review is important because otherwise the detention decision is made solely by law enforcement agents or administrative personnel in the juvenile court. Unfortunately this review does not always balance police recommendations; in fact, there is evidence that in many cases the court staff accommodates police opinions about whether to place a child in detention.[38]

After judicial review, some states limit the length of time that a juvenile can be detained. For example, New York requires a hearing on the case within 3 days and Ohio sets a maximum of 90 days for detention.[39] Most states do not have such time limitations, which can lead to very long periods of detention; one survey indicated that one in about six or seven juveniles was detained for more than one year.[40] The amount of time that children are held does vary greatly, but *most* facilities hold juveniles for less than one month.[41]

The conditions that exist in detention facilities are usually not beneficial to the child. Many children are held in adult jails where they become the victims of other inmates. Although they may be kept in separate cells or wings of the jail, overcrowding and the physical layout of the jails often make segregation impossible. It is estimated that as many as 500,000 children are held in jails each year, but exact statistics are difficult to obtain since many jails do not keep records.[42] One survey in New York State found that 43 percent of the youngsters held in local jails were PINS offenders (persons in need of supervision).[43]

Detention practices unfortunately have resulted in tragedies such as the following:

In Iowa a girl was thrown into jail because she ran away to get married: she hanged herself. She was 16 years old.

In Missouri, a 17-year-old boy was homosexually assaulted and kicked to death by jail cellmates.

Another 17-year-old boy was murdered in a Miami jail.[44]

Conditions in detention facilities that house only juveniles are not significantly better. Understaffed and overcrowded, detention facilities often place a major emphasis on control of the children. Punishment of uncooperative youngsters ranges from solitary confinement to physical blows, and is frequently administered for infractions of rules. Substandard food, inadequate medical treatment, and a paucity of educational programs are often found in these facilities. Ironically, many detainees have been incarcerated for complaints stemming from problems in school yet once in the facility, they receive minimal educational instruction. In fact, many juvenile detention centers have no educational programs at all.[45] Excessive use of confinement is not needed and often children who were considered in need of detention are released back into the community following their court hearing. One must question whether detention was appropriate in such cases, for the courts did not find them delinquent or in need of confinement.[46] Status offenders are frequently confined, especially if they are female. A LEAA Survey of juvenile facilities in 1974 indicated that 49 percent of the females and 11 percent of the males were held for status offenses.[47] (See Table 8-1.) Status

**TABLE 8-1. OFFENSES OF JUVENILES HELD IN PUBLIC DETENTION AND
CORRECTIONAL FACILITIES: JUNE 30, 1974**

OFFENSE	MALE	FEMALE
Felony (except drug offense)	58% (8,022)	18% (568)
Misdemeanor (except drug offense)	25% (3,423)	25% (755)
Drug Offense	6% (909)	8% (252)
Status Offense	11% (1,537)	49% (1,483)
Total	100% (13,891)	100% (3,058)

n = 31,270

Data unavailable for 14,321 cases

Source: Adapted from data presented in *Children in Custody: Advance Report on the Juvenile Detention and Correctional Facility Census of 1974* (Washington, D.C.: Department of Justice, February 1977), pp. 48–49.

offenders are surely less in need of detention than are other children who come in contact with the court.

New Approaches to Detention

Status offenders and children from broken homes are likely to be incarcerated while waiting for a court hearing although they are the least in need of confinement. Children who are abused or neglected and children who are in need of foster home placements, medical care and psychiatric care may end up in county jails or juvenile centers. Sometimes they are held because of a lack of alternative programs or because of overloaded welfare and social agencies.

Some writers have encouraged the construction of new, modern detention facilities that are geared to rehabilitative care, but unfortunately when these new facilities are built they tend to be much like the old ones they were designed to replace. Overcrowding makes it necessary to convert recreation areas and classrooms into dormitories to accommodate the overflow of youngsters. In addition, there is evidence that the more detention facilities there are, the higher the percentage of children who are detained.[48] Thus building larger detention facilities may actually increase the number of children detained.

Another effort to change detention practices has been made through legal and financial funding channels. Under the Federal Juvenile Justice and Delinquency Prevention Act of 1974, states will be eligible for government funds if they take steps to provide new treatment for offenders in detention and incarceration.[49] Separate facilities are required for juvenile delinquents and status offenders, which, it is hoped, will help to decrease stigma for status offenders and will also enable them to receive more appropriate treatment.

Other efforts have been made to decrease the number of children held in detention. The National Council on Crime and Delinquency has stated that no more than 10 percent of all juveniles taken into custody require detention, and this 10 percent represents children who have been charged with serious offenses.[50] In order to decrease detention use, some areas have utilized professional intake staffs. Juvenile probation officers screen all cases referred to them and decide on appropriate action. In one city over half of the children originally held for detention were released prior to the detention hearing. Officers contacted parents, evaluated children, and sought noninstitutional placements.

Another program that has decreased detention use is that of "Home Detention." A Home Detention Program in St. Louis places children either in their own homes or in group homes to await trial. The program is much less costly than detention ($8.22 per child per day versus $17.54 per child per day) and of the first 157 juveniles who were involved in the program, none absconded.[51]

Detention of juveniles has been justified on the basis that it protects the community from delinquent crime and that it insures that the child will appear in court. But the reality of detention is incarceration, under abhorrent conditions, of children who often have committed only minor offenses. Changes in law enforcement and court policies are sorely needed to decrease the number of children held and to offer alternative treatment. Detention in the community offers a viable option that is effective and beneficial to the child. Although the child savers began their fight against the jailing of juveniles in the 1800s, today, almost one hundred years later, the jailing of children is still a major issue in the United States.

Intake Interview and Hearing

A juvenile who has been taken into custody by the police may be detained or released to his or her parents. In either situation, a preliminary investigation is performed by members of the probation department. This practice is referred to as the intake interview because it allows the probation officer to gather information needed to evaluate whether further court action is appropriate.

The child, parents, complainants, and intake worker (or probation officer) are present. The complaint against the child and the authority of the court to act in this case are outlined to the child and parents. Counsel for the juvenile is rarely present during this procedure, although this is an important point in the juvenile justice process since approximately one-half of the cases referred to the court are diverted at this stage.[52] The *Gault* decision provided right to counsel only at the adjudicatory hearing, and strict interpretations of *Gault* may contribute to the absence of defense attorneys at this stage. Also, public defenders with heavy caseloads have little time to devote to these preliminary stages, even when counsel is provided by state statute.

The intake worker has virtually unlimited discretion in these cases and has the potential to greatly reduce the case flow into the court. Diversion from the system at this time is very beneficial for some children, but the diversion of serious offenders may also occur. To control this discretion, some intake departments have developed standards for decision making by their staff. In New York City, the court requires adjudication (or a fact finding hearing) for all cases that are disputed, that involve crimes of violence or other serious offenses, or that involve children with extensive records.[53]

The expertise of intake staff has been acknowledged and relied upon by those involved in the juvenile justice system. Intake procedures are typically very informal and may be termed an interview or conference. Some courts routinely conduct intake hearings to determine whether a case should be dismissed, diverted, or held for adjudication. Although this hearing takes place in court, it is still informal and is often quite similar to the intake interview process.

The intake hearing is analogous to the stage in the criminal justice system known as the grand jury or preliminary hearing. In adult felony prosecutions a determination must be made prior to the trial that there is *probable cause* to believe the offense was committed by the defendant. The prosecutor presents enough evidence to show probable cause, and defense counsel attempts to show weaknesses in the case against his client. If the grand jury or the judge hearing the case decides there are not sufficient grounds for the probable cause standard, the case will be dropped and the defendant freed. In juvenile intake hearings, the probable cause standard is not required by juvenile codes, and the procedure is much less formal.[54] After the hearing, a petition may be filed and the case heard in court. But unlike adults, a child who has no petition filed may still be subject to treatment on an informal basis by the probation department or some other agency to which the child is referred.

The importance of the intake process for the child may increase the adversarial nature of this stage in the future. Defense counsel may become more involved at this point due to the increasing emphasis on due process for children and the inclusion of the district attorney at this stage in some states.[55] The district attorney may screen cases for determining the jurisdiction of the court, the seriousness of the charges, and sufficiency of evidence. Defense attorneys could use this opportunity to discover evidence in the case of the state and to begin negotiations for a particular disposition for their clients.

DISCUSSION QUESTIONS

1. Discuss some of the ways in which the school environment may be related to juvenile delinquency. What is the relationship between school performance and juvenile delinquency?

2. Police discretion may be most apparent with juvenile offenders. Why?

3. Why is the handling of juveniles in police custody an important issue for the juvenile court?

4. Discuss the importance of alternatives to detention for juveniles.

5. According to the data presented in Table 8-1, females are more likely than males to be detained for status offenses. Why?

NOTES

1. Ronald Goldfarb, *Jails* (New York: Anchor Books, 1975), p. 313.

2. Charles Murray, *The Link Between Learning Disabilities and Juvenile Delinquency* (Washington: Government Printing Office, 1976), p. 18.

3. See for example Albert Cohen, *Delinquent Boys: The Culture of the Gang* (Glencoe, Ill.: Free Press, 1955).

4. Ray Rist, "Social Class and Teacher Expectations: The Self-Fulfilling Prophecy in Ghetto Education," *Harvard Educational Review,* 40 (August 1970): 411–454.

5. Christopher Jencks et al., *Inequality* (New York: Basic Books, 1972); George W. Mayeske, *On the Explanation of Racial-Ethnic Group Differences in Achievement Test Scores* (Washington, D.C.: Office of Education, 1973).

6. Charles Willie and Anita Gershenovitz, "Juvenile Delinquency in Racially Mixed Areas," *American Sociological Review,* 29, no. 5 (1964): 740–744.

7. Roger Hood and Richard Sparks, *Key Issues in Criminology* (New York: World University Library, 1970), p. 23.

8. Ibid.

9. Malcolm Klein, "Issues in Police Diversion of Juvenile Offenders," in R. Carter and M. Klein, eds., *Back on the Street* (Englewood Cliffs, N.J.: Prentice- Hall, 1976), p. 77.

10. Ibid.

11. Richard Kobetz, *The Police Role and Juvenile Delinquency* (Gaithersburg, Md.: International Association of Chiefs of Police, 1971), p. 153.

12. Ibid., p. 57.

13. Ibid., pp. 51, 59.

14. Ibid., p. 175.

15. John G. Miles, David Richardson, and Anthony Scudellari, *The Law Officer's Pocket Manual* (Washington, D.C.: Bureau of National Affairs, 1977-78 edition), p. 6:2.

16. Joseph Senna and Larry Siegel, *Juvenile Law: Cases and Comments* (St. Paul, Minn.: West, 1976), p. 73.

17. Ibid.

18. Irving Piliavin and Scott Briar, "Police Encounters with Juveniles," *American Journal of Sociology* 70 (September 1964): 206–214.

19. Ibid.

20. George Bodine, "Factors Related to Police Dispositions of Juvenile Offenders" (Syracuse: Syracuse University Youth Development Center, 1964).

21. M. Wolfgang, R. Figlio, and T. Sellin, *Delinquency in a Birth Cohort* (Chicago: University of Chicago Press, 1972), pp. 241–255.

22. Ibid., p. 220; Piliavin and Briar, "Police Encounters." Nathan Goldman, *The Differential Selection of Juvenile Offenders for Court Appearance* (New York: National Council on Crime and Delinquency, 1963); Theodore Ferdinand and Elmer Luchterhand, "Inner-city Youth, the Police, the Juvenile Court, and Justice," *Social Problems,* 17 (Spring 1970): 510–527.

23. Goldman, *Differential Selection.*

24. Goldman, *Differential Selection.* Piliavin and Briar, "Police Encounters."

25. For an example of the effects of departmental policy, see James Q. Wilson, "The Police and the Delinquent in Two Cities," in Stanton Wheeler, ed., *Controlling Delinquents* (New York: John Wiley, 1968), pp. 9–30.

26. Richard Kobetz and Betty Bosarge, *Juvenile Justice Administration* (Gaithersburg, Md.: International Association of Chiefs of Police, 1973), pp. 144–145.

27. *In re Gault,* 387 U. S. 1 (1967).

28. Among the states that include the Miranda warning or a similar warning in their statutes are California, Colorado, Connecticut, and Oklahoma. See Samuel M. Davis, *Rights of Juveniles: The Juvenile Justice System* (New York: Clark Boardman Company, 1974), pp. 38–104.

29. Senna and Sigel, *Juvenile Law,* p. 75.

30. Ibid., p. 75.

31. Ibid., p. 73.

32. Ibid., p. 75.

33. Mark Levin and Rosemary Sarri, *Juvenile Delinquency: A Comparative Analysis of Legal Codes in the United States* (Ann Arbor, Mich.: National Assessment of Juvenile Corrections, University of Michigan, 1974), p. 29.

34. *In re Whittington,* 391 U. S. 341 (1968).

35. Elyce Ferster, Edith Snethen, and Thomas Courtless, "Juvenile Detention: Protection, Prevention or Punishment?", in R. Carter and M. Klein, eds., *Back on the Street* (Englewood Cliffs, N.J.: Prentice-Hall, 1976), pp. 179–196.

36. Levin and Sarri, *Juvenile Delinquency,* p. 29.

37. Ibid, p. 30.

38. Ibid., p. 32.

39. Ibid., p. 21.

40. Goldfarb, *Jails,* p. 317.

41. Rosemary Sarri, *Under Lock and Key: Juveniles in Jails and Detention* (Ann Arbor, Mich.: National Assesment of Juvenile Corrections, University of Michigan, 1974), p. 45.

42. Ibid.

43. Ibid., p. 9.

44. Excerpts from "This Child is Rated X," an NBC News White Paper on juvenile justice, 1971.

45. Goldfarb, *Jails,* p. 331.

46. Lawrence Cohen, "Delinquency Dispositions: An Empirical Analysis of Processing Decisions in Three Juvenile Courts," *Analytic Report 9* (Washington, D.C.: Government Printing Office, 1975), p. 51.

47. Lawrence Cohen, "Preadjudicatory Detention in Three Juvenile Courts," *Analytic Report 8* (Washington, D.C.: Government Printing Office, 1975).

48. Robert B. Coates, Alden D. Miller, and Lloyd Ohlin, "Juvenile Detention and Its Consequences," Unpublished Report, Center for Criminal Justice, Law School of Harvard University.

49. Public Law 93–415, 93rd Congress, S. 821, September 7, 1974.

50. National Council on Crime and Delinquency, *Standards and Guides for Detention of Children and Youth* 2nd ed. (Hackensack, N.J.: NCCD, 1961).

51. Goldfarb, *Jails,* p. 361.

52. Sanford Fox, *The Law of Juvenile Courts in a Nutshell* (St. Paul, Minn.: West, 1976), p. 147.

53. Frank Miller, P. Dawson, G. Dix, and R. Parnas, *The Juvenile Justice Process* (Mineola, N.Y.: The Foundation Press, 1976), p. 201.

54. Levin and Sarri, *Juvenile Delinquency*, p. 26.

55. Ibid., p. 27.

9 Adjudication Hearing

In the juvenile justice process, initial case screening is performed at the juvenile court intake stage. Cases are referred to the court or diverted by probation officers who assess the facts of the case and choose between a number of possible responses. Many children are sent home, diverted to community agencies, or given pre-court probation. These options channel juveniles out of the court prior to a hearing. Youngsters who are not channeled out of the process are given an intake hearing to determine whether a formal petition should be filed. If a petition is filed, the juvenile's case moves to the next stage in the juvenile court called the adjudication hearing. At this stage a review of the facts of the case will take place and a decision on the guilt of the child will be made.

Petitions and Determination of Jurisdiction

The adjudication hearing follows the filing of a petition (Figure 9-1) by the intake staff. This petition is the formal document which states the complaint against the child, the facts of the case which have brought the child before the court, the names and address of the child and his guardian or parents, and the time and place of detention. The petition is filed with the court, a hearing time is set, and the child and his parents are notified of the charges and the time of the hearing. Many children who are arrested and detained do not have a petition filed, which implies that the filing of a petition itself indicates that the case is considered serious.

COURT OF COMMON PLEAS _____ COUNTY
PENNSYLVANIA

PETITION

In the Interest of: JUVENILE
PAT _____   No. _____
A Minor

(Form 1)
TO THE HONORABLE JUDGE OF SAID COURT

Your petitioner, _____ , _____ , _____ County, Pennsylvania,
respectfully represents that Pat _____ , born October 6, 19—, about the
age of 14 years is in the opinion of the petitioner a delinquent minor child under
the age of 18 years of age and is the son of _____ , father, and _____ ,
mother, _____ Street, _____ County, Pennsylvania.

That on Tuesday, January 23, 19—, around the hour of 7:30 A.M., Pat
_____ left the home of his parents. Pat _____ was absent from his
home without parental permission, knowledge or consent until Thursday,
January 25, 19—, when he did return about the hour of 7 P.M. On that date Pat
_____ was brought to _____ Detention Home, _____ ,
Pennsylvania, by Officer _____ of the _____ Police Department and he
was detained.

And that on December 28, 19—, Pat _____ did leave the home of his
parents without their permission, knowledge or consent, and he did not return
home. On January 4, 19— Pat _____ was apprehended in _____ ,
Pennsylvania, by Officer _____ of the _____ Police Department and he
was brought to _____ Detention Home, _____ , Pennsylvania, and he
was detained.

And that on about December 15 or 16, 19—, Pat _____ did leave the
home of his parents without their permission, knowledge or consent and he did
not return home until December 21, 19—.

And that Pat _____ is habitually disobedient and uncontrolled by his
parents.

Source: John Palmieri, *Pennsylvania Law of Juvenile Delinquency and Deprivation*
(Philadelphia: George T. Bisel, 1976), p. 199.

Figure 9-1. Sample court petition.

Prior to adjudication, the petition is reviewed to determine whether there
is sufficient evidence to warrant a hearing. At this point some states implement a *consent decree*. A consent decree is a negotiated agreement that provides for supervision of the child in his or her home. The agreement is made
between the child, the parents, probation staff, defense counsel, and a prosecutor.[1] If the agreement is broken, the juvenile can be brought into court
under the original charges, or new charges may be filed.

The original petition may also be deemed inappropriate and the child may be diverted out of the court. This review of petitions is performed by a district attorney in some courts, but in others probation officers continue to perform this task.[2] This dismissal of the petition may result from a weak case against the child or a decision that alternative handling would be more beneficial to the juvenile.

The jurisdiction, or authority of the court to hear the case, must also be determined. If the court is to have power to hear the case, statutory requirements must be met in relation to the age of the child, the type of offense committed, and the place where the offense occurred. Waiver of jurisdiction must also be considered, for under state laws some types of offenses must be dealt with by the adult criminal court.

Statutes include the upper age limit for children who are to be tried as juveniles, and original jurisdiction depends primarily on the age of the youngster. Minimum age limitations are rare in state statutes, but the common law standard of seven years of age is frequently referred to in adult penal codes. Maximum age for jurisdiction is typically 17 (see Figure 9- 2).

Specific offenses are sometimes indicated as appropriate for trial in adult criminal court, or a juvenile judge may waive jurisdiction and transfer the juvenile to the adult criminal justice system. Eight states provide for a criminal trial, regardless of age, for a juvenile charged with homicide or other capital offenses.[3] Waiver of jurisdiction by the juvenile judge is often limited by the age of the child. For example, minimum ages may be specified for transfer to adult court, as in Pennsylvania where transfer for offenses other than murder can occur only with children 14 or older.[4]

There are also established procedural requirements for waiver of jurisdiction in many states, which are in part a response to the U. S. Supreme Court's decision in *Kent* v. *U. S.* Statutes call for hearing or investigation before a waiver decision is made.[5] Waiver decisions must also be made prior to adjudication in juvenile court. Under the decision of *Breed* v. *Jones,* waiver to adult court after a delinquency hearing violates protections against double jeopardy.[6]

Waiver of jurisdiction is an extremely important decision for some juveniles. The Kent case provides a good example of this: Morris Kent faced a possible maximum sentence of 5 years confinement if tried as a juvenile and

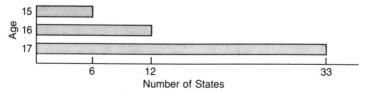

Source: Mark Levin and Rosemary Sarri, *Juvenile Delinquency: A Comparative Analysis of Legal Codes in the United States* (Ann Arbor, Mich.: National Assessment of Juvenile Corrections, University of Michigan, 1974), p. 13.

Figure 9-2. Maximum age for continuing jurisdiction.

a maximum sentence of death if tried as an adult.[7] In addition to the issue of sentence, an adult trial may be more detrimental to the child's future because of its public nature and the resulting criminal record. On the other hand, some observers have decried the inability to transfer very young but serious offenders who may commit felonies and receive the relative leniency of the juvenile court.

Hearing: The Participants

The participants in the juvenile court hearing typically include the child, the parents, defense counsel, the judge, probation staff, the prosecutor, and witnesses and complainants. The number of people involved in this proceeding has increased as a result of U. S. Supreme Court decisions, and today there is a formality that was unknown during the early days of the juvenile court.

Parents and the Child

Parents may encourage their child to admit his or her guilt at the adjudicatory hearing. The child who admits to having committed a delinquent act does not usually have a hearing but proceeds directly to the dispositional stage. Although this admission is virtually the same as a guilty plea, it is frequently called "submitted to a finding" or "did not deny the petition."[8] Most cases in juvenile court are uncontested, and a full hearing is not held.[9]

The child and the parents also may decide to waive the right to counsel and the protection against self-incrimination. Waiver of these rights must be intelligent and voluntary, meaning that the significance of waiver is understood and that the decision is made without pressure or coercion. There is evidence that pressure is applied to encourage waiver in some courts. Research conducted in three cities in the United States indicated that some juvenile judges influence the decision to waive counsel in a variety of ways.[10] In some cases, either no mention was made of the right to counsel or only partial advice was given. Partial advice consisted of a statement to the parents that they had a right to a lawyer but no mention was made of court appointed counsel for indigents. Other examples of inappropriate advice were noted, as is illustrated in the following conversation between a judge and the father of a child who had been charged with possession of narcotics.

> After hearing some of the evidence during which time the boy denied that he had smoked marijuana, the judge turned to the father and said, "Now sir, I am prepared today to place this boy on probation and let him go home. If you want to come back here next week and have this detective . . ." He continued on to say that if he wanted to come back here and say the same thing over while the father had an attorney he may do so. The judge then said that he didn't know what he would do next week, however. [After some more conversation

the judge said], "We can go through the mechanics of the court and have cross examination and all the rest, but this court's interest is what is best for the boy . . . I think what I'm trying to do is save everybody's time." The father then said that probation would be all right. The judge stated that he could sign the waiver.[11]

Waiver forms (see Figure 9-3) are often utilized in the juvenile court. These forms, which are signed by the parent and the child, confirm that the meaning of the waiver decision is understood. It must be emphasized that waiver of the right to counsel may occur when the parents and the child have been informed of this right in an impartial and thorough manner, and is certainly not always an indicator of insufficient information or inappropriate encouragement by juvenile court personnel.

The privilege against self-incrimination may also be unclear to children and their parents. They may be given (or already have) the impression that an admission of guilt will guarantee a minimal court delay and a more lenient disposition. Remaining silent may be seen as a lack of cooperation or remorse, so parents may encourage a confession from their children.

Witnesses and Complainants

Witnesses and complainants may testify if a hearing is held for the juvenile. Since the *Gault* decision, confrontation and cross-examination of witnesses are considered necessary in the hearing. The testimony of a witness or complainant may be discredited in the same way that it is in a criminal trial—that is, by bringing to light a past criminal record.[12] A common problem with both witnesses and complainants is failure to appear for the hearing, which may result from postponements of the hearing, fear of retaliation by the defendant, or an unwillingness to become involved.

Probation Staff and Prosecutor

The probation officer presents the case for the state when a prosecutor is not included in the hearing; not all courts require a prosecutor. Pertinent information about the child's background may be presented at this time as well as the facts of the present charges.

Probation personnel do not have the expertise in court procedure and points of law that defense attorneys have and thus are at a great disadvantage in performing prosecutorial functions. In response to these problems, judges began to utilize prosecutors in the court, especially in delinquency cases. Some juvenile courts employ full-time prosecutors and others appoint prosecutors for specific cases.[13] In cases in which prosecutors are involved, the role of the probation officer in adjudication is minimized considerably.

The prosecutor's role in juvenile proceedings is frequently less extensive than that of prosecutors in adult criminal trials. Many courts do not require

IN THE COURT OF COMMON PLEAS OF
_____ COUNTY, PENNSYLVANIA
JUVENILE DIVISION

IN RE: NO.

a Juvenile

CHARGE

REFUSAL OF RIGHT OF COUNSEL

I have had my rights to a lawyer fully explained to me. I do not want to have a lawyer represent me. I know that I have the right to have a lawyer that I can choose myself and pay for myself; or, the right to have a lawyer chosen to represent me by the Court without any payment of money by me or by my parents.

This writing and signing of my name to this paper is a legal refusal to have a lawyer help me.

I have signed this paper without any offers or promises of any kind and freely without fear or favor.

I read and write the English language and I know how important what I am doing is and that this paper will mean I will have no lawyer take care of my case.

_____
(Juvenile)

_____

_____
(Parents or guardian)
Dated:

Source: John Palmieri, *Pennsylvania Law of Juvenile Delinquency and Deprivation* (Philadelphia: George T. Bisel, 1976), p. 219

Figure 9-3. Sample form for refusal of right of counsel.

a prosecutor to be present at the intake stage when cases are screened, and petitions are sometimes reviewed by other court personnel. A survey of juvenile courts in 1972 indicated that the prosecutor's major function occurred at the adjudication stage, with minimal involvement at intake and disposition.[14] Resources have been concentrated at the adjudicatory stage because it is here that issues such as Fourth, Fifth, and Sixth Amendment requirements concerning arrest, search and seizure, stop and frisk, detention, and interrogation must be dealt with. Cross-examination of witnesses and presentation of evidence must be conducted by the prosecution to prove the child's guilt beyond a reasonable doubt.

Defense Counsel

The presence of prosecutors in court may also be advantageous to the child since it could encourage more vigorous representation by defense counsel. The increased adversarial nature of the hearing should provide a more thorough examination of facts and points of law. Although the *Gault* decision required that counsel be present at the adjudicatory stage, this right can be waived. Even if counsel is present, a thorough defense is not always presented. A study of juvenile adjudicatory hearings investigated "contested cases," or cases in which the child did not plead guilty. According to the findings,

> . . . most of the contested cases are only nominally contested. It is the typical pattern in a "contested" case for the public defender to cross-examine the prosecution witnesses, to present no witnesses on the defendant's behalf and then to state that the government has not proved its case. Even the cross-examination is frequently perfunctory and reveals no design or rationale on the part of the defense attorney.[15]

Public defenders are often defense attorneys owing to the impoverished condition of many of the defendants in juvenile court. But because public defenders have heavy case loads, the time available for case preparation is often minimal.[16] There is some reason to believe that the actions of defense counsel may be influenced by the behavior of other court personnel. Unless the prosecutor's case is unusually weak or the charges against the child are extremely serious, the defense may tend to rely on the benevolence and good judgment of other court personnel and contest the case in a less than vigorous fashion.[17]

The *Gault* decision attempted to protect children from unnecessary intervention in their lives through the implementation of due process rights. The right to counsel was seen as the key to insuring such due process, but unfortunately the right to counsel does not always produce the results envisioned by the Supreme Court. As was noted earlier, waiver of the right to a lawyer may even be encouraged in some courts.

Another aspect of legal representation concerns how the presence of defense counsel affects the ultimate outcome of the case. One study of the effects of counsel on disposition indicated that those juveniles who had a lawyer were more likely to be incarcerated (see Table 9-1). The authors of the study

TABLE 9-1. REPRESENTATION AND DISPOSITION BY OFFENSE SERIOUSNESS

		LAWYER	WAIVER
Major Crime	Dismissal	9%	38%
	Probation	56%	62%
	Incarceration	35%	0%
		100% (43)	100% (60)
	N = x^2 = 29.1262 103	Df = 2	PL.01
Minor Crime	Dismissal	8%	50%
	Probation	58%	50%
	Incarceration	34%	0%
		100% (12)	100% (42)
	N = 54 x^2 = 18.1035	Df = 2	PL.01
PINS (persons in need of supervision	Dismissal	12%	27%
	Probation	52%	50%
	Incarceration	36%	23%
		100% (25)	100% (26)
	N = 51 x^2 = 2.2820	Df = 2	Not significant

Source: David Duffee and Larry Siegel, "The Organization Man: Legal Counsel in the Juvenile Court." Reprinted from *Criminal Law Bulletin*, Vol. 7, No. 6, July–August 1971. Copyright 1971 by Warren, Gorham, and Lamont, Inc., 210 South Street, Boston, Mass. All rights reserved.

suggest that their findings indicate two possible conclusions: either that lawyers are not genuine advocates for the child or that the court is more likely to incarcerate children who have had the "appearance of due process."[18]

Other studies of the effects of legal counsel on the outcome of cases have found some conflicting evidence, but generally these studies have questioned the assumption that the exercise of one's right to counsel in juvenile court is always beneficial. [19] Perhaps this is a function of problems in role definition faced by these attorneys. Effective functioning may be hampered by the lack of a clearly defined set of expectations about the role of defense counsel in juvenile proceedings.[20] For example, lawyers may adopt the rehabilitative philosophy of the court since a strictly legal approach does not seem appropriate and may even be resisted by the judge. Lawyers who work primarily in juvenile court may compromise themselves into a position in which they become, in effect, adjuncts to the court.[21]

Indeed one study of juvenile court concluded that informal bargaining arrangements between defense attorneys and prosecutors were not encouraged because the general atmosphere of the court was one of cooperation, which precluded the need for negotiation between adversaries.[22] Even if an attorney does present a vigorous defense, it may be discouraged by the reactions of the judge; for example, continuances may not be granted to the attorney and his or her clients may suffer more severe dispositions.[23]

Another problem for attorneys in juvenile court involves conflict over whom the lawyer is to represent. Are the parent's demands to be given primary consideration? Should counsel perform as an advocate for the client as in adult cases? Should community welfare be a factor in counsel's approach to the defense?

Even if these questions are resolved by an individual attorney, the juvenile court presents many difficulties. Not only is legal expertise expected, but attorneys often need to act as liaisons between various court personnel. Here a lawyer who writes of these difficulties describes the role of the juvenile court attorney.

> Juvenile Court proceedings cause defense counsel to become a liaison interpreter among the Juvenile Court, the probationary authorities, the psychiatrist, and to the extent that he is able, the child himself. The attorney must also serve at various times as a type of judge, social worker, probation officer, psychiatrist and sociologist—the demands are almost overwhelming.[24]

Judge

The judge presiding over juvenile cases is usually a lawyer, although a few states do not require that a judge have a law degree.[25] They are elected to their positions in 38 states and appointed to their positions in the remaining 12 states. The role of the judge at the adjudicatory stage of a juvenile case is to preside over the hearing and to insure that the proceedings meet statutory and Constitutional requirements. The vast majority of the cases heard are not adversarial and the hearings are very informal.[26]

The presiding judge is a powerful figure since he or she alone makes the decisions in each case. There is usually no jury to make decisions on guilt or innocence. The judge may either: 1) dismiss the case by having it "continued without a finding"; 2) remand the child to adult criminal court; or 3) adjudge the juvenile to be delinquent.[27] The judge may discuss the situation with the child and the parents and advise them of their rights or, in some cases, attempt to expedite the procedures by influencing them to waive right to counsel or other rights. The judge may exert influence over the presentation of the case by the prosecutor and the response by the defense attorney.

Although the discretionary power of the judge is most extensive at the dispositional stage, much of the adjudication stage is affected both directly and indirectly by the judge. The judge's position will have enabled him or her to communicate which actions are acceptable and which are not to defense attorneys and other court personnel. Prosecutors may recognize that one judge is very hard on drug cases whereas another feels that drug cases are less serious than sexual delinquency. Probation staff members learn which types of cases are typically dismissed in court and which are frequently found to require some type of rehabilitative care. Defense counsel may realize that the judge tolerates few technical arguments. Through such interactions, roles become established. These roles, when followed, make the day-to-day running of the court more harmonious. But it is the judge who exercises the primary control over these patterns of interactions. Clearly, judicial influence in the juvenile court extends beyond the questions of legal standards and guilt or innocence.[28]

Hearing: The Procedure

The steps in the hearing of juvenile cases usually include the plea of the child, presentation of evidence by the prosecution and by the defense, cross-examination of witnesses, and the finding by the judge. Many hearings are brief since most defendants confess to the charges.

The prosecutor presents the case of the state. This includes testimony by the arresting officer and witnesses at the scene of the crime, as well as any other evidence that has been legally obtained. Cross-examination of witnesses may be conducted by the defense attorney. At the conclusion of this presentation, defense counsel has the opportunity to introduce evidence and witnesses favorable to the child, and the child may testify in his or her own behalf. Cross-examination of defense witnesses is then conducted by the prosecutor. Summaries of the case are then presented by both the prosecution and the defense to the judge, who will reach a finding or verdict. Below are some other aspects of the hearing.

1. *Burden of proof.* Under the *Winship* decision, proof beyond a reasonable doubt is necessary for a finding of delinquency. Whether this burden of proof applies to other juvenile proceedings, such as those concerning incorrigibility, is unclear. Generally, statutes have utilized the standard of preponderance of the evidence for this latter type of case.[29]

2. *Rules of evidence.* The *Gault* decision required sworn testimony, confrontation, and cross-examination of witnesses in juvenile court. Other rules of evidence are often adhered to in juvenile hearings, although state statutes are silent on how these rules apply to juvenile court. Hearsay, irrelevant evidence, and illegally obtained evidence may be excluded following a motion by defense counsel. Indeed, some juvenile statutes require evidence that is "material, competent, and relevant" at the fact finding hearing.[30]

3. *Jury trial.* Although the *McKeiver* decision denied the right to jury trials to juveniles, ten states provide for this; however, jury trials are seldom demanded.[31]

4. *Privacy.* Statutory provisions often close juvenile hearings to the public. This is done to mitigate the negative effects of publicity on the child. The judge is often given discretionary power to admit "interested parties," but the general public is not permitted to view the hearing.[32]
5. *Speedy trial.* The right to a speedy trial is provided by state court decisions and by those statutes that limit the amount of time that may elapse between the filing of a complaint and the actual hearing.[33]

The judge must insure that the hearing conforms to statutory and Constitutional standards of due process. Efforts should be made to inform the child and his parents of their rights and to ascertain that they understand the effects of waiver of these rights. Ultimately the judge also decides if the prosecution has proved the case of the state with proof beyond a reasonable doubt. If the judge arrives at a finding of delinquency or that the child is in need of treatment, the disposition of the case will be considered. It is also possible that the case will either be dismissed or continued without a finding. The case that is continued without a finding may involve an agreement or contract between the court, the child, and the parents regarding voluntary participation in a community-based treatment center or some other activity deemed appropriate. This practice is also called a suspended judgment, and is thought to be less stigmatizing in that the court has not actually found the child to be delinquent.

After a decision has been reached regarding the youngster's delinquency, the disposition of the case must be considered. This stage is called sentencing in the criminal justice system, but in the juvenile court it is referred to as the dispositional stage.

Many courts conduct a separate hearing to determine what treatment measures are needed for the juvenile. This bifurcated hearing, one in which there are separate stages for adjudication and disposition, has been advocated as more fair to the child and more consistent with juvenile justice philosophy.[34] There are courts that routinely determine disposition at the end of the adjudicatory hearing, and it may be that this practice has detrimental results.

Without a bifurcated hearing procedure, the welfare of the child may become a secondary concern in the choice of disposition. Evidence that is presented during adjudication may encourage a more punitive approach by the judge. The social investigation reports normally written by the probation officer are made available prior to the formal finding on the facts of the case. These reports often include a suggested disposition, which may influence the decision on both disposition and guilt since guilt is more or less implied in the way reports are written.

Social investigations consist of information on the child's school records, family background, reputation, and any other facts or statements thought to be relevant to the case. The use of such information was advocated under *parens patriae,* which encouraged the court to consider the general welfare

of the child in addition to the facts of the case. Status offenders are tried on
the basis of their condition—such as incorrigibility or beyond the control of
their parents—and so these reports are needed for prosecution of their cases.
However, the use of these reports prior to a finding of fact has been questioned, and some states have enacted statutes that prohibit the use of these
reports prior to disposition.[35]

Appeals

Until the *Gault* decision in 1967, appeals of cases disposed of in the juvenile
court were rare because of the absence of legal counsel.[36] After this Supreme
Court decision, the likelihood of appeals from juvenile court decisions was
greatly increased. Through appellate review, actions by police, prosecutors,
and judges may be controlled since decisions in which they have acted inappropriately will be overturned. Without review, inappropriate and illegal
practices in the juvenile court can remain uncurbed.

Provisions for appeal vary by state statute. In some states there is no such
provision, but the majority authorize higher trial courts or appellate courts
to review juvenile court decisions.[37] The review frequently involves questions
of law rather than a complete redetermination of the case. Some statutes provide for a trial *de novo,* which means that the original juvenile court proceedings are given no weight and the case is completely retried in adult
court.[38]

Adjudication: Conflicting Perspectives

As has been noted previously, various perspectives may be utilized in a critique of the court. Advocates of a Constitutional approach point to the need
for legal safeguards, proper trial procedure, and vigorous defense. Those who
favor the "treatment philosophy" of the court desire to emphasize the child's
total condition rather than the particular offense that has brought him to the
attention of authorities. Another perspective emphasizes the need to protect
society and to apply punishment that befits the crime; in addition, it stresses
how manipulation of legal technicalities by defense counsel can be to the
client's benefit and can effect leniency on the part of the court when trying
serious offenders.

From the review of United States Supreme Court decisions in Chapter 7,
it is easy to see that the court has made rapid progress in its practices since
the 1960s. It is also apparent that practices that circumvent the rights granted
to defendants have developed in some courts and should be changed. Rights
in and of themselves are meaningless without administrative procedures
which require notification of these rights to the defendant and parents.

Other critics describe the increased formality of the court proceedings as
dangerous to society and harmful to juveniles. The suppression of illegally

obtained evidence or confessions, or some other legal technicality may result in the release of a juvenile offender who is a threat to members of society. Juveniles who have been through the court many times often become quite sophisticated in utilizing the provisions of the law to their advantage. As a police lieutenant in San Francisco stated, "It fosters the kid's belief that he can beat the system. He goes through the court, comes back to the neighborhood, and he's a hero."[39] The treatment orientation of the court is also criticized for downplaying the responsibility of the juvenile and concentrating on therapeutic intervention. The amount of time that a youngster remains incarcerated may be quite short even for hardened offenders who have committed crimes ranging from murder, to armed robbery, to rape.

Legal rights and responsibility for criminal acts are not the answer to the problem of delinquency, according to still other critics of the juvenile court. They see the trend of Supreme Court decisions as undermining the benefits of this specialized court. They feel that the juvenile hearing has become the equivalent of a criminal trial, with its stigmatizing effects. Concern for the welfare of the child has become obscured by concerns for either punishment or Constitutional rights.

It is unlikely that these three perspectives—the Constitutional approach, treatment, and the protection of society—will be reconciled in the near future. To do so would require a substantial change in the philosophy of the juvenile court. Trends toward increased formality continue, such as the more extensive utilization of prosecuting attorneys, and cynicism about the efficacy of the treatment perspective grows as research shows that most treatment techniques have failed to achieve change in the offender's future behavior.[40] Yet the Supreme Court maintains an unwillingness to completely abandon the philosophy of the juvenile court and the unique role it plays in our society, as can be seen in the *McKeiver* decision.

DISCUSSION QUESTIONS

1. What is meant by jurisdiction of the court and waiver of jurisdiction?

2. Why do so many children plead guilty to the charges at the adjudication hearing?

3. Discuss steps that could be taken to insure that the right to counsel for juveniles is upheld in juvenile court.

4. Why is the judge in juvenile court powerful? What aspects of the court does the judge control?

5. Why is a bifurcated hearing procedure considered better for the child?

NOTES

1. M. Finkelstein et al., *Prosecution in the Juvenile Courts: Guidelines for the Future* (Washington, D.C.: Department of Justice, 1973), pp. xiv–xv.

2. Mark Levin and Rosemary C. Sarri, *Juvenile Delinquency: A Comparative Analysis of Legal Codes in the United States* (Ann Arbor, Mich.: National Assessment of Juvenile Corrections, University of Michigan, 1974), p. 13.

3. These states are Colorado, Delaware, Florida, Indiana, Mississippi, North Carolina, Pennsylvania, and West Virginia, according to Levin and Sarri, *Comparative Analysis of Legal Codes*, p. 17.

4. Laws of Pennsylvania, Act No. 333, Section 28 (1).

5. Levin and Sarri, *Comparative Analysis of Legal Codes*, p. 21.

6. *Breed* v. *Jones*, 421 U. S. 519 (1975).

7. *Kent* v. *U. S.*, 383 U. S. 541 (1966).

8. Sanford Fox, *The Law of Juvenile Courts in a Nutshell* (St. Paul, Minn.: West, 1971), p. 157.

9. Joseph Senna and Larry Siegel, *Juvenile Law: Cases and Comments* (St. Paul, Minn.: West, 1976), p. 187.

10. Norman Lefstein, Vaughan Stapleton, and Lee Teitelbaum, "In Search of Juvenile Justice—Gault and Its Implementation," in Frederic Faust and Paul J. Brantingham, eds., *Juvenile Justice Philosophy* (St. Paul, Minn.: West, 1974), p. 441.

11. Ibid., p. 446.

12. Sanford Fox, *Law of Juvenile Courts*, p. 184.

13. Finkelstein et al., *Prosecution in the Juvenile Courts*, pp. 9–26.

14. Ibid., p. xi.

15. Ibid., p. 51.

16. J. Glen and R. Weber, *The Juvenile Court: A Status Report* (Rockville, Md.: Center for Studies of Crime and Delinquency, National Institute of Mental Health, 1971).

17. Finkelstein et al., *Prosecution in the Juvenile Courts*, p. 52.

18. David Duffee and Larry Siegel, "The Organization Man: Legal Counsel in the Juvenile Court," *Criminal Law Bulletin*, 7, no. 6 (1971): 552.

19. See for example: Anthony Platt and Ruth Friedman, "The Limits of Advocacy: Occupational Hazards in the Juvenile Court," *University of Pennsylvania Law Review*, 116, no. 7 (1968): 1156–1184; Anthony Platt, Howard Schecter, and Phyllis Tiffany, "In Defense of Youth: A Case Study of the Public Defender in Juvenile Court," *Indiana Law Journal*, 43, no. 3 (1968): 619–640; Jackwell Susman, "Juvenile Justice: Even-handed or Many-handed?", *Crime and Delinquency* (October 1973): 493–507.

20. Susman, "Even-handed or Many-handed?", p. 502.

21. Fred Cohen, "A Lawyer Looks at Juvenile Justice," *Criminal Law Bulletin*, 7, no. 6 (1971), pp. 513–529.

22. Platt and Friedman, "Limits of Advocacy," pp. 1156–1184.

23. William Stapleton and Lee Teitelbaum, *In Defense of Youth* (New York: Russell Sage Foundation, 1972), pp. 111–153.

24. John Palmieri, *Pennsylvania Law of Juvenile Delinquency and Deprivation* (Philadelphia: George T. Bisel, 1976), p. 197.

25. Levin and Sarri, *Comparative Analysis of Legal Codes,* p. 44.

26. Ibid., p. 48.

27. Finkelstein et al., *Prosecution in the Juvenile Courts,* p. 37.

28. Susman, "Even-handed or Many-handed?", p. 495.

29. A survey of state statutes conducted in 1976 indicated that only thirteen states used the evidentiary standard of proof beyond a reasonable doubt for status offenders. L. Teitelbaum and A. Gough, *Beyond Control: Status Offenders in the Juvenile Court* (Cambridge, Mass.: Ballinger, 1977), pp. 297–309.

30. See the Texas Family Code in *Vernon's Texas Code Annotated,* Title 3, § 54.03 (d) and the New York Family Court Act, *McKinney's Consolidated Laws of New York Ann.,* § 744 (a).

31. Fox, *Law of Juvenile Courts,* p. 170.

32. Levin and Sarri, *Comparative Analysis of Legal Codes,* p. 49.

33. Laws of Pennsylvania, Act No. 333, Section 18 a. (A hearing date within 10 days after the filing of a petition is required.)

34. President's Commission on Law Enforcement and Administration of Justice, *Task Force Report: Juvenile Delinquency and Youth Crime* (Washington, D.C.: Government Printing Office, 1967).

35. Levin and Sarri, *Comparative Analysis of Legal Codes,* p. 50.

36. J. Norman McDonough, D. R. King, and James E. Garrett, *Juvenile Court Handbook* (South Hackensack, N.J.: Fred B. Rothman, 1970), p. 47.

37. Ibid., p. 38.

38. Fox, *Law of Juvenile Courts,* pp. 56, 57.

39. "The Youth Crime Plague," *Time,* (July 11, 1977), p. 26.

40. See for example D. Lipton, R. Martinson, and J. Wilks, *The Effectiveness of Correctional Treatment* (New York: Praeger Publishers, 1974).

10 Disposition

For the juvenile who has been adjudicated as a delinquent or found to be deprived, neglected, or in need of supervision, the dispositional stage of the juvenile court process is perhaps the most significant one. The decision made at this stage will greatly affect the child's future because it determines whether the youngster will remain at home on probation, be incarcerated in an institution for a period of months or years, be released, or be completely discharged from any type of supervision.

Several points must be considered in relation to disposition. First of all, how are these decisions made? The judge typically presents the disposition, but what are the specific factors that influence the choice? Another issue involves the types of dispositional alternatives that are utilized: What types of disposition are most frequently used and what effects do they have on the child? Finally, what criticisms have been made of the treatment efficacy of these dispositional alternatives?

The Decision-Making Process

The disposition of a juvenile case is influenced by a number of factors. The resources of the community vary greatly from court to court; some judges have a wide variety of private agencies and institutions from which to choose in addition to state facilities. In other areas, there are few alternatives to probation or incarceration, and overcrowding in institutions further reduces the number of possible choices.

Naturally the severity of disposition is extremely important. The degree of intervention in the child's life may be minimal, as in community supervision, or it may be extensive, as in incarceration. Several researchers have noted that racial and socioeconomic status biases influence the severity of dispositional choices; for example, black youngsters and the poor have been found to receive harsher treatment, regardless of prior record or the severity of the offense.[1] The home background, sex, and age of the offender have also been found to be related to disposition. In some courts females are more frequently incarcerated than in other courts.[2] Juveniles from broken homes are more likely to be treated severely.[3]

Recent research conducted in the juvenile courts of Denver County, Colorado; Montgomery County, Pennsylvania; and Memphis-Shelby County, Tennessee, has uncovered another influential variable in dispositional decision making; namely, that prior decisions by juvenile court personnel can often affect the severity of the disposition.[4] For example, children who are detained prior to their hearing are more likely to be incarcerated or transferred to adult court. Although other variables, such as seriousness of offense, prior contacts, and coming from a broken home, were also found to be related, prior processing decisions in the court system were more strongly related to disposition.

This suggests that to a large extent initial decisions in the juvenile court process influence later ones. Because some of the detained children are the most serious offenders more severe dispositions are to be expected, but among those who are detained, there are many who have committed no offense, or only a status offense. Given findings such as these, one must conclude that even nonoffenders and status offenders are more likely to be incarcerated. Judicial decisions, then, reflect considerations of both the particular child *and* the prior judgments of other persons in the juvenile court process. Unfortunately these prior decisions about the child are not always the most appropriate, and reliance on them at disposition may only serve to exacerbate an earlier mistake.

The judge's final disposition of the case may be influenced by other members of the juvenile court in addition to those who make intake and detention decisions. Defense counsel and the prosecutor (if one is present) may present disposition proposals to the court. Although this part of the court procedure has not involved attorneys in the past, it is obvious that there is a strong need for additional points of view. The defense counsel may be most effective in securing a less restrictive treatment option for a client when efforts have been made to gain knowledge of local programs geared to the client's needs. A definite alternative plan may sway the court in the child's favor.

The prosecutor's role may be that of advocate for society as well as for the rehabilitation of the child. Protecting citizens from violent juveniles and selecting appropriate treatment programs can be encouraged at this stage, especially if the judge attempts to negotiate a disposition that is acceptable to both the defense and the prosecution. Given the growing concern about the leniency afforded the dangerous juvenile in court, the prosecuting attorney may be called upon to contest dispositions that fail to require incarceration of serious offenders. Clearly, the role of the defense and the prosecution at disposition, which is minimal in many courts, could be greatly expanded.

There is evidence that the probation officer is the most influential person at this stage. Attorneys tend to rely on the expertise of probation personnel in making suggestions about the treatment needs of a particular juvenile.[5] This may in part be a result of the fact that many lawyers are simply unfamiliar with juvenile court philosophy, and thus view their role as a strictly legal one.

The probation officer presents a social investigation of each case to the judge. This investigation includes information about the child's school performance, family life, and prior record. In addition, a psychological or psychiatric evaluation of the juvenile may be included. Once an analysis of the child's situation has been made, a suggested disposition is presented. Figure 10-1 is an example of a probation report.

Ideally the social investigation provides information that will enable the probation officer to recommend the most appropriate and constructive disposition of the case. The judge will also utilize this information to arrive at a final decision. Many of these reports contain considerably more information than is provided in this example; the quality of these reports also tends to vary from one place to another.

Studies of the practices of probation officers have shown that the objective information contained in the social investigation is not necessarily the most influential factor in determining what recommendations will be made to the judge. The child's personality, family relationships, and overall social adjustment were frequently cited by probation officers as important in their decisions, although this information is the sketchiest in the reports.[6] Emphasis is often placed on recording objective data, but when these data are used, they are sometimes used inappropriately. Again the sex, age, and race of the child inspire discriminatory practices by some officers who recommend more serious dispositions for older children, females, or minority group members.[7]

The question of whether the child and the defense counsel should have access to the social investigation is governed by the Supreme Court decision of *Kent* v. *U. S.*[8] Although this case was concerned with the staff report relating to waiver of jurisdiction, the ruling is not distinguishable from access to the social study report at disposition.[9] Under *Kent*, counsel is allowed to see the reports and to challenge the information contained in them; in this way, information of questionable accuracy or relevance can be deleted.

Dispositional Alternatives

In order to provide juveniles with effective individualized treatment, it is necessary to have access to a variety of dispositional alternatives.[10] Although

PROBATION REPORT

Name: Kathy Johnson
Address: 4412 Cuthbert Road
Height: 5′4″   Weight: 117
Age: 15
Health: Good
Eyes: Hazel   Hair: Blonde
Race: Caucasian

Present Referral:	Referred by:	Disposition
Shoplifting	Police	

Subject and a friend were apprehended by store security guard with a bag containing a hair brush, slippers, Barbie doll clothing, and underwear.

Prior Referrals:

1975 Chronic Truancy	School	Informal Supervision
1976 Juvenile Drinking	Police	Informal Supervision

Family:	Age	Address	Occupation
Father, John	40	Northfield	Excavating
Mother, Alice	44	4412 Cuthbert Rd.	Welfare Recipient
Siblings: Robert	21		Married
Donna	13		8th grade
Tom	7		1st grade
Dennis	19 months		

Parents have been divorced for six years. Her mother states that Kathy was more affected by the divorce than the other children since she was very attached to her father. The father has not been in contact with his children in over two years, although he lives in the same town.

Mrs. Johnson describes Kathy as quiet and withdrawn, preferring to be alone in her own room rather than with people. She also notes that Kathy was very helpful with housework (scrubbing floors, baking, taking care of the youngest child) when she was not attending school. In the interview, it appeared that Mrs. Johnson preferred for Kathy to miss school.

Mrs. Johnson stated that she has tried to get Kathy to attend school and to stay out of trouble but that she "can't do anything with her." She emphasized the trouble that Kathy makes for her with the school and the probation department. She suggested that if only she would attend school it would be enough and that Kathy didn't even have to pay attention or study.

Figure 10-1. Sample probation report.

Mrs. Johnson expressed concern over the shoplifting incident. Her older son works in a Shop-Rite store in the same shopping center and she is worried that Kathy's shoplifting may endanger his job.

Kathy's younger sister, Donna, is attractive and intelligent. Her mother described her as an excellent student. There appears to be rivalry between Donna and Kathy.

Kathy Johnson:

During the interview, Kathy was cooperative but not spontaneous. She appeared socially withdrawn and emotionally flat. She stated that there is nothing about school that she likes and notes feelings of exclusion from peers as a possible source of her difficulties.

Kathy's attitude about the shoplifting incident was not very remorseful. She seemed to have difficulty expressing herself about this incident as well as other topics.

Kathy appears to be of average size and is fairly well groomed. She has bleached platinum blonde hair and wears a great deal of makeup.

She seems to be of normal intelligence, and there is no evidence of thought disorder.

School Report:

Kathy is in the eighth grade at Winslow Junior High School. Her attendance record is poor (30 absences during the present year), as is her overall academic performance. Achievement test scores indicate that she is functioning below the eighth-grade level.

Her teacher described Kathy as a quiet and withdrawn youngster who appears bored and indifferent. Although of normal intelligence, she rarely uses her abilities.

Recommendation:

Kathy has progressed from truancy to underage drinking to shoplifting. Although these offenses have not been serious they do indicate a lack of change in her attitudes and behavior.

She suffers from a disorganized and emotionally unsupportive family background, which includes a self-concerned mother and an absent father. Her delinquent behavior may be an attempt to compensate for her loneliness and to obtain attention from Mrs. Johnson.

Kathy has been placed on informal supervision two previous times. At this point it is necessary to increase the amount of supervision and to emphasize the need for change in the family and her behavior. Formal probation is recommended, with a referral to the Family Counseling Center. Mrs. Johnson's active involvement is needed to help Kathy, and she must be made aware of her role in this situation.[6]

the most commonly used dispositions are probation and incarceration, judges may also choose from several other alternatives.

1. *Informal handling.* This involves disposition without a dispositional hearing and often provides informal probation, with the consent of the child and his or her parents.

2. *Probation.* The most frequently used disposition, probation is often set for a specific period of time, usually a maximum of two years.

3. *Foster home placement.* A juvenile may be placed in a foster home if it is deemed necessary. Such foster homes are approved by the state, the court, or local agencies.

4. *Fines and restitution to the victim.* Fines can be imposed by a judge, and a youth may be directed to pay restitution for damage inflicted.

5. *Private institutions.* Various types of private homes and institutions may be chosen for treating the child. Institutions run by private foundations and religious groups often receive dispositions from the court if space is available and the institutions are willing to accept the child.

6. *Public institutions.* These institutions are run by the state and include training schools, industrial schools, and forestry camps. Although many commitments to these institutions are indeterminate (ending at the age of majority), newly enacted juvenile codes usually set maximum limits. Eight states set the maximum length of incarceration at two years, with possible two-year extensions following a rehearing.[12] Decisions to release a juvenile are made by the institution, a juvenile parole board, or the court.

7. *Other options.* Counties with large populations have their own facilities and juveniles may be sent to institutions within their communities. In some states, a juvenile may be committed to an adult correctional facility if it is deemed appropriate for the child's needs. This may occur when a juvenile has committed a serious offense or has been very difficult for staff members to handle. After a psychiatric evaluation of the juvenile has been made, a recommendation for the initiation of proceedings for commitment to a mental institution may be made.

8. *Dismissal.* A juvenile may be dismissed from the court without a formally mandated treatment prescription.

Probation

It is estimated that 90 percent of all children who go through the disposition process are placed on probation.[13] The extensive use of supervision in the community has become a distinguishing characteristic of the juvenile justice system. The child savers originally advocated this approach, because they felt that in order to detect problems and prevent delinquent behavior it was necessary to develop an intervention technique that would help the child become reintegrated into the home environment and the community.

Although probation typically results from a court disposition, it may also occur at an earlier stage in the juvenile justice process. Diversion at the intake stage may place the child on "informal probation," which involves a limited period of supervision prior to a hearing. If problems persist, the youngster may be brought back into court for a fact-finding hearing and disposition.

The probation officer performs many duties in the juvenile justice process, and it is precisely this diversity of functions that at times leads to conflicts. Initially, the probation staff screens all cases referred to the court and assists in detention decisions. The child may be diverted at the officer's discretion, or a formal petition may be filed. Prosecutorial functions can then be performed during hearings. The social investigation report and recommendation for disposition require diagnostic skills. The final duty of client supervision requires a therapeutic approach but may also involve a law enforcement role. Juveniles who break the rules of probation or commit additional offenses may be arrested by a probation officer and returned to court.[14]

Probation personnel, then, may be called upon to perform law enforcement, prosecutorial, diagnostic, and therapeutic tasks. In large departments these tasks are usually assigned to staff members on a permanent basis, so that intake officers are responsible for making intake decisions while other officers are in charge of compiling social investigations and supervising caseloads.[15] In smaller organizations such specialization is not possible, and one person may have to assume a variety of responsibilities.

Supervision

Ideally during the supervision of a caseload, a probation officer develops a relationship with clients that facilitates free expression of feelings and trust. This relationship is based on the concept of casework treatment, which encourages the use of intensive interviews that will ultimately give the client some insight into his or her behavior.[16] Naturally, this "ideal" relationship is rarely attained. Because probation officers typically have large caseloads and limited time, intensive supervision or counseling cannot occur. One writer has described a probation department in which over half of the staff members were working full time with only 30 to 40 percent of their total caseload.[17]

It is not unheard of for a single probation officer to have over one hundred cases at one time. (See Table 10-1.) Traditionally, the ideal caseload size has been described as ranging from 35 to 50 cases. In 1967, the President's Commission on Law Enforcement and Administration of Justice proposed a different technique for calculating caseloads. The Commission suggested that

TABLE 10-1. PERCENTAGE OF JUVENILES ON PROBATION BY OFFICER CASELOAD

CASELOAD	PERCENTAGE
0–50 cases	11.76
51–71 cases	31.15
71–100 cases	46.14
Over 100 cases	10.68

Source: National Corrections Survey. The President's Commission on Law Enforcement and Administration of Justice, *Task Force Report: Corrections* (Washington, D.C.: Government Printing Office, 1967), pp. 98–99.

each officer carry 50 units per month. Under probation supervision each case counts as one unit, and each new diagnostic investigation counts as five units.[18] Officers conducting social investigations would then be expected to do less supervision. This proposed system reflects today's growing concern with upgrading screening, investigation, and diagnostic techniques.

Unfortunately the relationship between caseload size and the amount of contact an officer has with probationers has not been clarified by empirical studies. In some instances a reduction in caseload size apparently led to increased numbers of probation revocations.[19] Caseload size does not always determine the amount of supervision, and some critics have noted that the *number* of actual contacts with the probation officer may be the key variable in probation success. But, again, research has indicated that the number of contacts between staff and probationer has little effect on whether probationers commit additional offenses or break their probation rules. Perhaps the *quality* of the relationship between the probation officer and his or her clients should be examined instead of the caseload and number of clients.

The casework approach to probation has been discouraged in recent years due to large caseloads, and service delivery has been stressed. Some departments have experimented with classifying probationers and then assigning them to appropriate specialized treatment programs. These specialized programs include guided group interaction, intensive supervision, delinquent peer group programs, residential treatment, and group home placement.[20]

Others have advocated the role of *community resource managers* for staff members.[21] Instead of acting as the sole provider of resources, the officer works to coordinate the probationer's needs with appropriate services available within the community. In this way, a wider variety of services can be made available to each client; this is extremely helpful since it would be impossible for a single probation officer to provide such a wide range of services to his or her probationers.

Another role that has emerged for probation officers is that of counselor to the client's family. The casework method emphasizes individual characteristics and change, but some people involved in treatment believe that it is not possible to effectively treat a single member of a family.[22] According to this point of view, what is needed is diagnosis and counseling of the *entire* family. This family therapy is often practiced on a limited basis by probation officers, and they often refer families to a family therapy clinic for more intensive help.

The probationer and his family are often resistant to this approach, and naturally it takes considerable skill on the part of the counselor to meet this resistance.[23] Theoretically, once resistance is successfully overcome, the family can begin working together to decrease or even eradicate delinquent behavior. By changing long-established patterns of interactions within the family, juveniles can learn to fill their needs without having to resort to deviance, and the family can learn to communicate more openly and give each other needed support.

Revocation

One aspect of the supervision of clients involves the revocation of probation for juveniles who commit new offenses or who break the rules of probation. Probation departments formulate rules that must be agreed to and followed by all persons placed on probation. Additional rules may be included for offenders who have had particular problems. For example, a rule may specifically prohibit association with other delinquents or gang members.

Conditions of probation have been upheld by the courts even when they are as vague as that the child must "stay out of trouble."[24] Other specific conditions have been ruled inappropriate, such as a requirement that the child attend church and Sunday School for a period of one year.[25] Of course whether the juvenile complies with these conditions depends to a large extent on the amount of supervision he or she receives. Again, this supervision is often minimal. If a probationer does violate these conditions or other laws, the probation officer may initiate revocation proceedings.

This role of surveillance of clients and law enforcement makes the therapeutic or counseling aspect of the probation officer's task difficult. Probationers are often very reluctant to confide in their probation officers and may try to present an image that they feel will be acceptable to the officer.

If revocation does occur, a hearing must be held to determine whether there is sufficient evidence to prove that the violation occurred. In *Gagnon* v. *Scarpelli,* the Supreme Court ruled that an adult probationer is entitled to a preliminary hearing in order to determine whether there is probable cause to believe that the probationer has in fact violated the conditions of probation.[26] The probationer is also entitled to a final revocation hearing. Following this court decision, many states provided notice, a hearing, right to counsel, and other safeguards for due process for juveniles during revocation.[27]

The Future of Probation

Although probation is by no means a panacea for the problem of juvenile delinquency, there is reason to encourage its continued use and expansion.

_____ COUNTY JUVENILE COURT
RULES OF PROBATION

Rules to be followed while you are on probation.

1. You are to obey the laws of every state, township or borough.

2. You are to stay away from all undesirable places, keep good company and good hours. During week days you must be home by _____ o'clock P.M. On Saturdays and Sundays by _____ o'clock.

3. You must not leave the county, without obtaining permission from your probation officer.

4. You must not apply for an operator's permit or license, or come into ownership of a motor vehicle without permission from your probation officer.

5. You must not change your address, quit school or your job without permission from your probation officer.

6. Your probation officer may visit your home, school, or place of employment at any time.

7. WHEN YOU ARE NOT SURE WHAT IS EXPECTED OF YOU, FEEL FREE TO CALL YOUR PROBATION OFFICER AT ANY TIME.

8. ADDITIONAL RULES:

IF YOU VIOLATE ANY OF THE ABOVE RULES, YOU WILL BE RETURNED TO JUVENILE COURT FOR ANOTHER HEARING BEFORE THE JUDGE WHO PLACED YOU ON PROBATION.

We, the parents of _____ , agree to enforce the above rules.

_____   _____

I have read the above rules and understand them. While on probation, I agree to abide by them.

_____   _____
                                                            Date

Source: John Palmieri, *Pennsylvania Law of Juvenile Delinquency and Deprivation* (Philadelphia: George T. Bisel, 1976), p. 251.

Figure 10-2. Sample of court rules of probation.

Recidivism rates are as low or lower for children placed on probation as for children who are incarcerated.[28] Probation is also much less expensive as a treatment intervention than is incarceration. In fact, the overall daily cost for a juvenile who is incarcerated is *ten* times greater than that for a child on probation.[29]

In addition to considerations of cost and recidivism, probation can be advocated as a technique that has the potential to offer a means by which the juvenile can be reintegrated into the community. The probation officer's referrals and assistance can locate community services for both the child and the family. The juvenile's life is not disrupted to any great extent, and he or she may learn more adaptive and socially acceptable methods of attaining desired goals. Institutionalization does not offer these advantages and may actually be very detrimental to children. Not only is the institutional setting disruptive, but it fails to offer any real opportunities for children to develop the necessary skills for community adjustment. Moreover, incarceration inevitably means that the child will be exposed to an array of negative experiences.

Programs have been developed to encourage the use of probation. One of these is the probation subsidy program currently in effect in California. To encourage the use of probation and to discourage institutionalization, the state of California actually pays counties to reduce the number of juveniles committed to state institutions. This money can then be channelled back into expanded probation programs. Not only does this method save the state money, but it also makes it possible for large numbers of less serious offenders to remain in the community. The success of this program is evidenced by the fact that California is presently in the process of closing some institutions and two of its new institutions are not in use.[30]

Another effort to improve probation services has relied on volunteer probation officers. These volunteers, who are drawn from the community, are trained as adjuncts to probation staff and then assigned a probationer. Citizen volunteers are helpful in several ways: they ease probation caseloads, offer needed expertise, and establish one-to-one relationships with the juveniles. There is some evidence that antisocial attitudes decrease in offenders who are assigned to a volunteer whereas offenders who are assigned to regular probation do not show this change.[31]

Institutionalization

Placement in some type of institution is the second most frequently used disposition by the juvenile court. State, county, and private facilities are utilized; these institutions are frequently called training schools, industrial schools, or reformatories. Because they are designed to serve the dual purpose of custody and treatment, youngsters who are thought to be in need of greater external control are sent to them for rehabilitative care. In recent years institutionalization has been used less and less, but nonetheless many youngsters today do find their way into some type of secure facility. (See Table 10-2.)

Juvenile institutions evolved as an alternative to incarcerating children in the same facilities with adults. The House of Refuge was established in New

TABLE 10-2. TYPES OF JUVENILE INSTITUTIONS AND THEIR POPULATIONS*

Detention Centers	10,782
Shelters	190
Reception and diagnostic centers	1,734
Training Schools	26,427
Ranches and forestry camps	4,959
Half-way houses	713
Group homes	889
Total	45,694

Source: National Criminal Justice Information and Statistic Service, *Children In Custody,* Law Enforcement Assistance Administration, Department of Justice, Washington, D.C., May 1975.

*Substantially higher figures are reported by others. The U.S. Senate Subcommittee to Investigate Juvenile Delinquency estimates *10 percent* of the *one million* children who enter the juvenile justice system will be incarcerated. Subcommittee to Investigate Juvenile Delinquency, Committee on the Judiciary, *Juvenile Delinquency,* (Washington, D.C.: U.S. Senate, Report No. 93-K124, Dec. 19, 1974), p. 2.

York City in 1825 to provide shelter and care for youngsters, and other states soon followed suit, opening similar institutions for children. The goals of these early institutions were to provide instruction and reformation rather than to administer punishment.[32]

Training schools and reformatories were also set up in many states. Located in rural areas and emphasizing a return to agricultural skills, these schools were designed to provide a healthier atmosphere for children from urban areas. A cottage layout was employed to make the institutions more home-like; discipline, hard work, morality, vocational training and formal education (if possible) were stressed. It was hoped that the teachings of these institutions would help alter attitudes and future behavior and thereby prevent further delinquency.

Eventually criticism of the wide use of training schools and reformatories led many to question the efficacy of incarceration.[33] Delinquent behavior was not eliminated despite the fact that children spent many years in a training school. Today the same criticisms are made of juvenile correctional programs, which has led to the implementation of community-based programs that serve as alternatives to incarceration.

Philosophy of Institutionalization

In theory juvenile institutions are concerned primarily with the treatment and rehabilitation of youngsters. Unlike prisons, deterrence and retribution are not among their major goals. Theoretically, juvenile institutions are specialized institutions designed to rehabilitate children who are hardened delinquent offenders.

But in reality these institutions bear little resemblance to what their original founders envisioned them to be. Overcrowding and insufficient funds are common problems, as are heterogeneous client populations and a paucity of treatment personnel. Custodial, or security, concerns are often given priority, and may serve to inhibit treatment efforts. Although staff members advocate treatment or rehabilitation as a major goal, they also acknowledge the need for de-emphasis on custodial concerns.[34]

Custodial concerns focus on institutional practices that will tighten the security of the facility. Uniforms, perimeter fencing, regular population counts, and extensive rules governing the movement of juveniles within the training school make it easier for officials to detect potential runaways. Not only do these practices lead to regimentation and lack of individuality among those incarcerated, but they also interfere with the therapeutic process.

This concern with custody has developed in response to many factors. Community fear of victimization by escaped delinquents may result in pressure on the institution to control its population. The ratio of children to staff members may be very large and necessitate a reliance on custodial methods of control. Naturally, children who are incarcerated want to return to their homes and regain their freedom; thus certain security measures are needed, but training schools often respond to these needs by making security an end in itself.

Custodial issues do not present the only impediment to a successful treatment philosophy. Organizational patterns and the large population of children also contribute to the difficulty of developing therapeutically oriented training schools and reformatories.

Organization

The training school or reformatory is itself a community and requires a wide range of services. These institutions are "total institutions" in that they encompass the juvenile's entire daily activities—from sleeping and eating to working and learning.[35] A variety of staff positions is required to oversee and provide these services. These positions are briefly described below.

1. *Superintendent.* The superintendent is the head of the organization and is often appointed to this position. Frequently he or she has little relevant experience prior to appointment, but some jurisdictions do require that superintendents have an established professional career in corrections.[36]

2. *Assistant superintendent.* This person is capable of taking over the operation of the institution if necessary; other duties include specialized functions such as personnel management and inmate discipline.

3. *Housekeeping staff.* These staff members are responsible for maintenance of the physical plant and provision of clothing and food for the inmates.

4. *Custodial staff.* These employees supervise the inmates in their living quarters and in activities not covered by professional specialists.

5. *Educational staff.* Educational programs are conducted by qualified teachers and provide schooling for children who still require compulsory education as well as for older juveniles who wish to continue their education. Members of the educational staff may also be responsible for vocational training programs.

6. *Medical services.* Medical treatment is provided by nurses and doctors who may be assigned to the institution on a full-time or part-time basis.

7. *Treatment staff.* These staff members have backgrounds in social work, psychology, and counseling. They devise and implement treatment strategies within the institution.

The major expenditure within correctional institutions is for custody and administration, which account for 80 to 90 percent of the total annual expenditure. Treatment personnel account for approximately 20 percent of all personnel.[37] So although there is a diversity of personnel in these institutions, resources are mostly channeled into the areas of custody, administration, and housekeeping. Thus treatment, which is in theory the primary goal of these institutions, is given little real support.

Further analysis of institutional staff may be obtained from Table 10-3. The juvenile programs surveyed by the National Assessment of Juvenile Corrections indicated that staff members are most frequently young, white, and male. Their educational backgrounds tend to be more extensive than those of personnel found in adult institutions.[38]

TABLE 10-3. STAFF CHARACTERISTICS BY OCCUPATIONAL SUBGROUPS

	MEDIAN AGE	MALE (%)	FEMALE (%)	WHITE (%)	NONWHITE (%)	WITH DEGREE (%)
Executive (n = 48)	34	80	20	84	16	63
Treatment (n = 213)	30	68	32	68	32	72
Teaching (n = 196)	35	56	44	70	30	73
Living Unit (custodial) (n = 260)	34	52	48	68	32	29
Clerical and Maintenance (n = 162)	39	43	57	76	24	19

Source: Reprinted from "Justice for Whom? Varieties of Juvenile Correctional Approaches" by Rosemary C. Sarri and Robert D. Vinter in *The Juvenile Justice System,* Sage Criminal Justice System Annuals, Volume V, Malcolm W. Klein, Editor © 1976 p. 182 by permission of the Publisher, Sage Publications, Inc. (Beverly Hills/London).

Population

It is often assumed that the juveniles who are incarcerated are the most serious offenders and to some extent this is true. But surveys have found that many of the children in training schools and reformatories are actually status offenders. One study of 19 major cities in the United States found that 40 to 50 percent of the residents of institutions were juveniles who had not committed offenses that would be criminal for an adult.[39]

The practice of holding delinquents and status offenders together in the same facility is a common one, although it is surely detrimental to the less serious offender. Not only can children learn new techniques for committing offenses, but antisocial attitudes are also reinforced through constant daily exposure to hardened delinquents. There is also the possibility that juveniles who are neither hardened nor delinquent will become stigmatized as a result of their having been assigned to institutions for delinquents. Today some jurisdictions provide separate facilities for delinquents and status offenders so that only those youngsters who have committed crimes will be housed together.[40]

Table 10-4 shows the types of commitments given to children who had committed various offenses. This study indicated that the severity of the offense is not necessarily related to the type of disposition. Note the high proportion of female status offenders who were institutionalized, as well as the percentage of juveniles who had committed crimes against the person who were placed in day treatment or community residences. The authors of the study suggest that these data might lead one to conclude that the concept of diversion has not been supported in practice. This is particularly obvious

TABLE 10-4. COMMITMENT OFFENSE, BY PROGRAM TYPE AND SEX (IN PERCENTAGES)

	STATUS OFFENSE	PROBATION OR PAROLE VIOLATION	MISDE-MEANOR	DRUGS OR ALCOHOL	PROPERTY	PERSON	n
Institution							
Male	23	4	2	6	46	18	(832)
Female	50	1	3	18	14	14	(349)
Community Residential							
Male	50	3	1	10	26	10	(70)
Female	67	3	0	14	12	3	(58)
Day Treatment							
Male	45	3	4	6	30	12	(164)
Female	87	0	0	5	3	5	(37)

Source: Reprinted from "Justice for Whom? Varieties of Juvenile Correctional Approaches" by Rosemary C. Sarri and Robert D. Vinter in The Juvenile Justice System, Sage Criminal Justice System Annuals, Volume V, Malcolm W. Klein, Editor © 1976 p. 181 by permission of the Publisher, Sage Publications, Inc. (Beverly Hills/London).

when we consider how many children are still being committed to secure facilities.

Other descriptions of training school populations point out that many of these children have educational deficiencies and come from disrupted family backgrounds. They also tend to be older juveniles, and those who have either committed several offenses or have been brought into juvenile court on more than one occasion.[41] But generalizations about incarcerated children are difficult to make with accuracy, because there is a wide variation of opinion among jurisdictions about what types of offenses require institutionalization.

As we discussed earlier the heterogeneity of the population may have detrimental effects on children who are introduced to hardened offenders. It also makes treatment techniques difficult to implement because different approaches may be required for different types of juveniles. An effort to improve this situation has centered around the use of diagnostic and classification units within a state juvenile correctional system. At the beginning of the child's commitment, an extensive evaluation of the child is conducted, and an appropriate institution and treatment program is recommended. By separating or classifying offenders, those who respond most favorably to a specific therapy technique may be incarcerated together. Unfortunately, classification must also contend with practical considerations such as the amount of available space. For example, a juvenile may be sent to a particular state facility only because there is space for her there, but in fact another facility would actually be more appropriate for her needs.

Another aspect of the inmate population that creates problems for both treatment and custodial staff is the evolution of a subculture within the institution. These subcultures are most frequent in institutions that have longer terms of commitment and the largest number of recidivists.[42] The subculture is a system of roles set up by the inmates and used to obtain desired goods (such as drugs or extra food), emotional support, and status.

Male institutions have subcultures based on dominance and aggression, with the largest or strongest juvenile acting as the leader. In female institutions a different type of subculture often evolves. This subculture is characterized by the establishment of family structures in which other females play the roles of family members. Some girls are mothers or fathers, others are children, and there may be aunts, uncles, and cousins.[43] This family structure provides emotional support and security during the juvenile's stay in the institution.

The subculture may help facilitate the distribution of contraband and the proliferation of homosexual behavior, which are both areas of concern for custodial staff. For treatment staff the difficulty lies in resistance to treatment by the subculture. Solidarity among the juveniles may be reinforced by the subculture, which makes it difficult for a counselor to establish a rapport with individual children. Reprisals may occur when members of the subculture cooperate with the institution staff. Although not *all* of the inmates are involved in the subculture, this situation nonetheless creates difficulties for the day-to-day operation of the institution and impedes its rehabilitative goals.

Length of Commitment and Release

The early juvenile court committed children to institutions for indeterminate lengths of time. For example, a youngster who was sent to a reformatory would be committed until his majority age (usually 21) or until he showed improvement. Today, states are placing maximum limits on the period of incarceration. Eight states currently have these limits, which usually provide a maximum time of two years with possible extensions.[44] The authority to release children is often given to the individual institution, but practices vary from one place to another. Juvenile parole boards operate in some areas, and in others the court must approve release.[45]

The amount of time that juveniles are held in confinement ranges from 4 to 24 months, with a median length of stay of about 9 months.[46] Efforts have been made to reduce the length of incarceration owing to the deleterious effects of long periods of confinement. The cost of incarceration and overcrowding of institutions also have contributed to shorter training school terms.

Ideally, release from confinement indicates significant improvement in the child's attitudes and behavior, which was the original rationale behind giving the institution the authority to terminate incarceration. Such improvement is extremely difficult to measure, and because many institutions provide minimal treatment, this improvement may not occur at all. In many cases, release is not related to treatment success but results from a need for additional space or the requirement of a statutory maximum limit. Thus those institutions that *do* provide therapy may be hindered by statutory or administrative limitations on the length of confinement.

Treatment Techniques

Although a wide variety of techniques is employed in juvenile facilities, there are specific types of therapy that are used most frequently. Three types of approaches will be described here. Each of these techniques is based on different assumptions about the causes of and remedies for delinquent behavior and consequently focus on different issues. Although they are presented separately, it is possible to find institutions in which several different types of therapy are being administered. Indeed, an eclectic approach, which draws from many schools of therapy, may be the most effective in treating juveniles since it would allow for truly individualized treatment.

Guided Group Interaction   Guided group interaction was developed at the Highfields Project for the short-term treatment of young offenders in the early 1950s.[47] It is a group therapy technique that is administered to delinquents in a group home setting.

Guided group interaction and other types of group therapy work within the peer group to help members gain an understanding of their behavior and to change attitudes. Because delinquency is often described as a group phenomenon, group therapy is considered particularly effective in that it employs group influence in a positive manner.

The group leader or trainer begins the group sessions and helps establish the basic rules for group behavior, which must be enforced by the group members. The leader initiates and guides the interactions between the group members until the group begins to take a more active role, at which point the leader can assume a more passive one.

This type of therapy extends the role of a single therapist to many more children than could be reached on a one-to-one basis. It also decreases the role of the leader (or authority figure) so that the youngsters are forced to help each other. Discipline may be administered by the group members; in one program group members could deny release to a peer if they found it necessary.[48]

Evaluations of the effectiveness of guided group interaction have indicated that the Highfield's Project had lower recidivism rates than a state reformatory.[49] Unfortunately a reanalysis of this information conducted by Lerman showed that differences between Highfields and the reformatory were not as significant as had originally been thought.[50]

Behavior Modification   Behavior modification is a technique used to eliminate undesirable behavior or actions. Unlike traditional therapies, behavior modification does not focus on internal conflicts or the underlying causes of the behavior pattern, but rather seeks to modify the behavior and to replace it with socially acceptable patterns.

To change behavior, the therapist manipulates environmental contingencies. For example, a juvenile may earn a specific number of points for 30 minutes of studying or for keeping her room in the institution clean. Other privileges can be purchased with these points. Some programs use a "token economy"; here the inmate earns tokens for desired behaviors, which in turn can be used to purchase goods (like candy) or privileges (such as extra television viewing time).

Behavior modification typically attempts to reinforce desirable behaviors through a system of rewards, but there must also be some technique for extinguishing undesirable behavior. This may be accomplished by ignoring the behavior (not rewarding) or by punishing it with a negative stimulus.[51] Through these techniques appropriate behaviors can be learned and inappropriate behaviors can be eliminated.

The Robert F. Kennedy Youth Center in Morgantown, West Virginia is a correctional institution that utilizes behavior modification extensively in its treatment program.[52] Many aspects of inmate activity are included in the behavior modification strategy. Youths can progress within a class-level system from trainee to apprentice to honor student. This is accomplished by achieving progressively higher goals. As the child progresses to higher class levels, living quarters, pay, clothing, jobs, and recreation improve.

Juveniles can also earn points (one point equals one cent) for accomplishments in other areas. At the end of each week, a paycheck equalling the number of accumulated points is received, and youngsters can buy desired goods. The paycheck must also be used to pay room rent and other expenses within the institution, as well as any fines incurred. The rate of pay accumulation and room rent vary by class level, so that honor students earn points at the highest rate and also have the highest expenses and fines, and apprentices have higher rates than trainees.

Although there is evidence that behavior modification can decrease recidivism rates (at least in the first years following release), this treatment approach has been sharply criticized.[53] The use of certain unethical "punishments" in the guise of behavior modification caused widespread concern about the ways in which this type of program could be abused. It was found, for example, that electric shocks and a drug called succinylcholine, which simulates dying, were being used in some "behavior modification" programs. State and federal institutions moved to change their treatment techniques after these instances of abuse had been publicized, and today only a handful of institutions are using behavior modification treatment programs exclusively.[54]

Reality Therapy   Reality therapy was developed by Dr. William Glasser as an alternative to traditional forms of therapy.[55] According to Glasser, all people seek to fulfill two basic needs: to love and be loved; and to feel worthwhile to one's self and to others. In Glasser's view, the delinquent attempts to fulfill these needs in an irresponsible way and thus has little or no awareness of the effects of his or her actions on others. Reality therapy helps the patient learn how to fill these needs in a responsible way.

The therapy process contrasts sharply with that used in psychotherapeutic methods. First, the patient's past is considered insignificant in dealing with present behavior; instead present problems and actions are the focus of treatment. Delving into past family relationships and environmental influences enables the patients to rationalize their present behavior. Second, patients are encouraged to accept full responsibility for their actions. *Why* the act was performed is not significant; what is significant is that the act was committed and that there is no way to absolve oneself from this responsibility. And third, the therapy process requires a warm, supportive, involved relationship between therapist and patient. The therapist must reinforce responsible behavior, set appropriate standards of behavior for the youngster, and not reject the patient if he should behave in an irresponsible manner.

Glasser has used this technique in a treatment program for delinquent girls in the Ventura School for Girls in California. The program includes educational and vocational training in addition to reality therapy, but the basic philosophy of reality therapy underlies *all* treatment. High standards of behavior are expected from the girls, and discipline for rule infractions consists of exclusion from the usual day-to-day program. No excuses are accepted for misbehavior, and problems are dealt with in a manner that encourages the development of more acceptable behaviors in the future.

A comparison between juveniles who were treated in an institution stressing responsible behavior and those who were treated with standard psychiatric techniques indicated that the violation of parole after release was lower among girls in the first group. Glasser interprets this as support for reality therapy and also notes that the recidivism rate at Ventura is approximately 20 percent.[56] This is considerably lower than that found in most juvenile institutions.

The Future of Institutionalization

The many problems that exist in institutions can have profound effects on children who are incarcerated. Recidivism rates are extremely high; figures of 50 percent are not uncommon in studies of the proportion of inmates who will return to an institution.[57] There is also evidence that institutionalization exacerbates the problem of delinquency. The cohort study conducted by Wolfgang et al., which has been discussed in previous chapters, revealed that juveniles who received the most serious dispositions not only continued to commit delinquent acts but went on to commit even more serious crimes.[58]

Training schools and reformatories have been criticized for their emphasis on custody as opposed to treatment, their impersonality, and their punitive practices. Large institutions with limited staff often resort to corporal punishment to control the population, and the possibility of abuse is all too likely. Solitary confinement is a common punishment for runaways, which again underscores the emphasis placed on custody-related problems.[59] Institutions often formulate rules that govern the most minute details of a child's day in order to maintain a smoothly running facility. But practices such as these actually inhibit the learning of self-control and independence since so much external control is exerted.

Proponents of institutionalization explain its failure to reform in terms of insufficient funding for adequate treatment programs and well-trained staff. They also note the need for incarceration of dangerous offenders who may harm more citizens if they are allowed to remain in the community. Surely such offenders do exist, but experts estimate that only 20 to 30 percent of all offenders presently incarcerated present this type of danger.[60]

The culmination of all of these problems has been a move in some states toward deinstitutionalization of offenders. Deinstitutionalization includes the use of a variety of alternative institutions within the community, such as half-way houses and group homes. These treatment alternatives are much less expensive than incarceration and are surely more humane. (Innovations in juvenile corrections will be discussed in greater detail in the next chapter.) But the dominant trend throughout the United States is not deinstitutionalization; reorganization and centralization of existing juvenile systems are much more common phenomena.[61] In light of all of the criticisms of institutions, one must question the value of these developments.

The position of the federal courts in establishing the right to treatment for juveniles will also have an effect on the way in which juvenile institutions are run in the future.[62] If states continue to incarcerate juveniles in training schools and reformatories, they will have to provide trained personnel, treatment, and educational programs for the youngsters held in these facilities. Failure to do so may result in the release of the juveniles.

Aftercare

Upon release from an institution, juveniles are frequently placed in aftercare, which is analogous to parole for adults. The term *aftercare* has been advocated by persons who wish to separate juvenile programs from the legalistic language and concept of adult parole.[63] Although this term is not always utilized, the idea that juveniles need specialized supervision and counseling to facilitate their reintegration into the community is widely accepted today.

Juvenile aftercare first appeared in the United States in the early nineteenth century, but it was not until recent years that it has become a common aspect of rehabilitation efforts for juveniles.[64] The President's Commission on Law Enforcement and Administration of Justice described juvenile aftercare as the least developed aspect of rehabilitation for children in 1967,[65] but by 1973 nearly all juveniles were released under some type of supervision, and distinct programs for juvenile parole supervision had emerged in many states.[66]

Ideally aftercare provides counseling, school referral, vocational training, and supervision for juveniles released from institutions. A juvenile is assigned to a juvenile aftercare worker who is to provide assistance to the child in his adjustment to the community and monitor his behavior. Unfortunately juvenile aftercare suffers from many of the same problems found in juvenile probation. Heavy caseloads and inadequate training of aftercare workers are common problems in aftercare programs. These problems have been pointed to as explanations of the relative ineffectiveness of aftercare or parole in reducing recidivism, but research findings on the effects of this type of community supervision have not been very promising, even when caseloads are reduced.[67]

The child who is placed on aftercare can be returned to the institution if parole rules are broken or a new offense is committed. In recent years the United States Supreme Court has provided some due process rights for adult parolees in the parole revocation procedures.[68] Although the court has not yet extended these rights to juveniles, many states have voluntarily extended some due process procedures to juveniles.[69] These often include notice of the revocation proceedings, a revocation hearing, and in some states representation by an attorney is provided.[70]

DISCUSSION QUESTIONS

1. What are the most important factors that influence the decision of the judge at disposition?

2. Why does the probation staff play such an influential role at this stage of the juvenile justice process?

3. Why is probation the most common disposition in juvenile court?

4. What are the characteristics of many institutions for juveniles that make them failures at rehabilitation?

5. What is the purpose of aftercare for juveniles?

NOTES

1. Terence Thornberry, "Race, Socioeconomic Status, and Sentencing in the Juvenile Justice System," *Journal of Criminal Law and Criminology* 64, no. 1 (1973): 90–98; William R. Arnold, "Race and Ethnicity Relative to Other Factors in Juvenile Court Dispositions," *American Journal of Sociology,* 77, no. 2 (1971): 211–227.

2. William H. Barton, "Discretionary Decision Making in Juvenile Justice," *Crime and Delinquency,* 22, no. 4 (1976): 470–480.

3. Lawrence Cohen, "Delinquency Dispositions: An Empirical Analysis of Processing Decisions in Three Juvenile Courts," *Analytic Report 9* (Washington, D.C.: Department of Justice, 1975), p. 51.

4. Ibid.

5. M. Finkelstein, E. Weiss, and S. Cohen, *Prosecution in the Juvenile Courts: Guidelines for the Future* (Washington, D.C.: Department of Justice, 1973), p. xv.

6. Yona Cohn, "Criteria for the Probation Officers' Recommendation to the Juvenile Court Judge," *Crime and Delinquency,* 9 (July 1963): 262–275.

7. Ibid.

8. *Kent* v. *U.S.*, 383 U.S. 541 (1966).

9. Sanford Fox, *The Law of Juvenile Courts in a Nutshell* (St. Paul, Minn.: West, 1971), p. 209.

10. Mark Levin and Rosemary Sarri, *Juvenile Delinquency: A Comparative Analysis of Legal Codes in the United States* (Ann Arbor, Mich.: National Assessment of Juvenile Corrections, University of Michigan, 1974), pp. 52–57.

11. The information in this report has been changed to protect identities.

12. Ibid. The states are Colorado, Connecticut, Georgia, Maryland, New York, North Dakota, Wisconsin, as well as the District of Columbia.

13. Joseph Senna and Larry Siegel, *Juvenile Law* (St. Paul, Minn.: West, 1976), p. 379.

14. Lewis Diana, "What Is Probation?" in R. Carter and L. Wilkins, eds., *Probation and Parole: Selected Readings* (New York: John Wiley, 1970), pp. 39–56.

15. Jackwell Susman, "Juvenile Justice: Even-handed or Many-handed?" *Crime and Delinquency,* October 1973, pp. 493–507.

16. Diana, "What Is Probation?" p. 52.

17. President's Commission on Law Enforcement and Administration of Justice, *Task Force Report: Corrections* (Washington, D.C.: Government Printing Office, 1967), p. 207.

18. National Advisory Commission on Criminal Justice Standards and Goals, *Corrections* (Washington, D.C.: Government Printing Office, 1973), pp. 318–319.

19. Ibid.

20. Ibid., p. 320.

21. Ibid., pp. 322, 323.

22. Virginia Satir, *Conjoint Family Therapy,* rev. ed. (Palo Alto, Calif.: Science and Behavior Books, 1967), pp. 1–7.

23. For a good description of family resistance to counseling, see Warren Walker, "Games Families of Delinquents Play," *Federal Probation,* 36, no. 4 (December 1972): 20–24.

24. *Interest of Green,* 203 So. 2d 470 (Miss. 1967).

25. *Jones* v. *Commonwealth,* 185 Va. 335, 38 S. E. 2d 444 (1946).

26. *Gagnon* v. *Scarpelli* 411 U.S. 778 (1973).

27. Senna and Siegel, *Juvenile Law,* p. 380.

28. Carl W. Nelson, "Cost-Benefit Analysis and Alternatives to Incarceration," *Federal Probation,* 39, no. 4 (1970): 45–50.

29. Robert Smith, "A Quiet Revolution: Probation Subsidy," *Delinquency Prevention Report,* 1971, pp. 3–7.

30. Ibid.

31. Ivan H. Scheier, "The Professional and the Volunteer in Probation: An Emerging Relationship," *Federal Probation* 34, no. 2 (June 1970): 12–18.

32. Hassim Solomon, *Community Corrections* (Boston: Holbrook Press, 1976), p. 43.

33. Frederic Faust and Paul J. Brantingham, *Juvenile Justice Philosophy* (St. Paul, Minn.: West, 1974), pp. 206–355.

34. Rosemary Sarri and Robert D. Vinter, "Justice for Whom? Varieties of Juvenile Correctional Approaches," in M. Klein, ed., *The Juvenile Justice System* (Beverly Hills, Calif.: Sage, 1976), pp. 161–200.

35. Erving Goffman, *Asylums* (Garden City, N.Y.: Anchor Books, 1961), pp. 4–12.

36. R. Carter, R. McGee, and E. Nelson *Corrections in America*, (Philadelphia: Lippincott, 1975), p. 53.

37. Henry Burns, *Corrections, Organization and Administration*, (St. Paul, Minn.: West, 1975), p. 358.

38. Sarri and Vinter, "Justice for Whom?", p. 181.

39. Hassim Solomon, *Community Corrections*, p. 109.

40. Joseph Senna and Larry Siegel, *Juvenile Law*, p. 380.

41. Ruth Cavan and Theodore Ferdinand, *Juvenile Delinquency*, 3rd ed. (Philadelphia: Lippincott, 1975), pp. 401–404.

42. D. Clemmer, *The Prison Community* (New York: Holt, Rinehart & Winston, 1958), pp. 298–304.

43. Rose Giallombardo, *The Social World of Imprisoned Girls* (New York: John Wiley, 1974), pp. 145–239.

44. Levin and Sarri, *Comparative Analysis of Legal Codes*, p. 55.

45. Ibid., p. 56.

46. President's Commission on Law Enforcement and Administration of Justice, *Corrections*.

47. H. Weeks, "The Highfields Project," in R. Giallombardo, ed., *Juvenile Delinquency* (New York: John Wiley 1972), pp. 551–564.

48. L. Empey and J. Rabow, "The Provo Experiment in Delinquency Rehabilitation," in Giallombardo, *Juvenile Delinquency*, pp. 531–550.

49. Weeks, "Highfields Project," pp. 551–564.

50. Paul Lerman, "Evaluative Studies of Institutions for Delinquents: Implications for Research and Social Policy," *Social Work*, 13 (1968): 55–64.

51. Robert Wicks, *Correctional Psychology* (San Francisco: Canfield Press, 1974), p. 57.

52. Roy Gerard, "Institutional Innovations in Juvenile Corrections," *Federal Probation*, 34, no. 4 (1970): 37–44.

53. H. Cohen and J. Filipczak, *A New Learning Environment* (San Francisco: Jossey-Bass, 1971).

54. Dale Mann, *Intervening with Convicted Serious Juvenile Offenders* (Washington, D.C.: National Institute for Juvenile Justice and Delinquency Prevention, Department of Justice, 1976), p. 28.

55. William Glasser, *Reality Therapy* (New York: Harper Colophon Books, 1975).

56. Ibid., pp. 104–106.

57. Solomon, *Community Corrections,* pp. 107–108.

58. M. Wolfgang, R. Figlio, and T. Sellin, *Delinquency in a Birth Cohort* (Chicago: University of Chicago Press, 1972), p. 252.

59. Giallombardo, *Social World of Imprisoned Girls,* pp. 121–144.

60. Solomon, *Community Corrections,* p. 104.

61. Sarri and Vinter, "Justice for Whom?", p. 70.

62. *Inmates* v. *Affleck,* 346 F. Supp. 1354 (D.P.I. 1972); *Morales* v. *Turman,* 364 F. Supp. 166 (Tex. 1973); *Nelson* v. *Heyne,* 491 F.2d 352 (7th Cir., 1974).

63. President's Commission on Law Enforcement and Administration of Justice, *Corrections,* pp. 149–150.

64. Ibid.

65. Ibid.

66. National Advisory Commission, *Corrections,* pp. 389–408.

67. Marc Riedel and Terence Thornberry, "The Effectiveness of Correctional Programs: An Assessment of the Field," in B. Krisberg and J. Austin, eds. *The Children of Ishmael* (Palo Alto, Calif.: Mayfield Publishing, 1978), pp. 418–432.

68. *Morrissey* v. *Brewer,* 408 U.S. 471 (1972).

69. Malcolm Goddard, "Juvenile Parole Revocation Hearings: The New York State Experience," *Criminal Law Bulletin,* 13 (1973):553.

70. Senna and Siegel, *Juvenile Law,* p. 421.

11 Innovations in the Juvenile Justice Process

In recent years, the juvenile justice process has come under serious critical examination in the United States. Empirical studies and reports from individuals who have extensive contact with the juvenile court have emphasized the court's shortcomings and have called for some major changes. Some have suggested abolishing the juvenile court altogether; others have proposed stricter due process protections; still others have advocated a decrease in the use of the juvenile court in dealing with deviant youngsters.

This chapter examines four current areas of innovation in juvenile justice: *removal of status offenders from the juvenile court, child advocacy, deinstitutionalization,* and *diversion.* The first three areas involve change within the juvenile court itself. By removing status offenders from the jurisdiction of the court, for example, alternative forms of treatment that are less stigmatizing and less punitive could be employed. This would reduce the number of juveniles who are processed through the court and possibly be of more benefit to both the child and the community.

The second area, child advocacy, involves increased representation of individual children who come into contact with the juvenile justice system and other child-welfare agencies. Child advocacy emphasizes the right of the child to be handled in a just manner, and supports assertive efforts to insure that the rights of children are not violated. Thus, for example, in court proceedings, advocacy by the defense attorney would require a vigorous defense of the client's interests.

Deinstitutionalization and community-based corrections are aimed at developing alternatives to incarceration. Instead of relying on training schools and reformatories for juvenile care, alternatives such as half-way houses and group homes are used. Community-based corrections programs are thought to be more humane and more therapeutic than traditional institutions.

The final area, diversion, is concerned with the implementation of programs that will divert juveniles away from the juvenile justice system either before they are arrested or after they have been officially taken into custody. Diversion projects have burgeoned in the last few years in response to growing evidence that contact with the juvenile justice process can have detrimental effects on many youngsters.

This chapter does not cover all of the current trends in the United States but rather describes the most important new approaches to the problem of delinquency. It should be noted that underlying all of these innovations is the belief that children are harmed by the present juvenile justice system, especially juveniles who have committed only minor offenses. All the new ideas presented in this chapter represent attempts to alter the existing situation and to implement programs that will avoid the type of damage that has been done to juveniles in the past.

Removal of Status Offenders from the Juvenile Court

In December 1974, the Directors of the National Council on Crime and Delinquency (NCCD) adopted a policy that calls for the removal of status offenders from the jurisdiction of the juvenile court. This policy recognized the failure of the court to rehabilitate status offenders and acknowledged the unwarranted punishment suffered by these children. Research on status offenders has indicated the following.

1. Juvenile status offenders are incarcerated as long as or longer than children who are committed for rape, aggravated assault, and other felonies classified as 'FBI index crimes.'
2. The younger the offender, the longer the period of institutionalization.
3. Classification for rehabilitation lengthens the period of institutionalization and does not reduce the rate of recidivism.
4. Children with the longest institutional sentences have the highest rate of parole revocation.[1]

Clearly, there is no justification for the incarceration of juveniles who have committed noncriminal offenses. The NCCD policy calls for the utilization of noncoercive community services in providing treatment for status offenders. Family counseling, youth service bureaus, and increased educational and employment opportunities are thought to be more beneficial to children than handling by the juvenile justice system.

Although the NCCD policy is gaining support, status offenders remain under the jurisdiction of the juvenile court. However, there has been some change in the type of treatment these juveniles receive while they are in custody, partly as a result of federal government requirements for funding. To qualify for federal monies for juvenile justice, states must provide separate facilities for children who have committed status offenses. (See Chapter 8.) This requirement will help put an end to the practice of holding children who have run away from home or broken curfew in the same facility with children who have committed crimes.

Diversion of offenders may also serve to keep many minor offenders out of the juvenile justice system. Alternative programs could provide status offenders with community-based services similar to those described by the NCCD. Unfortunately these programs do not always operate outside of the jurisdiction of the court. In some instances, difficult cases may be referred back to the court for adjudication or other action, but these programs do represent an important step in the direction of decreasing the number of juveniles who come into contact with the court.

Child Advocacy

Equality for blacks, women, and other minority groups was the central focus of social movements in the United States during the 1960s. As an offshoot of these growing demands for civil rights, an interest in the rights of children emerged. The current children's rights movement has stressed such issues as religious freedom, school desegregation, freedom of expression, school discipline, the right to education, and procedural due process in the courts.[2] Supreme Court decisions and legislation have greatly modified the position of children and have curtailed long-established practices in the treatment of the young.

Children constitute a large and very vulnerable minority group. They have no voice in the political and legal process and until recently, have had few advocates in their behalf. Even those groups that did claim to be working for the child's welfare often took steps that were harmful to children or that infringed on their rights, as has been the case in many procedures in the juvenile justice process in the past. The children's rights movement has sought to assert the rights of children by working with individuals, agencies, and public bodies that serve children, and to provide avenues for redress of grievances with the schools, child-care agencies, the police, and the courts. One of these avenues has been the establishment of child-advocate services. Child advocates represent children and *their* needs as opposed to the needs of the parents or the community. Through individual casework and community-action projects, the child advocate attempts to uphold the rights of the child.

Advocates of children's rights have also appeared in the juvenile court. Organizations lobby for changes in juvenile law and encourage change in the administration of the law in the juvenile justice system.[3] Alternatives to the juvenile justice system are also encouraged and developed by these organizations. Child advocacy has affected many of the attitudes of court personnel and has influenced the overall perspective on the treatment of juveniles.

One major change concerns the function of defense counsel in juvenile court proceedings. Traditionally, the role of defense counsel in the juvenile court has been a difficult one for many lawyers to fill. After the *Gault* decision, some people feared that the introduction of attorneys would completely undermine the humane and rehabilitative philosophy of the court. Many argued that the adversary role of defense counsel should be suppressed and that the goal of counsel should be to obtain appropriate and needed treatment for clients.

The problems that resulted from this interpretation have been discussed in a previous chapter, which emphasized the fact that juveniles are often given only minimal defense. Naturally, this weakens the rights of juveniles. Recently, many attorneys have adopted a different perspective on the defense of juveniles. This new stance is often referred to as *juvenile justice advocacy.*

Juvenile justice advocacy rejects the idea that a juvenile's defense should be different from that of an adult. Adopting an adversarial posture, the attorney works toward an adjudication that is favorable to the child. If the child is adjudged delinquent, defense counsel works to obtain a disposition that is acceptable to the child. Advocacy for juveniles rejects the assumption that counsel should serve as an adjunct to the court. Besharov makes the following observation:

> The pleasing but puerile notion that the attorney must act as the guardian of the objectives of the juvenile justice system should be put to rest. The court is the guardian of the values of the system. The defense attorney's role must be to represent his client vigorously and wholeheartedly.[4]

An adversarial stance has resulted from disillusionment with the ability of the juvenile court to help juveniles and a belief among some lawyers that minimal intervention into the child's life is most beneficial to both society and the child. The failure of the juvenile justice system to help children is widely acknowledged, and the fact that inappropriate detention or placement can actually harm juveniles is a major concern among child advocates. In recent years, there has been considerable evidence to suggest that children are in many cases better off if they are left alone; naturally, findings such as these have encouraged further critical appraisal of the supposedly benevolent juvenile justice system.

Others have explained an adversarial stance in terms of the professional and personal obligations required of attorneys under their Code of Professional Responsibility. The juvenile wants to be free, and the lawyer must represent him "zealously within the bounds of the law."[5] Defense counsel must be aware of ways to assert a client's rights without antagonizing the juvenile judge or other court personnel but does not have to abdicate the role of advocate for the child. Because good relations with the judge or probation officer are crucial and may enhance the receptiveness of the court to argument, it is very important for advocates to familiarize themselves with court procedures and philosophy and to reduce the chance of undue antagonism.

Besharov has summarized the role of defense counsel as advocate as follows:

> Advocacy, of any sort, is not gentle business. A person's freedom and integrity is at stake in *every* proceeding. Defense counsel must 'play rough' if that serves the need of his client. He must be careful not to confuse his young client's legal rights with his client's ultimate interests. Interests do not necessarily mean the need for treatment. In most cases the youth's interests are to get out of the system or to minimize intervention rather than to prove a legal point. At all stages defense counsel must be ready to take advantage of the systems commitment to diversion and non-judicial handling for his client's ultimate benefit. As one form of advocacy, counsel may assume the traditional role during the adjudicatory stage of putting the state to its proof and asserting an affirmative defense, if there is one. Counsel of course may be troubled if his client requires assistance or guidance—but that would be true of an attorney representing an adult defendant as well. There is no reason why counsel should see his role differently. If this client needs help and if his client is willing to accept it, help is just as available without formal court action.[6]

The children's rights movement is a relatively new movement in this country but eventually may have a great impact on many areas of children's rights. The changing role of defense counsel may well eliminate much of the informality previously found in juvenile court and also decrease the number of children who are adjudged delinquent and incarcerated. The practices of other child-welfare agencies may also change as they are given closer scrutiny and as legal statutes guaranteeing certain rights of children become more widespread.

Deinstitutionalization

A new philosophy of juvenile corrections is beginning to emerge in response to the strong criticism of today's juvenile institutions. This new philosophy, which is sometimes called *community-based corrections* or *deinstitutionalization,* emphasizes the need for treatment programs that will be located within the community and that will provide alternatives to existing juvenile institutions.

One of the most frequent challenges to traditional correctional programs has been the failure of training schools or other institutions to reform children who have been incarcerated. No doubt, the high recidivism rates of many institutions result from the fact that only limited efforts have been made to provide effective treatment. The following statement provides an accurate description of the types of practices that are commonly used in many training schools, reformatories, forestry camps, and other such institutions.

> Punishment is a key organizing principle of traditional training schools. There are efforts at vocational and general education in the training schools, but the institutions are basically custodial and authoritarian. Resocialization efforts are commonly reduced to instruments for creating conformity, deference to adult authority, and obedience to rules. Regimented marching formations, shaved heads and close haircuts, omnipresent officials, and punitive disciplinary measures have been the authoritative marks of the training school, along with the manipulation of privileges, such as cigarette smoking, television viewing, home visits, or release to reward compliance.[7]

Clearly, such an environment does little to encourage rehabilitation or reform and may even increase deviant behavior by exposing juveniles to other offenders who are more antisocial and more sophisticated in criminal behavior.

Perhaps the greatest irony of these institutions is that the expense of constructing and operating them is quite high. The cost of building a new institution is estimated at $20,000 per bed,[8] and the yearly cost per case for keeping a juvenile incarcerated is estimated at between $16,000 and $54,000.[9] The cost per case for probation, parole, or aftercare is approximately 10 percent of the cost of incarceration.[10] Incarceration, then, requires large allocations of funds but does *not* lead to appreciable improvements in behavior.

Another area of concern related to incarceration involves the effects of labeling on a youngster (see Chapter 3). Some researchers have suggested that any contact with the juvenile justice system may be stigmatizing to a child, and surely confinement in a training school or reformatory must be one of the *most* stigmatizing experiences. The fact is that all incarcerated youngsters suffer from the label of "delinquent," regardless of whether they are status offenders, have committed serious offenses, or are deprived. Then, even after the juvenile has been released, negative experiences with employers, school personnel, and members of the community may continue to reinforce the label, thus making it very difficult for the child to overcome the stigma of being a "delinquent."

An additional challenge to juvenile institutions comes from research that has exposed discriminatory practices in the way that decisions are made regarding which juveniles to incarcerate in the first place. As we have discussed in previous chapters, delinquent behavior is found throughout the social structure, but the poor and members of minority groups are much more likely to come into contact with the juvenile justice system than are other children. For example, when children from middle-class backgrounds commit offenses they are frequently diverted or treated by private agencies within the community. Recently, practitioners have begun to call for similar, community-based programs for the poor.

Another major criticism of juvenile institutions concerns protecting the civil rights of children. After Supreme Court decisions outlined the due process rights of juveniles, some courts began to focus on the "right to treatment" for youngsters. Cases in federal courts have examined the conditions that exist in institutions and have argued that rehabilitation must be the goal of these facilities. Practices such as corporal punishment, the administration of unauthorized tranquilizing drugs, the use of "strip-cells" and solitary confinement, and the lack of educational opportunities have been condemned in court decisions.[11] Minimum standards for care and treatment have been called for, instead of the systematic warehousing of juveniles that is so common today.

These challenges to institutions for juveniles have presented state correctional systems with the problem of implementing programs that will replace existing ones. This task has already been undertaken in some states and is beginning to be implemented in others. The wide variation among 46 states in developing community-based treatment programs is shown in Table 11-1. Surprisingly there are as many states showing an increase in the number of youths confined in institutions as there are states showing decreases.[12] Per-

TABLE 11-1. PERCENT OF JUVENILE OFFENDERS IN COMMUNITY-BASED PROGRAMS BY STATE, 1974

STATE	PERCENT	STATE	PERCENT
Massachusetts	86.6	Pennsylvania	11.7
South Dakota	59.1	Colorado	11.4
Minnesota	50.9	Kentucky	10.8
Utah	50.3	Mississippi	9.0
Oregon	48.6	West Virginia	8.8
North Dakota	43.4	Tennessee	8.6
Maryland	42.0	Oklahoma	8.3
Kansas	41.5	Illinois	8.2
Idaho	30.4	Rhode Island	7.4
Michigan	28.5	Ohio	6.3
Florida	25.2	Georgia	3.7
Montana	25.0	Delaware	3.6
Wyoming	24.7	South Carolina	3.5
Vermont	23.8	Arkansas	3.2
Arizona	20.8	California	2.9
Connecticut	20.6	Texas	2.8
New Jersey	17.7	Maine	2.0
Alabama	17.0	Nebraska	1.5
Missouri	14.8	Alaska	0
Hawaii	13.6	Indiana	0
Nevada	13.0	Louisiana	0
Wisconsin	12.4	New Mexico	0
Virginia	12.0	North Carolina	0

Source: Robert D. Vinter, George Downs, and John Hall, "Juvenile Corrections in the States: Residential Programs and Deinstitutionalization. A Preliminary Report." (Ann Arbor: National Assessment of Juvenile Corrections Project, University of Michigan, November 1975), p. 51.

haps the success of new programs will encourage deinstitutionalization in those states that have not yet begun to move away from training schools and reformatories.

Closing Institutions in Massachusetts

In 1969 Dr. Jerome Miller was appointed commissioner of the Massachusetts Department of Youth Services. Dr. Miller assumed the leadership of a system of juvenile correctional institutions that had been the subject of many critical studies and investigations. A mandate for reform had emerged, and within two years institutions in Massachusetts began to be closed.[13]

Initially, the new commissioner's intention was to humanize the treatment of offenders and to develop therapeutic communities within institutional facilities. Therapeutic communities required a small, democratically run unit in which staff and children would present and discuss all decisions at cottage meetings. This approach contrasted sharply with established training school policies and was resisted by many staff members. Resistance to change in the institutions ultimately led to deinstitutionalization.

The difficulties encountered in attempting to change the beliefs and philosophy of institutional staff led to the conclusion that the therapeutic community concept could only be implemented in a few select cottages. Miller suggested that such programs would be much more successful on the outside in a community setting. In the community, additional professional resources would be available for volunteer and purchased services, and there would not be the negative expectations typically found in correctional institutions. In 1971, major institutions in Massachusetts began to be closed, and alternative treatment programs based in the community were established.

One aspect of the community-based programs involved placing children in already-existing agencies in the community. Group homes were set up, and nonresidential programs were developed. Day or night programs allowed youngsters to participate while living at home or in some other setting. Nonresidential programs included Neighborhood Youth Corps, a recreation program at the Massachusetts Maritime Academy, and programs conducted in conjunction with colleges. Foster homes and parole were also used.

One problem that resulted from the deinstitutionalization process concerned the placement of dangerous and disturbed offenders. Obviously there are some juveniles who simply cannot be placed in community-based programs because they require a more secure setting. The department has tried to purchase services for these types of offenders in intensive-care placements. Custodial security is maintained, but treatment is handled by private agencies and by the Department of Mental Health.

The changes that were implemented in Massachusetts can serve as a model for other states that want to curtail the use of incarceration. Although the approach used in Massachusetts is not without flaws and problems, it does provide an example of the types of alternative programs that can be implemented and the types of resistance to deinstitutionalization that are typically encountered. Preliminary evaluation reveals lower recidivism rates for juveniles who are placed in the community and higher recidivism rates for those placed in secure facilities,[14] but there are some serious flaws in the way this evaluation was conducted.[15] Perhaps the only conclusion that can be drawn is that deinstitutionalization is at least as effective as incarceration, and considerably less expensive.

Community-Based Corrections: A Description

Community-based corrections include: 1) programs for juveniles who have not been incarcerated, such as probation and nonresidential care; 2) programs that are alternatives to incarceration, such as residential treatment; and 3) programs that serve juveniles after incarceration, such as half-way houses. All of these approaches are thought to offer more humane treatment, enable the offender to become reintegrated back into the community as a law-abiding citizen, and provide less expensive treatment than is available in secure institutions. Because steps must be taken to protect the community from potentially dangerous offenders, screening of juveniles is necessary. Yet many offenders who are not dangerous should and can be treated effectively in a local agency.

Community-based corrections can utilize citizen expertise on a volunteer or purchased service basis. Other community resources, such as vocational schools or the YMCA, may be enlisted to offer juveniles more effective treatment, recreation, and educational and vocational training. Efforts can be made to develop positive community ties, improve family relationships, and foster a sense of inclusion rather than one of exclusion among juveniles. Through this process the community can be actively involved in helping to solve the community problem of delinquency.

Several types of programs are common in community-based corrections. Nonresidential and group home programs are frequently used with juveniles, and an increasing number of half-way houses have been designed for juveniles who have been released from incarceration.

Nonresidential Programs   These are structured correctional programs that do not include "live-in" requirements but that do supervise substantial portions of the youngster's day. The clients usually need more intensive services than would be provided by probation but do not require institutionalization. Services include educational and vocational training, counseling, guided group interaction, and family therapy.

Foster and Group Homes   When difficulties in the home environment require that the child be taken out of it, foster and group homes are utilized. Foster homes are often considered to be less effective than group homes owing to the lack of training of foster parents and the absence of other supportive services.

Group homes are quasi-institutions with house parents who are actually paid staff members. The group home provides the child with semi-independence from the family but also offers a supportive environment. This setting is thought to be preferable to providing another family structure, for it offers emotional support and at the same time gives the child more freedom.

Group homes are usually small with six to ten juveniles living together with house "parents" who are actually counselors. Other community resources may be used when needed to supplement their skills.

Half-way Houses   Originally half-way houses were designed to treat offenders who were half way *out* of an institution. Today, half-way houses are also used for those who are half way *into* the juvenile justice system (or those who are on probation).

These homes are similar in structure to the group homes described earlier. They may provide a home for a juvenile with either no home or many family problems, an alternative to training school for other juveniles, or a prerelease community experience for those leaving institutions.[16]

The Future of Community Corrections

The move toward community-based treatment for juveniles is gaining momentum in the United States. There are still some states that plan to build more institutions for juveniles, but perhaps the success of deinstitutionalization efforts will discourage new construction.[17] Evaluation of community-based programs has been positive; they are at least as effective as incarceration and some studies have found them to be more effective.[18]

In addition to a desire to decrease recidivism rates, there are other considerations that must be taken into account. Increased citizen and community involvement with offenders is possible; existing community resources may be used to individualize treatment and expand services; and future adjustment in the community is enhanced by opportunities for juveniles to create or strengthen their ties to others. All these benefits should be considered when evaluating community treatment.

Community-based treatment is not without its own potential dangers, however, and care must be taken to monitor the functioning of these programs. Juveniles who really need intensive treatment may not receive it owing to overcrowded facilities or a lack of rigor in the administration of group homes or half-way houses. Often screening and surveillance of youth are inadequate, which exposes the community to unnecessary dangers. There is also the possibility that these techniques will be seen as so benign that children formerly diverted from the juvenile justice process will become subject to intervention by community-based treatment agencies.[19]

Other potential problems concern citizen reaction to the presence of offenders in the community. Juvenile delinquents are not readily accepted in quiet residential communities for a variety of reasons, ranging from fear of victimization to fear that neighborhood children will fall under the negative influence of offenders. Commercial-residential locations, areas adjoining light industrial sections, or areas in transition are the most receptive to half-way houses and group homes, but these areas are often disorganized and deteriorated and may expose children to deviant behavior and opportunities for illegal acts.[20]

Placing a group home in a community and calling it community based does not insure that it will adhere to the community-based philosophy. In reality, such programs may have virtually no ties to the community and thus suffer from the same kind of isolation found in traditional institutions.[21] Citizen involvement and good relations between the institution and the community must be actively cultivated if reintegration of juveniles is to be achieved.

Diversion

Throughout our discussion of juvenile justice the use of discretion in making decisions to divert juveniles out of the court has been noted. Police officers may choose to send a child home instead of to court; probation or intake staff may decide to divert rather than file a petition; in some cases, the judge may dismiss the charges. The number of youngsters who come into contact with the police is quite large in comparison to the number who are adjudicated delinquent and incarcerated. Figure 11-1 shows this estimated flow of cases from detection to disposition in the juvenile justice system during a one-year period.

Diversion of juveniles from the juvenile justice process has been possible due to the wide discretionary powers held by those involved in the system, the informality of the system, and the emphasis on treatment and rehabilitation. Because not all youngsters require formal treatment, the use of informal methods has been strongly encouraged. Recent analyses of the negative effects of the juvenile justice process on children have encouraged an even greater emphasis on dealing with juveniles outside of the court.

No one definition of diversion is used consistently across the United States, but generally the objectives of diversion are described in one of two ways. It is a process that 1) minimizes penetration of the client into the juvenile justice system; or 2) serves as an alternative to initial entry into the juvenile

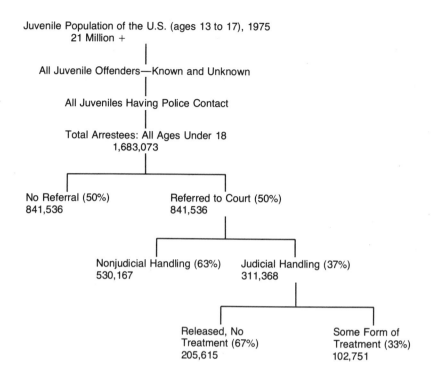

Juvenile Population of the U.S. (ages 13 to 17), 1975
21 Million +

All Juvenile Offenders—Known and Unknown

All Juveniles Having Police Contact

Total Arrestees: All Ages Under 18
1,683,073

No Referral (50%)
841,536

Referred to Court (50%)
841,536

Nonjudicial Handling (63%)
530,167

Judicial Handling (37%)
311,368

Released, No
Treatment (67%)
205,615

Some Form of
Treatment (33%)
102,751

Source: Dale Mann, *Intervening With Convicted Serious Juvenile Offenders* (National Institute for Juvenile Justice and Delinquency Prevention, Washington, D.C.: U.S. Government Printing Office, 1976), p. 8.

Figure 11-1. Juvenile population and offenders by types and stages of adjudication.

justice system.[22] Diversion tactics that minimize penetration would include referrals to agencies within the community or dismissal of charges. Those that provide alternatives to initial contact with the system center around diversion by police, schools, or welfare agencies. Instead of referring the juvenile to the intake staff of the juvenile court, the child would be released or dealt with by a non-court agency.

The concept of diversion is not a new one in juvenile justice. What is new, is the current diversion "explosion."[23] Efforts to vastly expand the volume of juvenile cases that are diverted have become widespread. Diversion programming was stimulated by the President's Commission on Law Enforcement and the Administration of Justice in 1967. These ideas were then further encouraged by the "national strategy" for delinquency prevention set up in the early 1970s.[24]

The arguments presented by advocates of diversion cover a wide range of concerns. Klein has suggested that the rationales are numerous and sometimes conflicting. He has described them as follows:

1. Diversion may override the biases in the juvenile justice system, since criteria for releasing or detaining suspects will be explicit and applied more equitably.
2. Diversion will decrease the volume of cases in the juvenile justice system by handling nonserious cases in alternative ways.
3. Diversion is less expensive than system processing.
4. Diversion will decrease the stigmatization of youngsters since negative labels such as "delinquent" are not applied.
5. Diversion protects naive young offenders from exposure to more hardened offenders.
6. Diversion to alternative treatment agencies may expose the child to effective treatment, rather than the ineffective programs of the juvenile court.[25]

Klein's description of diversion is commonly held by individuals who work in diversion projects or who advocate their adoption. Theoretically, there is good reason to believe that the benefits described above could be provided by diversion. Discriminatory practices in the use of discretion have been discussed previously in relation to police, probation officers, and judges. The overload of cases and the high cost of juvenile proceedings are realities in many courts. The negative effects that the juvenile justice process has on juveniles and the ineffectiveness of existing treatment programs have been underscored by the high recidivism rates of most training schools and reformatories. Diversion, or alternatives to the juvenile justice process, may help circumvent these problems.

Models of Diversion

Diversion may occur either prior to referral to the juvenile justice process or after the child has entered it. Communities, schools, parents, and the police may divert children rather than referring them to the court. And after referral to the court has occurred, a child may be diverted by a probation officer or the judge.

Diversion projects attempt to formalize these diversion decisions and to maximize the use of alternatives to official handling of cases. These projects do not fall into neat categories since there is much variation in their structure and functions, but there are two major locations for diversion projects. Projects are often part of the existing juvenile justice process. For example, police and probation diversion projects are developed and operated by branches of the juvenile system. Other diversion projects are externally located; these are often community-based programs designed to treat juveniles outside of the juvenile justice system.

Police Diversion   In Chapter 8, in which the intake stage of the juvenile court was discussed, the broad discretionary power of the police was described. Officers may choose to arrest, release, or refer juveniles, and it is estimated that at least 50 percent of their contacts with youngsters result in release.[26] This gate-keeping role of law enforcement personnel is extremely important in that it greatly affects the lives of many children and also determines the volume and type of cases that ultimately pass through the juvenile system.

Much research has been conducted to ascertain patterns in police decisions with juveniles, and there is evidence that their discretion is not always applied equitably. A multitude of factors influence the officer's evaluation of a case. Goldman specifies thirteen such factors which may come into play with police in a determination of how a particular child should be handled:

1. The police officer's opinion of and attitude toward the juvenile court.
2. The police officer's previous experiences with minority group members, parents of juveniles, or with the juvenile court.
3. Concern about possible criticism from the court.
4. Potential public reaction to informal handling of the case.
5. Concern for the police image in the community if disrespectful juveniles are treated too leniently.
6. Inconvenience for the officer, as in potential court appearances.
7. Interest group pressure.
8. The officer's personal evaluation of the particular offense.
9. The officer's evaluation of the juvenile's family situation.
10. The demeanor of the juvenile.
11. Perception of black children as more in need of formal handling.
12. Seriousness of the offense.
13. Each member of a group of juveniles will be handled similarly.[27]

From Goldman's analysis of police decision making, it can be seen that the offense, the characteristics of the child, the reputation of the juvenile court, and the officer's personal experiences are all important factors in evaluating a particular case. Additional influences that could be added to those listed above are departmental structure and policy.[28] These may encourage all officers to react to juvenile misconduct in a particular way, typically in either a treatment-oriented or punishment-oriented manner.

Although discretion is often looked upon with disdain, it is not necessarily a negative practice. Flexibility in the handling of juveniles is certainly desirable if the treatment philosophy of the juvenile justice system is to be realized. The problem with discretion then is really one concerning its application. Equitable decision making by police could decrease the stigmatizing effects of a delinquent label and discourage the adoption of deviant identities by juveniles.

Discretionary power in making arrest decisions concerning juveniles is not used in the same manner or with the same frequency in all police departments. There is variation across departments and even within departments. Certain officers in a given department may routinely release far more (or less) juveniles than their fellow officers.[29] Rates of diversion range from 95 percent of all cases handled informally to 2 percent (or lower).[30] Some police do not condone the use of diversion with juveniles for they see this alternative as antithetical to the police role—their rationale is that deterrence of future offenses may be undermined if children see that nothing will be done to them. Departments that do attempt to increase the use of diversion and that refer juveniles to agencies other than the juvenile court may encounter resistance from officers who do not support this philosophy.

Early efforts to establish a treatment-oriented approach to juveniles centered around juvenile units within police departments. Specialized training in the problems of adolescence and the nature of the juvenile justice system emphasized a role much more like that of a social worker. Instead of viewing the child as a "perpetrator," officers were to consider the needs of the child. Liaison procedures with public and private youth and family service agencies were established, as well as police-community relations programs.[31]

Today expansion of the police role in diversion of offenders is being encouraged throughout the United States. Diversion or release of juveniles is not sufficient, however, and police referral of children is being stressed. In the past some departments have utilized informal practices, such as a "police probation" system, which is actually an extension of their discretionary powers. Juveniles who are placed on "probation" are warned that another arrest will result in their adjudication as a delinquent.[32] This type of in-house treatment limits the range of services that can be offered to children. Programs have been developed to familiarize officers with resources available in the community and to encourage the use of these alternatives in lieu of formal handling of cases.

Police diversion projects have been established in many departments to develop appropriate diversion practices by officers. Such projects may originate within the department or result from initiatives by outside agencies, such as state planning boards. Funding of projects comes from the department, civic sources, or outside government and provides for additional staff and in-house counselors who handle referrals.

Diversion by law enforcement personnel provides youngsters with a second chance by referring them to an agency or treatment program that may help them avoid further delinquency. Formalized diversion programs encourage the use of alternatives to arrest, familiarize officers with what criteria should be used in making diversion decisions, and educate police about available community facilities. Hopefully, these practices will be beneficial to both the child and the community.

Police have also implemented programs designed to prevent delinquent behavior, which in a sense is another form of diversion. Police-community relations units often offer many police-sponsored activities for juveniles in the neighborhood. A survey by the International Association of Chiefs of Police found that the following programs were frequently used in police-community relations work with juveniles:

1. Recreational programs.
2. Public image improvement programs—these usually involve close work with juveniles in informal meetings, such as "rap" sessions, "hot lines," and hang-out patrols.
3. Community responsibility and awareness programs—these include public safety and crime prevention training and the organization of neighborhood groups of youth who take part in resolving community problems (gang truce meetings and tension patrols).
4. Traffic, personal, and general safety training.
5. Job counseling for teenagers.[33]

Many other programs are run by police throughout the United States to develop good relations between police and youngsters. Perhaps one of the best ways for officers to get to know juveniles is through police-school liaison programs.[34] Police serve as resource persons for school personnel and may counsel individual students, lecture classes, and investigate school vandalism. Working in the school on a full-time basis allows the officer to get to know the students and vice versa. It demonstrates that police have a sincere interest in young people and a willingness to become actively involved with them.

Diversion Based Outside of the Juvenile Justice Process

Police diversion projects are among the most popular diversion programs at present, although diversion may be conducted by probation officers or even public defenders in some courts.[35] Law enforcement agencies may prevent a child from entering the juvenile justice system and so there has been a concentration on diversion at this stage in the process. Programs developed by the juvenile court, such as probation diversion, can only minimize the amount of exposure a child has to the court.

Since referral is an integral part of the diversion process, organizations that will receive referrals from the police and the courts are needed. The following

section describes two such organizations, Youth Service Bureaus and the
Youth Development and Delinquency Prevention Administration.

Youth Service Bureaus   The development of Youth Service Bureaus
(YSB) as community agencies for the diversion of juveniles from the juvenile
justice system was recommended initially in 1967 by the President's Commission on Law Enforcement and the Administration of Justice. A year later,
the National Council on Crime and Delinquency conducted a major study of
this concept and offered a detailed outline of the structure and functioning
of Youth Service Bureaus.

These youth service agencies are to coordinate services for young people
in the community, to provide additional needed services for youth, and to
receive juveniles (both delinquent and nondelinquent) referred by the police,
court, parents, schools, or self-referrals. Youth Service Bureaus can then
perform three major functions.

1. *Service brokerage.* The YSB bridges the gap between available services
   and youth in need of them by referral, follow-up, and advocacy for the
   child on a voluntary basis.
2. *Resource development.* The YSB encourages citizens to participate in
   the development of new services for youth, contracts for services that
   would otherwise be unavailable, and encourages existing agencies to
   expand their services.
3. *Systems modification.* The YSB constructively evaluates existing attitudes and practices that may contribute to the antisocial behavior of
   youth and makes recommendations for improvement.[36]

These agencies would service youngsters between the ages of 7 and 18 and
would not be part of the juvenile justice system. Treatment of juveniles would
be noncoercive and aimed at preventing future delinquency.

Ideally the Youth Service Bureau would be sponsored by state or local
government and would operate as an independent, public agency. Citizen
input would be provided for by a supervisory board made up of members of
the community. This supervisory board would appoint and oversee staff in
the agency. Citizen volunteer programs and citizen committees would also
be directly involved in the functioning of the bureau.

The Youth Service Bureau would ideally accept *all* referrals, in order to
avoid unfair referral practices. Children who are referred to this agency participate on a voluntary basis and are included in the problem-identification
and problem-solving process. Efforts must be made to insure that appropriate
services are given to the child after referral and that information about the
case is disclosed to others only with the child's consent. Suggested services
include individual and group counseling, foster home and group home place-

ment, recreational and work programs, remedial or vocational education, and employment counseling.

Although the Youth Service Bureau concept emphasized voluntary and noncoercive practices, the 1967 President's Commission recommended the use of court referral for some cases. Juveniles who ignored available help or were not being effectively treated could be sent to the juvenile court by the Youth Service Bureau. These agencies, which are designed as alternatives to the juvenile justice process, could use the authority of the court to encourage cooperation from juveniles.

Youth Service Bureaus have been established across the United States in a wide range of communities. A national census in 1972 found 150 bureaus operating throughout the country, and it appeared that this type of program is a somewhat popular one in delinquency prevention.[37] The Youth Service Bureau concept has encouraged the proliferation of many other types of community-based alternatives to the juvenile justice process. The basic structure has been adapted to particular community needs in some diversion agencies.

Youth Development and Delinquency Prevention Administration   A national strategy for delinquency prevention that focuses on the diversion of juveniles in the community has been developed by the Youth Development and Delinquency Prevention Administration (YDDPA), a part of the U.S. Department of Health, Education, and Welfare. The strategy calls for nationwide youth services systems that will divert juveniles into community-based treatment programs.

YDDPA is the focal point for programs located *outside* of the juvenile justice process. The major functions of YDDPA have been outlined as follows.

1. Integration and improvement of existing programs and development of new programs
2. Acting as a youth advocate and providing technical assistance
3. Developing youth services systems.[38]

YDDPA helps communities plan, develop, and finance youth service systems. It can provide coordination with other federal departments and agencies affecting youth. It can help reduce negative labeling of juveniles by increasing the utilization of resources offered to the general youth population rather than relying on those that are specifically designed for delinquents.

This nationwide strategy seeks to bring about a basic change in society's reliance on institutionalization through the use of youth service systems. But in order to effectively decrease juvenile exposure to the juvenile justice system, alternative institutions must be available. If they were widespread and effectively utilized, youth service systems could greatly limit the flow of children into the juvenile court. The YDDPA approach seeks to expand and improve these youth service systems in order to reduce the number of children in the juvenile court and, in effect, limit the role of the juvenile institution in society.

Diversion: A Critical Appraisal

The diversion of juveniles out of the juvenile justice system has been encouraged to protect the welfare of both the child and society. Diversion is cheaper, is supposedly less stigmatizing for the child, and is thought to be more effective in curbing future delinquency than the traditional juvenile justice system. Various types of diversion programs have been implemented throughout the United States, as well as the YDDPA, which will oversee and encourage development of diversion programs on a national level. Diversion of offenders is perhaps the most popular concept in juvenile justice today, but no long-term evaluation of its actual effects has been conducted. However, some limited information is available, and it is important that these preliminary findings be closely examined.

First, diversion practices are based on the ideas of labeling theory, which assumes that contact with the juvenile justice process aggravates deviant behavior and encourages the adoption of deviant self-images by juveniles. The stigma, or negative labels, bestowed on ''official'' delinquents are thought to contribute to negative self-concepts, which in turn lead to increased delinquency. Diversion is thought to reduce this stigma while at the same time providing treatment that is more effective. The expected result of diversion would then be twofold: less negative labeling and reduced recidivism rates.

What are the actual results of diversion on negative labeling? Little research has been conducted comparing diverted juveniles with those who are referred to court, but one study has found that the self-esteem of diverted youngsters is lower than that of juveniles on probation. Another study of diverted youngsters indicated that these juveniles felt they had experienced more negative labeling.[39] Although more data is still needed on the issue of stigmatization, on the basis of what we do know we must question the assumption that diversion is less stigmatizing than contact with the juvenile justice system. Indeed, it has been pointed out that referral to a community agency may in fact be more stigmatizing since referral can be used as a method of social control and might be perceived by the child as an indication that he is somehow different from other juveniles. Carter and Klein have described this situation.

> What is the reaction of a youngster (and his family, his friends, his teachers) when he finds himself enrolled as a 'client' in something called the Community Mental Health Center, or Psychological Services, Inc., or The Youth Counseling Service, or the Drug Abuse Clinic, or The Family Therapy Group? May he not feel that he has left the frying pan for the fire, given up being 'bad' for being 'maladjusted'?[40]

The next issue to be considered is the effect of diversion on recidivism rates. Research results have been inconsistent, with some studies reporting no differences among diverted youngsters and others noting higher recidivism rates among juveniles who receive traditional treatment.[41] Comparisons between diverted and referred children and children released by the police indicated higher recidivism rates among the diverted subjects. This would seem to indicate that release with no referral is the most beneficial method of treating juveniles, diversion is the second most effective treatment, and traditional techniques are the least effective.

So far the data on the effects of diversion have not fully supported the claim that alternative methods are less stigmatizing or more effective in reducing recidivism. In attempting to appraise the value of diversion, we must ask several questions: Does diversion lead to effective treatment? How are diversion decisions made? Are some children diverted who previously would have gone to court? Is diversion substantially altering the population of juveniles in the juvenile justice system?

Diversion does not always mean that a juvenile will receive help. Referral is rare in some police agencies since there is a reluctance to turn the child over to another agency, such as a Youth Service Bureau. In addition, some law enforcement personnel are simply unaware of resources in the community that might assist a juvenile. Interviews with 31 juvenile officers in 2 large California police agencies showed that 25 percent of them could name no community resources and only 2 of them had used direct referral.[42]

When diversion and referral programs are utilized, follow-up examinations have not been encouraging in their implications about how these techniques are administered. The fact is that diversion is often applied to those youngsters who are least likely to commit new offenses in the future, and increased referral of these offenders appears to increase their recidivism rates.[43] In effect, diversion and referral of young minor offenders, who have little or no record, may do them more harm than good. The more serious offenders, those who traditionally have been referred to court, are still being sent to court.

Although the actual practice of diversion and referral of juveniles rarely conforms to recommended patterns, there are nonetheless many good reasons to support the use of alternatives to the juvenile justice process. *Efforts must be made to encourage referral of offenders who formerly would have been sent to court.* Diversion practices must *decrease* the amount of intervention in the lives of juveniles, not *increase* it.

Diversion practices must be carefully supervised to insure that they are not extending the reach of social control over the lives of young people. For some children, treatment by community agencies may not be beneficial and may intervene in their lives more than would traditional approaches. There is evidence that diversion and referral may be particularly damaging to minor offenders. One study found that diverted and referred offenders received between 7 and 12 hours of counseling. A group of similar offenders who had petitions filed were more likely to be released or given informal probation, which entailed minimal supervision and treatment.[44]

Diversion and referral services must concentrate on the treatment of children who otherwise would have a petition filed and who would possibly be incarcerated. Support for and commitment to alternative forms of handling must be encouraged among all individuals and agencies that refer children to the juvenile court. When this goal is accomplished, evaluations of how diversion is being implemented must be conducted so that any weaknesses and problems in these programs can be revealed and then altered.

DISCUSSION QUESTIONS

1. Discuss some possible reasons for the difficulty in having status offenders removed from the jurisdiction of the juvenile court.

2. Compare the role of an attorney who is a juvenile advocate with the description of typical legal representation in juvenile court, which has been presented in previous chapters.

3. Why is there resistance in some states to programs of deinstitutionalization for juveniles?

4. Discuss the positive attributes of community-based correctional programs.

5. Discuss the problems presented by diversion programs. What methods could be used to insure that juveniles who would typically go to court will be diverted?

NOTES

1. National Council on Crime and Delinquency, "Jurisdiction Over Status Offenses Should Be Removed from the Juvenile Court," NCCD Policy Statement (December 1974), p.3.

2. Beatrice Gross and Ronald Gross, *The Children's Rights Movement* (Garden City, N.Y.: Anchor Books, 1977), p. 204.

3. For example, both the Children's Defense Fund and the National Council on Crime and Delinquency perform these functions.

4. Douglas J. Besharov, *Juvenile Justice Advocacy* (New York: Practicing Law Institute, 1974), p. 50.

5. Ibid., p. 48.

6. Ibid., pp. 52–53.

7. Lloyd Ohlin, Alden Miller, and Robert Coates, *Juvenile Correctional Reform in Massachusetts* (Washington, D.C.: Government Printing Office), p. 1.

8. Robert L. Smith, "A Quiet Revolution: Probation Subsidy," in G. Perlstein and T. Phelps, eds., *Alternatives to Prison* (Pacific Palisades, Calif.: Goodyear Publishing, 1975), p. 140.

9. Robert Wagner, "The System Listens But Does Not Hear," *Criminology*, 15, no. 4 (Feb. 1978): 433.

10. Smith, "A Quiet Revolution," p. 139.

11. *Nelson* v. *Heyne*, 491 F. 2d 352 (7th cir., 1974); *Inmates* v. *Affleck*, 346 F. Supp. 1354 (D.R.I. 1972).

12. Ohlin et al., *Juvenile Correctional Reform*, p. 21.

13. Ibid., pp. 1–22.

14. Ibid., p. 78.

15. For a discussion of this evaluation, see Andrew T. Scull, *Decarceration* (Englewood Cliffs, N.J.: Prentice-Hall, 1977), pp. 101–102.

16. National Advisory Commission on Criminal Justice Standards and Goals, *Report of the Task Force on Corrections* (Washington, D.C.: Government Printing Office, 1973), pp. 232–236.

17. Ohlin et al., *Juvenile Correctional Reform*, pp. 23–34.

18. Ibid.

19. Ibid., p. 34.

20. Richard L. Rachin, "So You Want to Open a Half-way House," in Perlstein and Phelps, eds., *Alternatives to Prison*, p. 169.

21. Ohlin et al., p. 25.

22. Robert Carter and Malcolm Klein, eds., *Back on the Street* (Englewood Cliffs, N.J.: Prentice-Hall, 1976), p. xi.

23. Malcolm Klein et al., "The Explosion in Police Diversion Programs: Evaluating the Structural Dimensions of a Social Fad," in Malcolm Klein, ed., *The Juvenile Justice System* (Beverly Hills, Calif.: Sage, 1976), p. 106.

24. Ibid., p. 103.

25. Ibid., pp. 106–107.

26. Ibid., p. 109.

27. Nathan Goldman, "The Differential Selection of Juvenile Offenders for Court Appearance," in W. J. Chambliss, ed., *Crime and the Legal Process* (New York: McGraw-Hill, 1969), pp. 287–288.

28. James Q. Wilson, "The Police and the Delinquent in Two Cities," in Stanton Wheeler, ed., *Controlling Delinquents* (New York: John Wiley, 1968), pp. 9–30.

29. A. W. McEachern and Riva Bauzer, "Factors Related to Disposition in Juvenile Police Contacts," in Malcolm Klein, ed., *Juvenile Gangs in Context: Theory, Research and Action* (Englewood Cliffs, N.J.: Prentice-Hall, 1967), pp. 148–160.

30. Malcolm Klein, "Issues in Police Diversion of Juvenile Offenders," in Robert Carter and Malcolm Klein, eds., *Back on the Street* (Englewood Cliffs, N.J.: Prentice-Hall, 1976), p. 77.

31. Richard Kobetz, *The Police Role and Juvenile Delinquency* (Gaithersburg, Md.: International Association of Chiefs of Police, 1971), pp. 169–191.

32. Klein, "Police Diversion of Juvenile Offenders," p. 79.

33. Kobetz, *Police Role and Juvenile Delinquency*, p. 206.

34. Ibid., pp. 213–214.

35. Andrew Rutherford and Robert McDermott, *Juvenile Diversion* (Washington, D.C.: Government Printing Office, 1976).

36. Sherwood Norman, *The Youth Service Bureau: A Key to Delinquency Prevention* (Paramus, N.J.: National Council on Crime and Delinquency, 1972), pp. 12– 13.

37. National Advisory Commission on Criminal Justice Standards and Goals, *Report on Community Crime Prevention* (Washington, D.C.: Government Printing Office, 1973), p. 56.

38. R. Kobetz, *Police Role and Juvenile Delinquency*, p. 469.

39. D. S. Elliott and Fletcher Blanchard, "An Impact Study of Two Diversion Projects." (Paper delivered at the American Psychological Association Convention, Chicago, Illinois, 1975).

40. Carter and Klein, *Back on the Street*, p. 106.

41. Rutherford and McDermott, *Juvenile Diversion*, pp. 2– 11.

42. Klein, "Police Diversion of Juvenile Offenders," p. 83.

43. S. B. Lincoln, "Juvenile Referral and Recidivism," in Robert Carter and Malcolm Klein, eds., *Back on the Street* (Englewood Cliffs, N.J.: Prentice-Hall, 1976), pp. 321– 328.

44. Klein et al., "Explosion in Police Diversion Programs," p. 110.

12 Interview with Judge Richette
Judge of the Philadelphia Court of Common Pleas

Lisa Richette originally became involved in the area of juvenile delinquency and juvenile justice as a law student at Yale University. She worked as a cottage parent at the Children's Center of Hamden, Connecticut, while obtaining her law degree, and eventually entered the Philadelphia Family Court as an assistant district attorney. Her book, *The Throwaway Children,* is based on her experiences and the cases she handled in the juvenile court.

Although now a Judge in the Court of Common Pleas, Lisa Richette has maintained her involvement in the area of juvenile rights. She is presently active in a Philadelphia agency she founded to prevent and treat child abuse. She is also a professor at the Temple University Law School, where she teaches courses on juvenile justice and the rights of women.

INTERVIEWER: *If you could change the juvenile court, what would you do?*

RICHETTE: Well, I think the major thing that's wrong with juvenile court is that it isn't just a court, it's a social agency. It's a hybrid process with no real jurisprudence, with no real protection for kids.

I: *Do you think children would be better served by a system more like the criminal justice system? Perhaps take out the treatment-rehabilitative philosophy that many feel has been used to justify the lack of due process?*

R: Yes, it has been used to exclude due process. But take it out? No, I wouldn't take it out. But I would make very certain that the treatment of kids is handled appropriately. I would try to judicialize the juvenile justice system, but not to dehumanize it. I would try to keep the humanism intact, and have a much less subjective process. I think the adjudication of guilt or innocence is the area where more judicialization has occurred because of *Winship* and the other cases. The area of the sentencing of children and the actual treatment programs that the court engages in are where many problems exist. The classic exchange that everyone has talked about— where the child gives up the right to a jury trial and certain other rights in return for treatment—has not worked well. The mistake is for the court to deal in treatment; they should get out of the treatment business.

I: *So would you take all treatment services out of the juvenile court, such as probation which is used so frequently?*

R: Probation hasn't been very successful, but it isn't very popular to emphasize that point. Probation officers are a source of power for juvenile judges since they have a direct input into appointing probation staff. I am opposed to the creation of empires within the juvenile court and unfortunately it sometimes has been used for that purpose. I would be much happier to see ongoing, independent social agencies and institutions set up instead of short-lived or experimental programs created by the court. These agencies could have a very positive impact on childcare and child-rearing institutions in this society. For example, most children who come into court do have learning and reading problems. The court and the board of education could work together to develop programs within the schools. I would like to see the state get out of the rehabilitation of children, for I have little faith in the ability of the state to do it.

I: *So what you would propose is a system in which the child would go through the court and then the court would lose its power over him or her?*

R: No, not lose power. The court would supervise the child's progress. It would be a monitoring agency, but not a service-giving agency. Probation officers should be there as monitors. There is a terrible confusion and an ambivalence in probation. The probation officer is the arm of the court who watches over the child's behavior and at the same time is supposed to be the child's friend. It doesn't work out that way.

I: *So instead of having probation officers in a counseling role, they would oversee the progress of the child?*

R: They'd ensure that the child is getting the right services. They would be advocates for the child, instead of suppliers of services.

I: *In other words, they would play more of a broker role?*

R: Right. This is what the court hasn't done. That's why it has a paucity of services to offer to children. The court has really felt it can do the job of rehabilitation, but it hasn't.

I: *What do you think of the idea of the juvenile court as a system of social-class control?*

R: Well, it's a simplistic view of the process. There are increasing numbers of lower-class children who come into the juvenile court. That may be one of its bad products, but I don't think that's its ultimate goal. Its ultimate design is rehabilitation. Of course, one could be cynical and say that the rhetoric of rehabilitation is just that. But every society has to deal with lawbreakers, and if they happen to come from a certain social stratum, then to deal with them is social-class control. But that's not the chief function.

I: *What is the chief function? Dealing with lawbreakers?*

R: To actualize the community sense of horror and outrage when laws are broken. It's one of the mechanisms of a civilized society. The question is, who is going to deal with juvenile lawbreakers? Do you deal with them as adults or do you set up a separate system? And then, what is that separate system to do?

Once there is internal role confusion—the court acting as therapist, monitor, and the arm of social control—you run the risk of having all the hideous results that have occurred in the past. The only time the court should intervene is when there is no other community support system and the child must become a state ward. He or she is therefore either confined in an institution or is a homeless person and must be placed in a foster home. There should be a protector for the child's rights.

I: *What about the serious offender?*

R: The child who has committed a serious offense needs to be segregated, for a number of reasons. First, the community demands it. These children should be isolated and sent to institutions which are not hellholes, but places where they can work and learn and grow.

I have no doubt that the criminal justice system is coming more and more to the realization that prisons and places of quarantine are very much a part of our cultural response to crime. What I would do is institute something like what Sanford Fox talks about—fixed sentences. I would not allow the child's future to be determined by the people who run the institution.

I: *There has been increased criticism of the juvenile court for its lenient treatment of youngsters who are serious offenders. As a result, some people have advocated lowering the age of criminal responsibility. Do you see that as an unreasonable or a reasonable response?*

R: What I propose is that the age be lowered within the format of the juvenile court rather than handling young offenders in the criminal justice system. There should be a clear-cut philosophy of institutionalization for juveniles who have committed felonies or have displayed a harmful antisocial pattern. They should be sentenced to clearly defined terms which the court will be responsible for carrying out. The responsibility for management of the child would be in the hands of the court. I'm opposed to parole boards and administrative bodies who really don't know the children but nevertheless decide when they have been rehabilitated and when they can be sent home. It should remain a judicial decision, instead of a nebulous sociological appraisal of the child's growth and development. The court should take into account sociological input, but the court should exercise power over release from institutions. This may result in much longer detention for kids, because I think that courts tend to be more conservative and more concerned about public reaction. The way to get around this is not to place the burden of fixing the initial sentence on the judge, but to have statutory provisions that specify the length of incarceration for offenses. At present, the court is so distracted by trying to be a therapist that it really can't pay proper attention to the seriously disturbed child who is just going to grow up to be a full-blown criminal.

I: *You keep talking of judicial decision making. Do you think it is one of the major flaws in the juvenile system now? Would you say it is a problem in the way that the juvenile legal system has been set up?*

R: I think it's inherent in the court structure. People with power must have very rigid limits to their power, and they need very clear role definitions. We learned that from Watergate. There is no branch of the judiciary that has more power than the juvenile judge. They very strongly resist any infringement on that power. So they have more power than any judge in Anglo-American history has ever been given. There are very poor review procedures, and the appeals that are made about the use of discretion are very few. There is a serious problem with the use of discretion by judges.

I: *What about the other people in the juvenile court? For example, defense attorneys have been strongly criticized for not conducting vigorous defenses. Don't the public defenders have to be concerned about maintaining relationships with the judge or with other court personnel?*

R: That's only a problem because of the virtually unlimited powers that the judge has. I have public defenders who appear before me every day of the week in criminal court and they don't care if they antagonize me or vigorously press for defenses. They know that I'm operating within a very clearly defined framework. And if I do something wrong they can file an appeal. It all goes back to the autocracy of the juvenile court judge, which is why defenders who have to appear daily are concerned about ruffling feathers. If you are operating within a very clearly defined role, no matter how badly your feathers are ruffled you're not going to really step out of that role.

I: *There has been a real proliferation of diversion projects all throughout the United States. This has been primarily because of labeling theory and the popularity of that particular explanation of delinquency. What is your opinion of these projects?*

R: Diversion projects do have some beneficial effects. But we suffer from a lack of rigorous statistics. We don't really know how many of those kids in diversion projects have subsequently come back into the juvenile justice system. Have you seen any studies on this?

I: *There is some research to indicate that children who get diverted are the least serious cases, the ones that would probably have been dropped any-*

way. What seems to be happening is that some children are becoming more involved in the system as a result of diversion. They're going into diversion projects and getting 12 hours of counseling whereas before their cases would have been dismissed.

R: Is the counseling beneficial enough?

I: *There doesn't seem to be much difference in terms of recidivism between diverted and undiverted children. The initial studies don't look too promising.*

R: Let's face it. The real purpose of the juvenile justice system is to deal with lawbreakers in a coherent, responsible way. If the rhetoric of health is just that, I don't really believe that the ultimate goal is a realizable one under our present system. How can you take a child who is unhappy, who lives in a very difficult family situation, and change that? You can't. All you can do is to give that child a way of developing more appropriate behavior patterns and perhaps better controls. So much of what these kids are doing is part of the growth process—rebellion and experimentation. The idea of a total transformation of the child and a remolding of his personality—these are utopian and impossible goals.

I: *As I interpret the results so far it appears that the children may be better off left alone completely, which is Edwin Schur's idea of "radical nonintervention."*

R: I don't believe that because I think that the interventions that occur are so difficult to evaluate.

I: *Would you ever like to go back to work in juvenile court?*

R: I don't believe in the present system, but I would like to go if I could have some degree of authority and power to make some changes and improvements. I prefer to do creative work in the area of reducing the level of violence that takes place against children. I have this firm belief that child abuse is the largest single factor in creating violent, antisocial behavior in children and adults. I really believe that, and I think that until we do something in our juvenile courts to protect defenseless children and to deal very clearly with the problem of child abuse we are not going to decrease serious delinquency.

I: *I know you started an organization in Philadelphia to provide services for abusive parents and their children. What types of services do you hope to provide?*

R: We are going to set up a center where parents can come and leave their children, and we hope to make it a very beautiful and healthy place for children to play and relax and so forth. There are so few of those places where parents can just relieve pressures and where children can be in good, healthy atmospheres, other than the schools. Schools are available only to those children who have reached a certain age, and with the budget problems in Philadelphia we now have eliminated our preschool programs. We want to help those children who have suffered serious injury—

that's the long-range goal. And you run into problems because there are these institutionalized mechanisms that haven't been set up, such as public-defender advocacy projects for deprived children. The work that we do with the parents, no one else is doing. There are people who come to us and ask to be helped to change the way they treat their children.

I: *Do you provide other services and will you eventually offer services that go beyond simply providing a place to keep the children?*

R: We already offer counseling and group sessions, which are very important in helping people find solutions to real-life problems. In so many of the households in which child abuse occurs, there is also a problem with spouse abuse. A general atmosphere of violence exists in that home. So we help the woman remove herself, if she can, from that situation and take responsibility for what's happening to her children and herself. Generally I think what we've done, apart from the direct help we have given to the parents, is to sensitize the whole community to the problem. Our speaking programs and television campaign have helped. The National Council for Child Abuse, of which I am a board member, has undertaken a national advertising campaign, too. We are calling into question the whole concept of physical punishment in the schools, which was part of violence against children. We have to try to get legislation to prohibit corporal punishment. We have run into terrible problems because of the paucity of resources in the Department of Welfare and even in the probation department and the courts. There are simply not enough people to do the referral work and to take whatever steps need to be taken. So we are just a small growing effort, but I think what we are trying to do is what really needs to be done. I believe that this is the root cause of delinquency. I'm talking about the systematic brutalization of children. I think this occurs on many levels in our society. Probably the most abusing parent of all is the surrogate parent of television.

I: *I'm interested in this idea that brutalization of children is responsible for delinquency. Do you use that in a really broad sense, including television, or do you mean actual physical abuse?*

R: I mean actual physical abuse.

I: *So you feel that it's extremely widespread?*

R: Oh, yes. I see this in the adults that come before me. They are nothing more than late adolescents really—18 to 23—and the factors are all there. You read in their background about instances of severe beating, real physical beating. I now have a defendant on trial who rapes only old women. He is schizophrenic. A psychiatrist testified to this the other day. The daily beatings from his father from early childhood on were a very important factor in his learning problems and lack of ability to read as well as to develop a sense of identity. The raping and beating of old women was directly linked to the beatings from his father. This was his way of being a man.

I: *I know that other research has been conducted with murderers which indicates that brutal treatment is often found in their childhoods. I wonder if the same is true of more minor offenders–for example, people who commit property offenses.*

R: No, I'm talking specifically about violent offenders. We must be much more concerned about these. I think kids who steal *are* problems, but their behavior is less threatening and less worrisome to society. I guess the real failure of the juvenile court is that it is just a holding action, not probing the basic causes and certainly not taking a leadership role in society and transforming the conditions of childhood. This is particularly true for the children who don't have any real social-support systems. We need a rational and logical process to decide which children need help and which don't, and then we must make sure that the ones who do need help will get it. The court shouldn't offer the help, but should mobilize the institutions in society that can provide it. The most serious problem is isolation of the juvenile court from the other forces of society. It's not a very effective part of the justice system at all.

I: *I'm interested in what you said about the juvenile court mobilizing its resources to change the conditions of children on the societal level, because it's been suggested that, by the time the child gets incarcerated, it is too late.*

R: I don't think it's really ever too late. There are a great number of things that are effective and that can be done. What worries me is that we spend so much money so badly—operating detention centers, for example. It would be better to use that money to provide services that the child really needs. If the child can't read, there are wonderful places in the community where reading programs could be set up. That would be much more important than going to a probation officer every week.

I: *Something along the lines of a youth service bureau? Has that ever been tried in Philadelphia?*

R: Well, there was the Youth Services Commission, which was a total failure. There were many problems. First, the problem is taking in the philosophy of the judges who created a bureaucracy. Bureaucracies, as you know, do not easily give up their power. The second problem is that non-punitive treatment isn't a very popular thing to do. I think we live in an age of increasing terror, and the responses of people are really conditioned by a total disillusionment in the justice system and the courts. There is this widespread belief that judges are not really doing anything, and there is a hardening of attitudes toward kids. Certainly political leaders exploit that attitude. You can't be a candidate for anything today unless you take a very hard line.

What will happen in the next ten years is that as the LEAA programs come under increasing attack, and there are certain indications that this administration is not going to continue funding endlessly, and as the services dry up, you are going to be back with what existed in the past—a bewildering confusion of roles and the criminalization of the juvenile courts. Without the kinds of sensitive mechanisms and attitudes that I've been talking about, which would really sort out those kids who desperately need intervention, everyone is going to be processed on one level or another because the public is going to demand it. Then we will be right back to the reformatory mentality. If we could take treatment out of the court, widespread citizen participation could be generated.

I firmly believe that the community needs to become much more involved and much more sensitized.

Author Index

A

Adams, W., 106, 123
Adler, F., 108, 123
Ahrenfeldt, R., 52
Akers, R., 23
Appleby, M., 54
Arnold, N., 218
Asbury, H., 109, 125
Austin, J., 221

B

Bandura, A., 120, 123, 127
Barker, G., 106, 123
Barton, W., 104, 218
Baum, M., 68
Bauzer, R., 243
Beccaria, C., 148
Becker, H., 55, 67
Bee, H., 55
Bentham, J., 148
Besharov, D., 226, 242
Binet, A., 79
Blanchard, F., 244
Bloch, H., 25, 53
Bodine, G., 180
Bohlke, R., 102, 123

Bosage, B., 180
Bouma, D., 60, 68
Brady, N., 91
Brager, G., 53
Brantingham, P., 164, 195, 220
Briar, S., 47, 54, 180
Briggs, P., 82, 97
Brown, M., 96
Burgess, E., 27
Burns, H., 220

C

Campbell, A., 68
Caplan, N., 80, 96, 97
Carter, R., 179, 219, 220, 240, 243, 244
Cartwright, D., 126
Cavan, R., 22, 220
Chambliss, W., 243
Chapman, A., 68
Chilton, R., 122
Cicourel, A., 22, 67
Clemmer, D., 220
Clinard, M., 124
Cloward, R., 35, 40, 51, 52, 53, 110, 122

Coates, R., 181, 242
Cohen, A., 31, 37, 42, 52, 54, 96,
    100, 101, 110, 122, 123, 179
Cohen, F., 195
Cohen, H., 220
Cohen, L., 181, 218
Cohen, S., 218
Cohn, Y., 218
Cortes, J., 88, 97
Courtless, T., 180
Curran, J., 68

D
Davis, S., 180
Dawson, P., 181
Diana, L., 219
Dinitz, S., 68
Dix, G., 181
Downs, G., 228
Duffee, D., 189, 195
Durkheim, E., 32, 53

E
Eisenberg, L., 94, 97
Eisenstadt, S., 52
Elliott, D., 244
Elman, R., 53
Empey, L., 220
England, R., 102, 123
Epps, P., 97
Erikson, K., 53
Ervin, R., 121, 127
Eysenck, H., 89, 95, 97, 121, 127,
    140

F
Facella, C., 123
Farrington, S., 68
Faust, F., 164, 195, 220
Ferdinand, T., 22, 180, 220
Ferracuti, F., 43, 54, 116, 119, 126
Ferrero, W., 123
Ferri, E., 148
Ferster, E., 180
Figlio, R., 68, 122, 180, 221
Filipczak, J., 220
Finkelstein, M., 194, 218
Foster, J., 68

Fowler, A., 68
Fox, S., 181, 195, 219
Franks, C., 97
Freud, S., 71
Friedman, R., 195

G
Garrett, J., 196
Gatti, F., 88, 97
Geis, G., 25, 53
Gelles, R., 127
Gerard, R., 220
Gershenovitz, A., 179
Giallombardo, R., 220
Gibbens, T., 52, 97
Gibbons, D., 22, 53, 106, 123, 124,
    164
Glasser, W., 140, 215, 220
Glen, J., 195
Glick, S., 83
Gligor, A., 97
Glueck, E., 82, 88, 96, 97, 104, 120,
    123, 127
Glueck, S., 82, 88, 96, 97, 104, 120,
    123, 127
Goddard, H., 79, 96
Goddard, M., 221
Goffman, E., 58, 68, 220
Gold, M., 17, 23, 68, 104, 122, 123
Goldfarb, R., 22, 179
Goldman, N., 180, 235, 243
Goode, W., 52
Goodman, L., 52
Goring, G., 164
Gough, A., 22, 196
Gould, L., 69
Grams, P., 54
Griswold, M., 106, 123
Gross, B., 242
Gross, R., 242

H
Hall, J., 228
Hall, M., 68
Hall, P., 63, 68
Handy, W., 118, 126
Hathaway, S., 82, 97
Heifetz, H., 54

Henry, A., 120, 126
Henry, C., 97
Hindelang, M., 23, 106, 124, 125
Hirschi, T., 23, 26, 44, 47, 51, 52,
    54, 99, 101, 103, 122, 123
Hodges, E., 85
Hoffman, L., 55
Hoffman, M., 55
Hood, R., 22, 122, 179
Hook, E., 127

J
Jeffrey, C., 164
Jencks, C., 179
Jensen, G., 69

K
Karacki, L., 100, 122
King, D., 196
King, J., 3
Kitsuse, J., 22
Kittrie, N., 165
Klein, M., 111, 114, 117, 125, 179,
    210, 220, 233, 240, 243, 244
Kobetz, R., 179, 180, 243
Kobrin, S., 32, 53
Konopka, G., 124
Krisberg, B., 221
Kvaraceus, W., 102, 123

L
Lefstein, N., 195
Lemert, E., 58, 68
Lerman, P., 220
Levin, M., 180, 184, 195, 219
Lewin, R., 122
Lichtenstein, M., 96
Lincoln, S., 244
Lindsley, D., 97
Lipton, D., 196
Lombroso, C., 103, 106, 123, 148,
    164
Luchterhand, E., 180

M
McDermott, R., 244
McDonough, J., 196
McEachern, A., 243

McGee, R., 220
McKay, H., 27, 31, 40, 53
Mack, J., 165
Maher, B., 68
Mahoney, A., 68
Mann, D., 220, 233
Mark, V., 121, 127
Martinson, R., 196
Matza, D., 31, 53, 54, 67
Mayeske, G., 179
Meade, A., 68
Megargee, E., 75, 96, 118, 126
Mennel, R., 164
Merton, R., 33, 36, 51, 53
Miles, J., 179
Miller, A., 181, 242
Miller, F., 181
Miller, J., 229
Miller, W., 31, 40, 42, 52, 54, 102,
    110, 117, 119, 123, 126, 138
Monachesi, E., 82, 97
Morris, R., 124
Murray, C., 179
Myerhoff, B., 122
Myerhoff, H., 122

N
Nelson, C., 219
Nelson, E., 220
Newman, G., 22
Norman, S., 244
Nye, F., 23, 122

O
Ogburn, W., 52
Ohlin, L., 35, 40, 51, 52, 53, 110,
    122, 181, 242

P
Paddock, A., 122
Palmer, S., 76, 96, 120, 127
Palmieri, J., 187, 196, 206
Parnas, R., 181
Parnell, R., 97
Parsons, T., 101, 123
Perkins, R., 22
Perlstein, G., 242
Phelps, T., 242

Piliavin, I., 47, 54, 180
Pittman, D., 118, 126
Platt, A., 22, 164, 165, 195
Polk, K., 54, 69
Pollak, O., 107, 124
Porterfield, A., 15
Porteus, S., 97
Purcell, F., 53

Q

Quay, H., 81, 85, 95, 97
Quinney, R., 51, 55, 67, 124

R

Rabow, J., 220
Rachin R., 243
Radzinowicz, L., 3
Redl, F., 73, 96
Reiss, A., 53
Remington, F., 68
Rendleman, D., 164
Richardson, D., 179
Richette, L., 245
Riedel, M., 221
Rist, R., 179
Rhodes, A., 53
Robins, L., 96
Rodman, H., 54
Rothman, D., 165
Rubin, S., 22
Ruchelman, L., 68
Rutherford, A., 244

S

Sanders, W., 164
Sarri, R., 180, 181, 184, 195, 210,
    219, 220
Satir, V., 219
Saunders, F., 106, 123
Scarr, S., 89, 97
Schafer, W., 54, 69
Schecter, H., 195
Scheier, I., 219
Schramm, G., 165
Schur, E., 55, 66, 67, 68, 69
Schwartz, H., 126
Scudellari, A., 179

Scull, A., 243
Sellin, T., 68, 122, 180, 221
Senna, J., 179, 195, 219
Shaw, C., 27, 31, 40, 53
Sheldon, W., 87, 95, 97
Shields, J., 90
Shipler, D., 55
Short, J., 23, 64, 69, 101, 120, 123,
    125, 126
Shuman, H., 68
Siebert, L., 80, 96
Siegel, L., 179, 189, 195, 219
Simon, R., 105
Smith, R., 219, 242
Snethen, E., 180
Solomon, H., 219
Sparks, R., 22, 122, 179
Spitzer, S., 55
Stapleton, V., 195
Stapleton, W., 195
Stein, E., 68
Steinmetz, S., 127
Straus, M., 127
Strodtbeck, F., 64, 69, 125
Susman, J., 195, 219
Sutherland, E., 30, 31, 53
Sykes, G., 54

T

Tait, C., 85
Tannenbaum, F., 67
Taylor, I., 55, 164
Teitelbaum, L., 22, 195, 196
Thomas, W., 107, 124
Thornberry, T., 218, 221
Thrasher, F., 26, 31, 39, 53, 109,
    110, 125
Toby, J., 52, 100, 101, 122, 123
Tognacci, L., 126
Toman, W., 96
Tomson, B., 126
Treaster, J., 157

V

Vaz, E., 101, 106, 122, 123
Vinter, R., 210, 220, 228
Vold, G., 164

W

Wagner, R., 243
Waldo, G., 68
Walker, W., 219
Walton, P., 55, 164
Ward, R., 68
Warren, M., 78, 96
Waters, M. van, 165
Walters, R., 123, 127
Wattenberg, W., 106, 123
Weber, R., 195
Weeks, H., 220
Weiss, E., 218
Weissman, H., 54
West, D., 68
Wheeler, S., 68, 180, 243
Wicks, R., 220

Wilkins, L., 219
Wilks, J., 196
Willie, C., 179
Wilson, J., 180, 243
Winch, R., 52
Wineman, D., 73, 96
Wintersmith, R., 68
Wirt, R., 82, 97
Wise, N., 104, 106, 123
Wolfgang, M., 3, 43, 54, 62, 68, 69,
    116, 118, 119, 122, 126, 180, 221

Y

Yablonsky, L., 113, 115, 125
Young, J., 55, 164

Subject Index

A

Adjudication, 182, 193
Affectional ties, 48
Affluence, 25
Aftercare, 217
Alcohol, 119
Amphetamines, 93
Anomie, 32, 34, 35
Appeals, 193
Arrest policies, 11, 170

B

Behavior Therapy, 93, 214
Bond, 44
Brain damage, 121
Breed v. *Jones,* 155, 184
Broken homes, 48

C

Cerebrotonia, 87
Chattel, 5
Chicago Area Project, 31
Child abuse, 120
Child advocate, 224
Child saving movement, 6, 147, 149, 203
Children's rights movement, 224

CHINS, 9, 168
Chivalry, 108
Classical conditioning, 91
Classification, 81, 212
Cliques, 112
College boy, 39
Communism, 50
Community-based corrections, 226
Complainant, 186
Conflict theory, 49
Conformist, 34
Congregate system, 151
Conscience, 92
Consensus, 50
Consent decree, 183
Control theory, 44
Counsel, 188
Crime trends, 12
Criminology, classical, 147, 150
Cultural assimilation, 27
Cultural transmission, 32

D

De-institutionalization, 217, 226
Detached workers, 37, 43
Detention, 174
Deterrence, 208

Differential association, 30
Discretion, police, 59
Disposition, 61, 63, 152, 197
Diversion, 66, 163, 169, 232
Diversion, police, 235
Divorce, 25

E
Ecological studies, 27
Ectomorph, 87
Education, 49
Ego, 72
Ego, delinquent, 73
Endomorph, 87
Enforcement, selective, 57
English law, 6
Etiology, 20, 24
Evidence, hearsay, 151
Evidence, preponderance, 151
Extraversion, 90, 140

F
Family, conjugal, 24
Family, extended, 24
Family, nuclear, 24, 100, 101
Family therapy, 204
Female delinquent, 103
Fingerprints, 173
Focal concerns, 40, 102, 138

G
Gagnon v. *Scarpelli*, 205
Gang, 36, 109
Gang, spontaneous, 111
Gang, traditional, 111
Gault, In re, 154, 188, 191, 193, 225
Genotype, 89
Gratification, delayed, 102
Guided group interaction (GGI), 213

H
Halfway house, 231
Hammurabi, code of, 6
Hearing, 152, 177, 185, 191
Hearing, adjudication, 182
Hearing, bifurcated, 192
Hearing, preliminary, 178
Home detention, 177

I
Id, 72
Immigrants, 26
Incarceration, 61
Industrialization, 100
Infanticide, 5
Innovator, 34
Institutionalization, 207
Intake, 152, 167, 177
Intelligence, 79
Internalization, 48
Interstitial areas, 26
Introversion, 140
Investigation, presentence, 152, 192

J
JINS, 9
Judge, 190, 198
Judgment, suspended, 192
Jurisdiction, 9, 184
Jurisdiction, waived, 184
Jury, grand, 178
Juvenile court, 147, 151
Juvenile delinquency, 2, 7
Juvenile officers, 60, 170

K
Kent v. *U.S.*, 153, 184, 199

L
Labeling theory, 21, 51, 56, 227
Leadership, 113

M
Masculinity, compulsive, 101
McKeiver v. *Pennsylvania*, 155, 191, 194
Mesomorph, 87
Midcity Project, 43
Middle Ages, 6
MINS, 168
Miranda v. *Arizona*, 173
MMPI, 84
Mobilization for Youth, 36

N
National Crime Panel, 19
Nelson v. *Heyne*, 156

Neurotic delinquent, 81
Neuroticism, 90
New York, 7
Nonutilitarian acts, 39

O

Official delinquents, 17, 26
Open-class system, 25
Opportunity, 32, 35, 139
Overcontrol, 75, 118

P

Parens patriae, 150, 156, 192
Parole, 218
Paterfamilias, 5
Pennsylvania, 7
Petition, 182
Physiological theories, 21, 86
PINS, 9, 168
Plea, guilty, 185
Positivism, 147
Predelinquent, 168
Predictors of adult criminality, 2, 81
Primary deviation, 58
Probable cause, 170, 178
Probation, 152, 186, 199, 202, 207
Probation, police, 236
Prosecutor, 186, 198
Psychoanalytic theory, 71
Psychological theories, 21, 70
Psychopath, 75, 113
Psychopath, unsocialized, 81
Punishment, consistent, 48
Punishment, love-oriented, 120
Punishment, physical, 6, 120

R

Race, 20, 171
Radical nonintervention, 51
Reaction Formation, 39
Reality therapy, 140, 215
Rebel, 34
Recidivism, 62, 171, 206
Referral, 167
Reformatories, 6, 150
Rehabilitation, 6
Release, 213

Responsibility, 6
Retreatist, 34
Retribution, 208
Revocation, 205
Ritualist, 34
Roman Law, 6
Ruling class, 50

S

Search and seizure, 173
Secondary deviation, 58
Self-incrimination, 185
Self-report, 15, 26, 45
Sentence, indeterminate, 148, 152, 213
Sex, 20
Sex-role identification, 101
Slum, 111
Social disorganization, 26, 32
Social organization, 31
Socio-economic status, 15, 20, 38, 39, 40, 42, 98, 171
Sociological theories, 21
Solidarity, 33, 113
Somatotonia, 87
Somatotype, 87
Stable-corner boy, 39
Status disequilibrium, 102
Status offenses, 9, 10, 223
Statutory definition, 7
Stigma, 58, 65
Stratification, 102
Structural strain, 35
Subcultural delinquent, 81, 92
Subculture, 31, 35, 36, 37, 43, 119, 138, 212
Superego, 72
Superego, delinquent, 74
Supervision, 203

T

Texas, 7
Token economy, 214
Training schools, 6
Treatment, 21, 31, 36, 43, 48, 50, 65, 77, 93, 213
Twins, 89

U
Undercontrol, 75, 118
Uniform Crime Reports, 11

V
Victim-precipitation, 119
Victimization, 15, 17, 169
Violent offenders, 116
Vlscerotonia, 87
Voir dire proceeding, 155
Volunteers, 207

W
Winship, In re, 154, 191
Witnesses, 186

X
XYY, 121

Y
Youth culture, 25, 101
Youth Development and Delinquency
    Prevention Administration, 239
Youth Services Bureau, 67, 238